UNIVERSAL SEMANTIC SYNTAX
Volume 160

Syntactic theory has been dominated in the last decades by theories that disregard semantics in their approach to syntax. Presenting a truly semantic approach to syntax, this book takes as its primary starting point the idea that syntax deals with the relations between meanings expressed by form-meaning elements and that the same types of relations can be found cross-linguistically. The theory provides a way to formalize the syntactic relations between meanings so that each fragment of grammar can be analysed in a clear-cut way. A comprehensive introduction into the theoretical concepts of the theory is provided, with analyses of numerous examples in English and various other languages, European and non-European, to illustrate the concepts. The theory discussed will enable linguists to look for similarities between languages, while at the same time acknowledging important language-specific features.

EGBERT FORTUIN is Associate Professor of Russian Linguistics at Leiden University. He has published numerous articles in journals such as *Lingua, Cognitive Linguistics* and *Russian Linguistics*. He is currently editor of the book series Studies in General and Slavic Linguistics.

HETTY GEERDINK-VERKOREN studied English and Japanese and completed her PhD in Japanese linguistics at Leiden University. She is the chief editor and content manager on a project for the compilation of a new Japanese–Dutch dictionary.

In this series

130 RACHEL WALKER *Vowel Patterns in Language*
131 MARY DALRYMPLE and IRINA NIKOLAEVA *Objects and Information Structure*
132 JERROLD M. SADOCK *The Modular Architecture of Grammar*
133 DUNSTAN BROWN and ANDREW HIPPISLEY *Network Morphology: A Defaults-based Theory of Word Structure*
134 BETTELOU LOS, CORRIEN BLOM, GEERT BOOIJ, MARION ELENBAAS and ANS VAN KEMENADE *Morphosyntactic Change: A Comparative Study of Particles and Prefixes*
135 STEPHEN CRAIN *The Emergence of Meaning*
136 HUBERT HAIDER *Symmetry Breaking in Syntax*
137 JOSÉ A. CAMACHO *Null Subjects*
138 GREGORY STUMP and RAPHAEL A. FINKEL *Morphological Typology: From Word to Paradigm*
139 BRUCE TESAR *Output-Driven Phonology: Theory and Learning*
140 ASIER ALCÁZAR and MARIO SALTARELLI *The Syntax of Imperatives*
141 MISHA BECKER *The Acquisition of Syntactic Structure: Animacy and Thematic Alignment*
142 MARTINA WILTSCHKO *The Universal Structure of Categories: Towards a Formal Typology*
143 FAHAD RASHED AL-MUTAIRI *The Minimalist Program: The Nature and Plausibility of Chomsky's Biolinguistics*
144 CEDRIC BOECKX *Elementary Syntactic Structures: Prospects of a Feature-Free Syntax*
145 PHOEVOS PANAGIOTIDIS *Categorial Features: A Generative Theory of Word Class Categories*
146 MARK BAKER *Case: Its Principles and Its Parameters*
147 WM. G. BENNETT *The Phonology of Consonants: Dissimilation, Harmony and Correspondence*
148 ANDREA SIMS *Inflectional Defectiveness*
149 GREGORY STUMP *Inflectional Paradigms: Content and Form at the Syntax-Morphology Interface*
150 ROCHELLE LIEBER *English Nouns: The Ecology of Nominalization*
151 JOHN BOWERS *Deriving Syntactic Relations*
152 ANA TERESA PÉREZ-LEROUX, MIHAELA PIRVULESCU and YVES ROBERGE *Direct Objects and Language Acquisition*
153 MATTHEW BAERMAN, DUNSTAN BROWN and GREVILLE G. CORBETT *Morphological Complexity*
154 MARCEL DEN DIKKEN *Dependency and Directionality*
155 LAURIE BAUER *Compounds and Compounding*
156 KLAUS J. KOHLER *Communicative Functions and Linguistic Forms in Speech Interaction*
157 KURT GOBLIRSCH *Gemination, Lenition, and Vowel Lengthening: On the History of Quantity in Germanic*
158 ANDREW RADFORD *Colloquial English: Structure and Variation*
159 MARIA POLINSKY *Heritage Languages and Their Speakers*
160 EGBERT FORTUIN and HETTY GEERDINK-VERKOREN *Universal Semantic Syntax: A Semiotactic Approach*

Earlier issues not listed are also available

CAMBRIDGE STUDIES IN LINGUISTICS

General Editors: P. AUSTIN, J. BRESNAN, B. COMRIE,
S. CRAIN, W. DRESSLER, C. J. EWEN, R. LASS,
D. LIGHTFOOT, K. RICE, I. ROBERTS, S. ROMAINE,
N. V. SMITH

Universal Semantic Syntax

UNIVERSAL SEMANTIC SYNTAX

A SEMIOTACTIC APPROACH

Volume 160

EGBERT FORTUIN
Leiden University

HETTY GEERDINK-VERKOREN
Leiden University

CAMBRIDGE
UNIVERSITY PRESS

University Printing House, Cambridge CB2 8BS, United Kingdom

One Liberty Plaza, 20th Floor, New York, NY 10006, USA

477 Williamstown Road, Port Melbourne, VIC 3207, Australia

314–321, 3rd Floor, Plot 3, Splendor Forum, Jasola District Centre, New Delhi – 110025, India

79 Anson Road, #06–04/06, Singapore 079906

Cambridge University Press is part of the University of Cambridge.

It furthers the University's mission by disseminating knowledge in the pursuit
of education, learning, and research at the highest international levels of excellence.

www.cambridge.org
Information on this title: www.cambridge.org/9781108476805
DOI: 10.1017/9781108658683

© Egbert Fortuin and Hetty Geerdink-Verkoren 2019

This publication is in copyright. Subject to statutory exception
and to the provisions of relevant collective licensing agreements,
no reproduction of any part may take place without the written
permission of Cambridge University Press.

First published 2019

Printed and bound in Great Britain by Clays Ltd, Elcograf S.p.A.

A catalogue record for this publication is available from the British Library.

Library of Congress Cataloging-in-Publication Data
Names: Fortuin, Egbert Lambertus Johan, author. | Geerdink-Verkoren, Hetty,
    1948- author.
Title: Universal semantic syntax : a semiotactic approach / Egbert Fortuin,
    Hetty Geerdink-Verkoren.
Description: New York : Cambridge University Press, 2019. | Series: Cambridge
    studies in linguistics ; 160
Identifiers: LCCN 2018041961 | ISBN 9781108476805 (hardback) |
    ISBN 9781108701587 (paperback)
Subjects: LCSH: Grammar, Comparative and general–Syntax. | BISAC:
    LANGUAGE ARTS & DISCIPLINES / General.
Classification: LCC P291 .F59 2019 | DDC 415.01–dc23
LC record available at https://lccn.loc.gov/2018041961

ISBN 978-1-108-47680-5 Hardback

Cambridge University Press has no responsibility for the persistence or accuracy
of URLs for external or third-party internet websites referred to in this publication
and does not guarantee that any content on such websites is, or will remain,
accurate or appropriate.

Exact definitions for each meaning can only be given after a detailed study of a great number of instances. This aspect of the analysis will never be reducible to the application of rules. Semantic description is not a mechanical affair; the only possible approach is one based on trial and error.

Ebeling (1978: 244)[1]

---

[1] C. L. Ebeling (1924–2017).

Contents

Acknowledgements	*page* xii
List of Abbreviations	xiii

Introduction	**1**

PART I THE SEMIOTACTIC THEORY

1	**Basic Theoretical Principles**	**5**
1.1	Form and Meaning	5
1.2	The Basis of Syntax: Entities and Syntactic Relations	8
	1.2.1 Entities	8
	1.2.2 Syntactic Relations	9
1.3	Language Structure and Syntactic Representation	11
1.4	Meaningful Elements	12

2	**Semiotactic Relations and Symbols**	**14**
2.1	Limitation Relation	15
	2.1.1 Convergent Limitation	15
	2.1.2 Divergent Limitation	18
	2.1.3 Temporal Limitation	19
2.2	Compounding Relation	20
	2.2.1 Convergent Compounding	21
	2.2.2 Divergent Compounding	22
2.3	Equipollent Relation	22
2.4	Stratification Relation	23
2.5	Gradation Relation	25
	2.5.1 Reversed Gradation	26
	2.5.2 Temporal Gradation	26

3	**Nexus: Subject-Predicate Relation**	**28**
3.1	Nexus Relation and the Verb 'Be'	29
3.2	'Σ' without Nexus	33
3.3	Notations in the Top Layer	35

x   *Contents*

4   Valences   39
4.1   What Is Valence?   39
4.2   How Many Valences?   42
        4.2.1   Valence and Case   48
        4.2.2   How to Represent Case?   50
4.3   A Special Type of Valence: Coordination   53
4.4   Non-Specified Element 'X'   56
4.5   Quasi-Divergence   57
4.6   Other Examples of Valence   60

5   Set Expression 'SE'   64

6   Nexus Relation as Entity (Bahuvrihi)   66

7   Negation   67

8   The Auxiliary Verb 'Do'   70

9   Appositions   73

10   Formal and Syntactic Sentences   74

11   Abstraction   76

12   The Basic Principles of the Formalization   77
12.1   Universal Syntactic Relations   77
12.2   Formalization and Form-Meaning Elements   83
12.3   Meaning, Interpretation, Polysemy and Formalization   85

PART II APPLICATION OF THE THEORY

13   Noun Modifications   91
13.1   Compound and Equipollent Junctions   91
13.2   Adjectives and Adverbs   92
13.3   Genitival Adjuncts   94
13.4   Genitival Compounds   96
13.5   Prepositional Phrases   96
13.6   Numerals and Quantities   97
13.7   Bahuvrihi and Other Nominal Constructions   100

14   Verb Constructions   105
14.1   Modal Verbs   105
14.2   Infinitive Constructions   109

14.3	Gerund Constructions	120
14.4	Progressive Form Constructions	122
14.5	Constructions with a Past Participle	124
	14.5.1 'Be' + Past Participle	124
	14.5.2 'Have' + Past Participle	127
	14.5.3 Other Past Participle Constructions	130

15   Impersonal Constructions   133

15.1	Impersonal and Existential Constructions in European Languages	133
15.2	Other Existential Constructions	139
15.3	Existential Constructions in Japanese and Lepcha	142

16   Other Constructions in Non-European Languages   145

16.1	Compound Verbs	145
16.2	Relative Clauses	149
16.3	Negation in Japanese	151
16.4	Transitive or Intransitive Constructions	152
16.5	Definite and Indefinite Constructions	154
	16 5.1 Turkish	154
	16 5.2 Manchu	156
	16.5.3 Classical Mongolian	157
	16.5.4 Oceanic Languages Mokilese, Ponapean and Tongan	158
	16.5.5 Alaskan Yup'ik	161
16.6	Serial Verb Constructions	162

17   Word Order and Propositional Contents   166

Conclusion: The Syntactic Theory from a Semantic Perspective   172

Appendix A	175
Relation Symbols	175
Analysed Examples	176
Appendix B	183
How to Construct a Semiotactic Representation	183
References	186
Index	191

Acknowledgements

This book could not have been written were it not for a number of people who helped us along the way. First of all, we would like to express our thanks to Frits Kortlandt, who was the first to suggest that we write a book on Semiotactics, and Lennart van der Velden, who helped us as an assistant during the very first stages of the book. We would also like to thank Andries van der Helden, whose stimulating conversations about the theory often helped us steer in the right direction. We are also very grateful to the various anonymous reviewers; their criticisms encouraged us to make a number of improvements to the book. We further wish to thank the *Croiset van der Kop Fund*, for helping us financially; Janet Taylor, who did an excellent job as copy editor; and Helen Barton, Commissioning Editor of Cambridge University Press, who helped us in the process of getting the book reviewed and accepted. Finally and foremost, we are greatly indebted to the late Carl Ebeling, with whom we had the pleasure of discussing various questions that came up while we were writing this book. He took the time to read our manuscript attentively, and in cases where we did not reach a unanimous conclusion, he always advised us to choose our own path, which we did. Without him the book would not have existed in the first place.

Abbreviations

ABS	absolutive case
ACC	accusative case
ADD	added information
ADV	adverbial case
AST	assertive particle
BNC	British National Corpus
COMP	comparative
COMPL	completion
COND	conditional
CONN	connective
CONTR	contrast
DAT	dative case
DECL	declarative
DEF	definite
EMPH	emphatic
ERG	ergative case
EXCL	exclamative
F	feminine
GEN	genitive case
HYP	hypothetic
IC	immediate constituent
IMP	imperative
IMPF	imperfective
INC	incomplete
INDEF	indefinite
INF	infinitive
INSTR	instrumental case
M	masculine
MUT	mutually
N	neutral

xiv *List of Abbreviations*

NO	none (zero)
NOM	nominative case
NON	negation
NONTHE	indefinite article
NP	noun phrase
PA	past tense
PF	perfective
PL	plural
POL	polite (Japanese)
PP	past participle
PR	present tense
PRED	predicative
PROGR	progressive
REL	relative case
RNC	Russian National Corpus
Q	question
SE	set expression
SG	(verb) singular (in glosses)
SING	singular
SOV	subject-object-verb
SVO	subject-verb-object
THE	definite article
TOP	topic

Introduction

Within linguistics there are various theories that describe syntax from a semantic point of view. To name a few: Lexical Functional Grammar (e.g. Bresnan 1982), Word Grammar (Hudson 1984), theories of Dependency Grammar, such as the work of Tesnière (1959) and the 'Meaning-Text' model of Mel'čuk (e.g. 1988), HPSG (Head-Driven Phrase Structure Grammar; e.g. Pollard and Sag 1994), strands of Generative Semantics (e.g. Seuren 1996), Dik's Functional Grammar (e.g. 1997; now Functional Discourse Grammar), strands of Cognitive Linguistics (see Croft and Cruse 2004) and various strands of Construction Grammar (see Hoffmann and Trousdale 2013). Besides these theories, there is also an older tradition of syntactic analysis within European Structuralism, which starts out from the idea of the Saussurian sign (form-meaning element) (de Saussure 1966). A notable example is the theory of *Semiotactics* developed by Carl Ebeling. This linguistic theory is based primarily on the work of Jespersen (in particular his *Analytic Syntax* of 1937) and on structuralist approaches to syntax (specifically the work of Jakobson and Martinet). The basic idea behind Semiotactics (in this name we find the Greek words *sēmeion* 'a sign' and *taktikós* 'fit for arranging') is that syntax concerns the relations between different form-meaning elements, and that these relations can be described with a limited set of syntactic relations, which are largely universal.

Ebeling explained his theory in various writings (including 'On the Semantic Structure of the Russian Sentence' 1954, *Syntax and Semantics* 1978, 'How Many Valences?' 1980, *Een inleiding tot de syntaxis* [An Introduction to Syntax] 1994 and *Semiotaxis* [Semiotactics] 2006). Most of these are of a rather technical nature or written in Dutch and therefore not accessible to a wider audience. Furthermore, the theory has been subject to ongoing development, and changes have been made in the practical application of the formalization (as well as the development in Ebeling's own works, culminating in his last book in 2006, see also e.g. the contributions of Kortlandt (1980, 2008) and Geerdink-Verkoren (2009), the various papers in Geerdink-Verkoren and van Engelenhoven (eds) 2011, and Fortuin 2014). In addition, there are many constructions in languages

2   *Introduction*

other than Dutch that have not yet been analysed using the semiotactic approach. The aim of this book is to fill this gap and present the first comprehensive introduction to Semiotactics. Although the universal semantic-syntax approach to language advocated here is based on various versions of Semiotactics as proposed by Carl Ebeling and other authors who have worked within this framework, we also offer own contributions to the semiotactic theory, which sometimes differ from the ideas put forward by Ebeling. To emphasize the broad typological scope and nature of the theory, we use the term *Universal Semantic Syntax* for the version of Semiotactics presented in this book.

Universal Semantic Syntax offers a truly semantic approach to syntax, taking as its primary starting point the idea that syntax deals with the relations between meanings and that the same types of relations can be found cross-linguistically. In indicating these relations, *Universal Semantic Syntax* abstracts from phrase structure, and focuses on the syntactic relations between the meanings of linguistic signs. As such, it differs from Chomskyan generative approaches to syntax and also from some functional approaches to syntax, such as the 'Meaning-Text' model of Igor Mel'čuk, which separate syntax from semantics and are primarily concerned with how words are arranged within a sentence. The theory presented in this book does not reject formal approaches to syntax, such as generative grammar, but rather presents another and perhaps complementary view on syntax. *Universal Semantic Syntax* is informed by various functionalist approaches to syntax, and is in some respects similar to syntactic theories, such as Construction Grammar. What makes it unique is that it provides a comprehensive way of both analysing and formalizing linguistic constructions across languages. At present there are few, if any, sign-based (form-meaning) theories of syntax that offer tools enabling us to take *any* fragment of the grammar of *any* language and to describe, analyse and formalize that fragment. Without such tools it is difficult to show the importance of the semantic approach to syntax. Therefore, *Universal Semantic Syntax* provides a genuinely unique approach to syntactic theory.

This book consists of two parts. In Part I we will discuss the theory, the formalization of the theory and our own views and contributions to the theory. In Part II the theory will be further illustrated by providing semantic-syntactic analyses and descriptions of numerous examples in English (many of them taken from Jespersen's *Analytic Syntax* and from The British National Corpus[1]) and various other languages, European and non-European.

---

[1] http://corpus.byu.edu/bnc.

PART I   The Semiotactic Theory

1 Basic Theoretical Principles

Before discussing the more technical aspects of Semiotactics in this chapter, namely the way in which the model represents syntax, we will first outline its basic theoretical principles.

1.1 Form and Meaning

The communicative basis of language explains the existence of the phoneme and the linguistic sign. The most important principle in Semiotactics is the Saussurian principle that a **linguistic sign** consists of two inseparable components: a form component and a meaning component, which correlate. Although the basic principle is that one form correlates with one meaning (**one form – one meaning**), many forms correlate with several interrelated meanings (i.e. they are **polysemous**) or with different non-related meanings (i.e. they are **homonymous**). In the case of polysemy, an important contributory factor is metaphoric and metonymic meaning transfer. Metaphor is based on comparison and similarity from a particular perspective (see e.g. Bartsch 1998). To give an example, we can use the word *wolf* to refer to a person because he is an aggressive and dangerous male. In that case there is a similarity from the perspective of character and behaviour. Metonymy involves a relation of contiguity between two concepts, such as 'part-whole' (e.g. *redhead* to refer to the person), 'institution-locality' (e.g. *university* to refer to the building where the university is located), and so on. In many cases one form is associated with several interrelated meanings that do not have clear boundaries between them. This often makes it difficult to postulate general meanings that can be seen as necessary and sufficient conditions for the correct use of a particular form (see e.g. Fortuin 2000: 52–54). We will come back to the issue of polysemy and metaphor and metonymy at several points in this book, because it also has consequences for the semiotactic analysis.

Another principle within the theory of Semiotactics is that meanings can be described in terms of **distinctive** (or **inherent**) **features** and the combination of

6   *Basic Theoretical Principles*

these features sets a meaning apart from other similar (oppositional) meanings. We should note that within the psychological literature it has been pointed out that some categories display a prototype structure. In such cases the meaning of a form cannot be defined in terms of necessary and sufficient conditions for the correct use of the form. Instead, similarity to the prototype of a category is sufficient for classification into the category if and only if similarity to the neighbouring (oppositional) prototypes is lower (see e.g. Rosch 1973 for the prototypical category of *bird*). Semiotactics does not a priori deny the existence of prototypical categories or other radial categories as proposed in cognitive linguistics but tries to define meanings in terms of necessary and sufficient conditions as much as possible (see also Fortuin 2000: 9–54 for a discussion).

Unlike formal semantic approaches and partly similar to cognitive linguistic approaches to semantics, Semiotactics does not describe meaning in terms of truth conditions. This view is reflected in two important features of the theory. First, there is a distinction between what is part of the **meaning** of a form (and therefore an inherent part of every use of the form) and what is part of the **interpretation** of a form used in a specific discourse context. Since the semantic-syntactic analysis deals with meanings and not with interpretations, a sentence such as *two men are carrying three tables* is analysed as having one complex meaning, even though it can have different interpretations depending on how the sentence is understood in the given speech context in which it occurs (two men together carrying three tables, or each of the two men carrying three tables, etc.). Semiotactics thus distinguishes semantics from **pragmatics**, despite the fact that the boundaries between these areas of linguistics are sometimes difficult to identify, as pointed out by Cognitive Linguistics frameworks, for example. Semiotactics is, however, primarily a semantic-syntactic theory.

Second, scenes that refer to the same entities but are conceptualized or 'construed' differently in language have different meanings (cf. Croft and Cruse 2004 within a Cognitive Linguistics framework, who discuss the notion of construal). To give an example, the passive voice and active voice in English are two different constructions with two different meanings. If we compare the following matching active and passive sentences, it is clear that in both (a) and (b) we find Peter and the book, both involved in a reading situation, but the meaning is different because of the passive or active construal (which, as we will explain later, is related to how the valences of the plurivalent verbal meaning are organized):

a)   *Peter is reading the book.*
b)   *The book is being read by Peter.*

1.1 Form and Meaning   7

The difference and similarity between these sentences can also be explained with the notion of **appropriate** referents. This term is used for the set of things (including situations, properties, etc., as experienced (or experienceable) by humans) that possess all the features expressed by the meaning of a given linguistic form. To illustrate this with an example, each tree in the world can be seen as an appropriate referent of the word *tree* as long as the speakers of the language community agree on the inclusion of this object as a tree. In the same vein, each set of properties is an appropriate referent of *cosy* if they are the properties that we agree on as being cosy. This shows that language must be flexible enough to categorize different experiences into one intersubjectively shared meaning. At the same time, what makes language special is that we can classify one and the same experienced situation with different meanings. This was illustrated with the passive and active sentences given above, where the same experience (including Peter, a book and a reading situation) can be materialized differently in language. In this case we find two constructions containing the same meanings ('Peter', 'book' and 'read'), which each have the same appropriate referents but the way in which these meanings are combined in the construction differs. The existence of such different meanings does, however, already influence our experience of reality from the start. Furthermore, the existence of separate constructions with the verbs *rob* and *steal* means that every experience where something is taken away without the owner's permission will probably be experienced immediately as either a robbing situation or a stealing situation. This indicates that the two verbs (or constructions containing these verbs) are each associated with different appropriate referents.

The flexibility of language also becomes clear in the case of metaphor and metonymy. For example, we can refer to a large, furry cat as *bear*, since from a particular perspective (i.e. appearance, especially of the fur and the relative size) there is a similarity between a bear and the cat. Similarly, we can refer to a building as *university* (e.g. *the university was painted white*) because it houses the institution named *university*. In both cases the meaning remains the same, but there is a **derived referent** to which the word refers. With conventionalized metaphors this need not necessarily be the case, since the direct relation between the original meaning and its metaphorical use is less transparent or not transparent at all. To give an example, in the case of a *mouse* (used for the computer) we do not necessarily think about an actual mouse. In such cases it is better to treat 'animal mouse' and 'computer mouse' as two separate, unrelated meanings.

8   *Basic Theoretical Principles*

1.2   The Basis of Syntax: Entities and Syntactic Relations

A language is a system where all elements are interrelated, and a complex meaning equals the constellation of its constituent meanings. That is, a meaning of a complex form can be completely and adequately described in terms of the meanings of the constituent forms and their interrelations. Semiotactics thus has a **compositional** approach to meaning, even though, as we will show, linguistic constructions may sometimes also display more or less idiomatic (i.e. non-compositional) features (as described in Construction Grammar, e.g. Fillmore, Kay and O'Connor 1988), and constructions may have a meaning of their own that influences the meanings of the individual parts (as described in Goldberg 1995). In this respect, Semiotactics is very akin to Construction Grammar. In our analyses we will also point out such instances of non-compositionality.

Syntax studies the relations between meanings in an utterance. Since in Semiotactics syntactic relations are inherently semantic, they are called **semiotactic**. The terms 'syntactic' and 'semiotactic' will therefore be used interchangeably here. In looking at syntax, the theory of Semiotactics focuses on two aspects:

a)   the way in which an utterance expresses one or more entities
b)   the type of semiotactic relation between the meanings (the theory proposes a limited set of such semiotactic relations)

1.2.1   Entities

An important feature of Semiotactics is that the syntactic theory should represent how linguistic utterances express relations between different entities. An **entity** is something that in principle is perceptible (directly or indirectly) to the senses or can be independently thought. It is real or only imagined and exists as a particular and discrete unit, considered apart from its properties. Entities are always linked to linguistic utterances (forms and their meaning). As such, the term 'entity' is a purely linguistic term.

The concept of an entity can be illustrated with some examples. First, in the sentence *John is walking* we can identify one entity, 'John', whereas in the sentence *John is reading a book* we can identify two entities, 'John' and 'book'. Also compare the phrases *red car* and *John's car*. In both cases the meaning 'car' is modified, but in the case of *red car* we find only one entity ('car') and a **property** ('red') of this entity, whereas in the case of *John's car* there are two entities – 'John' and 'car' – and one entity ('John') modifies the other ('car'). Even though the event associated with an entity (e.g. in *John is*

1.2 The Basis of Syntax: Entities and Syntactic Relations   9

walking) is not in itself an entity, there are cases where events can indeed be perceived as entities. Examples are the infinitive situations occurring as 'primaries' quoted by Jespersen, where an event is conceptualized as a 'thing' or rather as a 'situation', e.g. *to see is to believe*. Thus the term 'entity' is used with regard to both things and situations.

In Semiotactics the terms **convergence** and **divergence** are used to express whether meanings point to the same entity or not: if two meanings point to one entity they are called convergent (e.g. *red flower*), whereas if they do not point to the same entity they are called divergent (e.g. *John's car*); the flower is red but the car is not John. Another example is the phrase *very high trees*. In this phrase 'very' is divergent with respect to 'trees' because it does not modify 'trees', but rather modifies 'high'. In this case the **semantic immediate constituent** (for which we will use the common abbreviation IC) 'very high' taken together is convergent with 'trees'. This implies that if a language user communicates the idea of a very high tree, the resulting complex linguistic utterance *very high tree* consists of two semantic 'pieces': (i) 'tree', (ii) 'very high', the latter of which can be split again into two pieces (i) 'very' and (ii) 'high'.

1.2.2   Syntactic Relations

We now move on to the issue of the relations between meanings. Having a language enables us to conceptually split things that are not split in the world as we perceive it. To give an example, instead of having one word for the entity 'red flower', language enables us to conceptualize the entity 'flower' and its quality 'red' separately: *red flower*. In order to understand the phrase *red flower* we must know what the semantic-syntactic relation is between 'red' and 'flower'. In this case we understand that 'red' expresses a feature of the entity 'flower'. In terms of sets, if we think of the set of all possible flowers, we limit this set by selecting the subset of flowers that have the feature 'red'. This differs from the relation between 'flower' and 'one' in the phrase *one flower*. In this case 'one' does not express a feature of 'flower' but rather quantifies the number of 'flower'. We find an altogether different relation in *the flower is red*: a subject-predicate construction with a temporal dimension that is absent in *red flower*. In this construction 'red' does not modify 'flower' directly, but indirectly.

The theory of Semiotactics proposes that there is a limited set of syntactic, or rather semiotactic relations between meanings (an overview is given in this chapter and a list of the symbols in Appendix A). Note that many of these relations are identified in traditional grammars as well, and are also described

10   *Basic Theoretical Principles*

in detail by other linguists, such as Otto Jespersen (1965[1924], 1984[1937]). Furthermore, as we will also show in this book, these relations are universal in the sense that they occur in various (non-related) languages in the world. This probably follows from several factors: the communicative basis of language (what people want to communicate across cultures); the principle of 'least effort' (Zipf 1949), which explains, for example, why in English we have adjectives and nouns, i.e. a relation of modification (as explained above for *red flower*); and our cognitive make-up. Examples of such universal relations are several relations of modification (such as limitation, gradation, compounding) and the subject-predicate relation (nexus).

It should be noted that in the syntactic representation of a particular construction not only the relations between the meanings of words are represented, but also the relations between all the **semantic particles** expressed in the construction. A semantic particle is the smallest meaning element that is expressed by form. To give an example, in the phrase *red flowers*, we find TWO words but THREE semantic particles: 'red', 'flower' and 'plural'. The semiotactic representation must not only indicate the relation between the meanings 'red' and 'flower', but also between 'plural' and 'flower'.

One could also take a difference stance towards syntax and assert that syntactic structure is almost entirely language-specific (e.g. Croft 2001) and that it is not possible to postulate universal syntactic relations. In the same vein, one could also argue that each construction has its own semantic-syntactic relations and that it is not possible to use the same semiotactic relation for syntactic relations in different types of constructions. However, Semiotactics tries to abstract from differences between various languages and constructions as much as possible and to give a representation with universal semiotactic relations that is informative but not overinformative. To illustrate this with an example, the relation between 'red' and 'cat' in *red cat* and the relation between 'cat' and 'in the tree' in *cat in the tree* are both analysed in terms of a relation of limitation (modification), even though in the first example we find a combination of an adjective and a noun, and in the second we find a combination of a noun and a prepositional phrase. Semantically, however, in both instances 'cat' is limited (modified).

At this point we must admit that this approach may entail that some instances of particular syntactic relations are more prototypical or easily identified than others. To give an example, a typical and univocal instance of the relation of stratification can be found in the case of quantitative expressions with numerals (e.g. *two men*), where the meaning expressed by the noun is stratified by the meaning expressed by the numeral. However, the same stratification relation is used to represent the relation between the situation as a whole (expressing the proposition expressed by the construction) and semantic particles that further specify this entire situation, such as 'present' or 'past' (as will be further discussed in Section 3.3). In such cases the relation of stratification is also present but less self-evident, and therefore needs more explanation. In the end, we argue that the universal syntactic relations we propose must be seen both as abstractions from similar syntactic relations in various constructions across languages and as theoretical constructs, which do not necessarily have a *psychologically real* status.

We would also like to make an observation about the universality of meanings expressed by semantic particles, such as 'definite', 'singular', 'exclamative', 'emphasis' and so forth. These meanings are used as convenient labels for linguists to talk about comparable phenomena across languages and across constructions. As such, they abstract away from differences in meaning that may exist between form-meaning elements in different languages (or even within one language). Put differently, it may very well be that a meaning like 'definite' as expressed by the English definite article *the* is different from the meaning of a form expressing definiteness in another language. In this sense, the theory of meaning that we propose can be seen as essentially structuralist, since it acknowledges that meanings must always be studied within the larger structure of oppositional meanings in which they occur. If we consider it necessary for the syntactic analysis, we will discuss these meanings in this book, but in other instances we will not provide semantic analyses of the meanings used in our metalanguage, for example in the case of semantic particles that indicate e.g. definite ('DEF') or exclamative ('EXCL') meanings. This is because our focus is primarily on the syntactic relations between meanings, and not on the semantic contribution of the individual meanings as such.

1.3 Language Structure and Syntactic Representation

Like other theories of language, Semiotactics provides a specific **formalization** for the meanings of language utterances. The formal language of Semiotactics is an artificial metalanguage, which shows the syntactic relations between meanings and the way constructions express different entities. As a general rule, the syntactic relations between meanings are indicated by various symbols on a horizontal line, whereas the different entities (including different valences) that are associated with the utterance are presented in vertical columns. The advantage of using these semiotactic representations is that it

12   *Basic Theoretical Principles*

allows us to show how languages use different formal structures for expressing specific meanings; furthermore, the formalization is constructed in such a way that the semantic-syntactic relations must be defined distinctly and unambiguously, which also makes it possible to test them more univocally, and if necessary reject them as invalid.

Each semiotactic notation determines a set of appropriate referents, and each relation symbol designates an instruction of operation. The execution of such instructions, i.e. the reading of the notations, often has to proceed in a specific order. For example, if the meaning of *white flower* comprises the representation 'flower – white', there are two instructions implied in the semantic particles, i.e. 'find the set of appropriate referents of 'flower'' and 'find the set of appropriate referents of 'white'', and there is a further instruction in the relation symbol '–': 'select from the set of appropriate referents of 'flower' those members that are also members of the set of appropriate referents of 'white''. In some cases, two constructions have the same appropriate referents but differ in **assemblage**. We use the term 'assemblage' for the semantic constituents and their semiotactic relations, including the semantic IC structure of the construction. As an example of a meaning with the same appropriate referents but a different assemblage, we already mentioned the difference in meaning between active-passive pairs, such as: *the man is reading the book* v. *the book is being read by the man*. They are considered to have different meanings, even though the positions in the patterns are occupied by such elements that the interpretations coincide. The different positions of the elements in the patterns are indicated in the notations, resulting in different representations for these two example sentences, thus illustrating the two different meanings.

1.4   Meaningful Elements

The syntactic representation only deals with elements insofar as they contribute to meaning and do not represent mere form categories. To give an example, whether a language has an SVO or an SOV word order is not reflected in the syntactic representation, because for this representation it is only relevant to indicate what the subject is, and not how this is materialized formally in language. Similarly, the syntactic representation does not reflect whether a meaning is expressed by a separate word or by another morpheme, such as a suffix. Of course, one could provide cognitive or functional explanations as to why the subject occurs in the first position before the verb, but such explanations cannot be seen as syntactic rules, but rather as (synchronic or diachronic) reasons for linguistic patterns or regularities. As a result, the syntactic representation does not always provide a one-to-one representation of the form-meaning elements in the sentence and the order in which they occur. However, as we will show in other sections, word order – along with punctuation marks and intonation – is a form element that should be taken into account when analysing the meaning.

2 Semiotactic Relations and Symbols

In the following sections the formalization and the relation symbols used in the notations will be explained and illustrated with examples to demonstrate how the semiotactic representations are compiled and how they could be interpreted. The goal of the semiotactic formalization is to provide a formula for each construction. A **construction** consists of a number of semantic particles related to each other by semiotactic relations that can be formalized by using symbols. In the formalizations we will mainly use English as a metalanguage to refer to the meanings (semantic particles) of the construction, but in some instances we will also use the 'target language' as the metalanguage (e.g. French, Dutch, German, Russian and Japanese). It should be noted that in most cases we do not provide definitions of the meanings or discuss whether the meanings are polysemous or not.

Semantic particles (i.e. non-complex meanings) need not correlate only with words but may also correlate with (part of) the meaning expressed by a **morpheme**. To give an example, the English plural form -*s* is part of a word but has its own contribution to the meaning, which must be semiotactically represented so that a distinction can be made between, for example, *the dog* and *the dogs*. Another example is the English semantic particle 'un', expressed by the morpheme *un-* as in *unkind,* which does indeed contribute an added meaning to the word *kind*, i.e. a contrasting meaning. Of course, there are also many languages where a meaning that is expressed by a morpheme in English is expressed by a word, or vice versa. For the semiotactic representation it is irrelevant how a semantic particle is expressed (i.e. by a word or a morpheme), therefore this is not indicated in the formalization. At the same time, morphemes (or words) that do not contribute to meaning but have only a purely grammatical function are not semiotactically represented. An example is the English verb inflection -*s*, as in *he walks,* which does not indicate a difference in the meaning of 'walk' as compared with *I walk*, even though it only occurs in the case of a third person singular. For each element of an utterance the decision must be made as to whether and, if so, how it should be represented in the semiotactic notation. As the arguments presented in the following sections will show, such decisions are not always straightforward or easy to make, and in some cases more than one representation is possible, depending on how the construction is analysed.

2.1 Limitation Relation

Limitation is a relation between two meanings and is found when one word or word group modifies (qualifies) another in such a way that a subset is indicated. The relation of **limitation** may be convergent, divergent or temporal.

2.1.1 Convergent Limitation

(1) *old man*

 '*man – old*'

In the notation 'man – old', the use of the relation symbol '–' points to the fact that the set of appropriate referents of *old man* is a **subset** of those of *man*. The property expressed by 'old' modifies the entity expressed by 'man' by limiting or further specifying it. Additionally, it demonstrates convergence because there is only one entity. The **orientation** indicates that the representation is constructed from left to right: the headword 'man' is put first in the representation, then further specified (limited, modified) by 'old'. Note that 'old' is a relative feature, which presupposes a norm that is provided by its carrier ('old with respect to men'). However, the same notation is used in the case of adjectives that do not presuppose a norm of this kind, such as 'English' in *English breakfast*: 'breakfast – English'.

This order in the representation is maintained in the case of constructions with more than one adjective, as in the following example:

(2) *big young dog*

 '*dog – young – big*'

This should be read as ((dog – young) – big)), with the semantic immediate constituents indicated within brackets. This limitation relation '–' can therefore be seen as **progressive**, i.e. in the formula the splitting into ICs is done from left to right: 'x – y – z' is first split into the ICs 'x – y' and 'z', and secondly 'x – y' is split into 'x' and 'y'.

A question that arises in the case of the limitation relation as expressed by adjective-noun combinations, for example, is whether account must be taken of various **metonymic** relationships. To give an example, a phrase like *red pen*

16   *Semiotactic Relations and Symbols*

can be used for a pen that is red itself, but also for a pen that contains red ink (for a discussion, see Honselaar and Keizer 2011: 75). In the same vein, *red day* can be used to refer to a red object that is associated with a particular day (as in e.g. *I have red days and black days; today is a red day so I will wear a red dress*). In our view, it is difficult to account for such metonymic relationships in the syntactic representation. This is because the syntactic relation between what is expressed by the adjective and what is expressed by the noun is inherently flexible, and in all cases the basic meaning of the forms (noun, adjective) remains the same. However, Ebeling (2006: 130) discusses an example for which he proposes separate notations, i.e. *een oude vriend* 'an old friend', which may express four different meanings, namely 'a friend who is old', 'someone who has been a friend for a long time', 'an ex-friend' and 'a friend like friends used to be'. Ebeling proposes that the first meaning should be represented with the regular convergent limitation relation: 'friend – old', but that the other three meanings should be represented as 'friend > old'. According to Ebeling, the latter notation expresses 'someone in whom the feature 'friend' is old'. However, such a distinction in meaning cannot be made on the basis of the form (adjective + noun) but only on the basis of context, prior knowledge or interpretation, which are not taken into account in the semiotactic analyses we propose. To illustrate this with another example, in the case of a *hot day* one can argue that it is not the day itself that is hot, but rather *hot* refers to the temperature experienced during that day. We would argue, however, that it is a matter of interpretation how 'day' is perceived by a particular speaker, who may use this word to refer to a time stretch, a temperature, a mood or feeling ('black day', 'good day') or the way time is spent. The meaning of 'hot' and the meaning of 'day' are both inherently flexible and this is evident when the two meanings are combined. In all cases the same representation is given, i.e. with a limitation relation.

Another issue that we would like to raise here is that adjective modifiers can sometimes have both a **restrictive** and an **appositive** reading, as remarked by Hawkins (1978: 282). He quotes the example sentence *the rich Danes are well-educated*, which can either be used to indicate that all Danes are well-educated and rich (appositive reading), or to indicate that the property of being well-educated pertains only to the subset of rich Danes (restrictive reading). This difference can also be found if we analyse just the adjective-noun combination *the rich Danes*, which can be interpreted as referring to all Danes, who are all rich, or only to the Danes who are rich. The syntactic relation of limitation does not differentiate between these readings, since in both constructions a subset of Danes is selected, which in the case of the appositive reading is identical to the whole set; nevertheless, even in this case the use of the adjective is not superfluous, since it presents extra information for the hearer. As such, in the (intersubjective) communicative act the **potential referents** of Danes also include (imaginary) non-rich Danes. This means that the difference between 'apposition' and 'restriction' is here an interpretative phenomenon, which is not accounted for in the semiotactic representation, where the relation of limitation ('–') is used in both cases. Ebeling (2006: 303), who also proposes just one notation (with convergent limitation) for the example *the rich Danes are well-educated*, quotes a similar example that has only an appositive reading, i.e. *the Danes, rich, are well-educated*, which would be given a different representation, namely with the symbol '⊢' for apposition.[1] In this case a different representation (formalization) is necessary because of the difference in syntactic structure.

Although limitation is typical of adjective-noun relations, it also occurs in other contexts, for example with prepositional phrases (see Section 4.1) or with **definite or indefinite articles**, as in example (3) below, where *dog* is modified by the definite article *the*, which provides a further specification of 'dog' and is also a convergent limitation relation:

(3)   *the big dog*

        '*dog – big –* THE'

In his earlier work (1978: 165), Ebeling proposed the notation 'THE' to represent the **definite article**, and 'NONTHE' to represent the **indefinite article**. In his later book (2006: 111), he chose the notation 'DEF' for the Dutch definite articles *de* and *het*, and 'INDEF' for the indefinite article *een*. Furthermore, Ebeling (2006: 141) uses the same notation for occurrences of nouns without a definite or indefinite article, for example in the plural, where the (singular) indefinite article cannot be used, e.g. *drie vissen* ('three fish'): 'vis / 3 – INDEF' (*v. de drie vissen*: 'vis / 3 – DEF').

However, we see a problem with this latter notation; namely it is not consistent with the principle 'one form – one meaning' to use the same notation both for elements that are linguistically expressed (in this case the articles) and for the absence of such form elements. Moreover, in this way we cannot account for specific meanings of the articles, as it is only indicated that they signal definiteness or indefiniteness. In the literature, various meanings are attributed to these articles. For example, Shopen (1985: 285) writes that the

---

[1] See Chapter 9 on appositions, and relative clauses in Section 4.6.

18   Semiotactic Relations and Symbols

indefinite article in English can mark both referential and non-referential indefinite noun phrases. He quotes the sentence: *I'm looking for a snake*, which is ambiguous because it can have both the referential indefinite meaning ('specific') as in (a) below, where a certain snake with particular features is meant, and the non-referential meaning as in (b):

(a)   *I'm looking for a snake. It is 4 feet long and has red stripes.*
(b)   *I'm looking for a snake; any one will do.*

Furthermore, many languages have other structures to express definiteness and indefiniteness (as will be discussed in Section 16.5), i.e. constructions that do not necessarily indicate the same meaning as the definite and indefinite articles in the European languages. Therefore, we argue that separate notations are required for constructions with and constructions without definite or indefinite articles. We propose to use the notations 'THE' and 'NONTHE' for definite and indefinite articles respectively, and 'DEF' and 'INDEF' for other constructions that are taken to indicate definiteness and indefiniteness. Although we acknowledge that not all the (definite or indefinite) articles of different languages are used in the same way or express the same meaning,[2] and likewise not all constructions expressing definiteness or indefiniteness in other languages indicate the same meaning, we have concluded that in the scope of this present study it is not appropriate to further describe such individual meanings.

2.1.2   Divergent Limitation

In some cases we find a construction consisting of two words (or phrases) where the entity expressed by one word limits (modifies, qualifies) the entity expressed by the other. We then speak of divergent limitation, because there are two separate entities. In English this is the case in various possessive or possessive-like constructions, such as *my book* or *John's bicycle*. Divergent limitation is represented by means of the down arrow symbol, in combination with the symbol for limitation. Note that in the semiotactic notations only proper names and the English first person singular pronoun *I* are written with a capital letter.

(4)   *my book*

$$'book \downarrow \atop - I'$$

---

[2] For example, the Dutch equivalent for the English sentence *I play the piano* does not use a definite article: *Ik speel piano.*

2.1 Limitation Relation   19

(5)   *John's bicycle*

'*bicycle* ↓
         − John'

These representations show that in (4) a subset of books is created, i.e. books that are mine, and in (5) we find the subset of bicycles that belong to John. It should be emphasized here that in our representation for these English constructions we equate the relation that is linguistically expressed by a possessive pronoun or by the genitive'*s* with the relation of divergent limitation (or to put it differently, the meaning of the possessive construction is absorbed by the relation of divergent limitation). This means that we have chosen *not* to indicate the possessive meaning separately in the syntactic representation (*pace* Ebeling 2005, who represents these forms with the semantic bivalent particle 'x HAS y').[3] This is because we take the view that the semantic contribution of the second (pro)noun is specifically to modify (limit) the meaning of the first. Furthermore, the resulting combination may refer to an actual possessive relation, but not necessarily so. A phrase like *my book* may refer to the book owned by me, but also to the book written by me/about me, or to the book suitable for me, as in: *not really my book*.[4] Another use of the divergent limitation relation is for relative clauses, as analysed in Sections 4.6 and 16.2.

2.1.3   *Temporal Limitation*

A distinction must be made between temporal and non-temporal limitation. If we compare (6) and (7) we find that in both constructions the set of potential referents of *granddad* is limited, but in a different way: in the first example the granddad is opposed to other granddads that are not young, which is given the notation for convergent limitation; however, in (7), which has the meaning 'granddad when he was young', granddad is opposed to himself during other periods of his life. This relationship is called temporal limitation, which is represented with the symbol '~'. In English this temporal dimension is present only in constructions where the adjective occurs after the noun, implying a predicative reading.

---

[3] Ebeling (1978: 432) does not make a distinction in the syntactic representation between the genitive 's and the construction with *of* in English. However, we follow Ebeling (2006: 268) in making explicit the difference between these two constructions. Thus, 'the book of John' is given a different representation than 'John's book'. See also Section 13.5.

[4] According to Jespersen (1984: 108), the genitive does not only indicate possession; it merely denotes close relationship, but that relationship naturally varies according to the two (persons or things) that are connected by means of the genitive.

20   *Semiotactic Relations and Symbols*

(6)   *young granddad*

         '*granddad – young*'

(7)   (*this was*) *granddad young*

         '*granddad ~ young*'

2.2   Compounding Relation

The term **compounding** is used for the relation between two elements in a compound. This relation is represented with the symbol '∪'.[5] A compound consists of two words joined together, thus becoming one longer word. In general, there is assumed to be a word boundary between two elements if a third element can be inserted between them; if this is not the case, the unit is analysed as a compound. Compounds can be seen as borderline cases between syntax and morphology, because even though a compound functions as a single word, it can still be analysed as consisting of more than one form-meaning element. Not only are these form-meaning elements connected by the syntactic relation of compounding, it is also possible to establish whether the compound presupposes one or more entities.

A relation with a limitative (modifying) effect often occurs in two kinds of forms, i.e. as a full construction (e.g. the limitation relation described above) or as an incorporation. In a fully fledged construction every meaning is separately interpreted, whereas compounds are interpreted as units, so that there is a semantic difference between *tea from Ceylon* and *Ceylon tea*. While this difference is sometimes hardly noticeable, it is nevertheless maintained in the notation, to comply with the principle 'one form – one meaning'.

In a compound, the set of appropriate referents of the whole construction is commonly a subset of those of the headword in the compound. To illustrate this: *a blackbird* refers to a type of bird. A compound shares features with a regular adjective-noun construction with two words, such as *a black bird*. However, compared with the construction with two separate words, the modifying possibilities for the elements in a compound are much more limited. To give an example, if we compare *a blackbird* and *a black bird*, further specification, for instance with *very*, is possible for the adjective-noun construction (*a very black bird*) but not for the compound (**a very blackbird*). This is because in the compound *black* does not function as a separate word. Also note

---

[5] Ebeling refers to this relation with the terms close-knitting (1978) or incorporation (2006).

that even though *a blackbird* refers to a type of bird that is usually black, this is not necessarily the case (as in *that blackbird is actually white!*). Moreover, in spoken English the first element 'black' of the compound *blackbird* is stressed (BLACKbird), whereas in the adjective-noun construction *black bird* the word stress is on the second element 'bird' (black BIRD), implying that only the compound is conceptualized as one word.

2.2.1 Convergent Compounding

If the two elements of a compound are convergent, i.e. they point to the same entity, their relation is called convergent compounding. In the representation the second word is placed first, because in the semantic arrangement of a two-piece compound in English the second member dominates (or put in different terminology, the second member functions as the head), cf.:

(8)   *a blackbird*

        $'bird \cup black - \text{NONTHE}'$

(9)   *a black bird*

        $'bird - black - \text{NONTHE}'$

Also compare the following Dutch examples, which are different in form and meaning; the first example is a compound with the meaning of a non-alcoholic kind of drink (e.g. Coca-Cola), and the second phrase (11), consisting of an adjective and a noun, expresses a (non-specified kind of) drink with the property that it is refreshing:

(10)   *een frisdrank*
        'a soft drink'

        $'drank \cup fris - \text{NONTHE}'$

(11)   *een frisse drank*
        'a refreshing drink'

        $'drank - fris - \text{NONTHE}'$

This difference in meaning between the two phrases is evident, since not all *frisse dranken* ('refreshing drinks') are *frisdranken* ('soft drinks'), and *frisdrank* has more distinctive features than *frisse drank*.[6] However, the same

---

[6] See also Ebeling (2006: 56).

22 *Semiotactic Relations and Symbols*

argument does not always apply to such compounds; e.g. a specimen of *witvis* (a collective noun for a category of fish) is not by definition white and a *blackbird* is not always black. The question of whether such compounds should be regarded as expressions with an opaque structure (and hence as idiomatic expressions) or not will be discussed in Chapter 5.

2.2.2 *Divergent Compounding*

There are also compounds where the constituent parts are two entities that are divergent with respect to each other, e.g. (12) with the meaning 'a chair on/ with wheels' and (13) a silversmith, who is not 'silver' but is rather a person who makes silver articles. The same representation can be used for *a blacksmith* (a person who works with black metals).

(12)　　*a wheelchair*

　　　　'*chair* ↓ − NONTHE
　　　　　∪ *wheel*'

(13)　　*a silversmith*

　　　　'*smith* ↓ − NONTHE
　　　　　∪ *silver*'

In our analysis of compounds, we provide the syntactic relations between the component parts of the compound, but these relations may well not exist for some speakers of the language, if the compounds are stored as single units in the speaker's brain.

2.3　　**Equipollent Relation**

Following Jespersen (1984: 11), we use the term **equipollent** relation for constructions consisting of two parts where one word does not dominate the other. They are represented in the notations in their original word order, with the symbol '•' between them, e.g.:

(14)　　*Samuel Johnson*

　　　　'*Samuel • Johnson*'

These constructions have the character of a compound because no linguistic material can be inserted between the words, but in contrast to compounds there is no 'modifier-head' relation between the two nouns, since they have equal syntactic rank, i.e. they are equipollent. This relation will be further discussed in Section 13.1.

2.4   Stratification Relation

Stratification is the name for the relation that exists between elements on the basis of their set level (i.e. the level of the set as a whole). Unlike other modifications that connect entities and properties, in the case of **stratification** an entire set is specified. What is to the left of the symbol for stratification '/' can best be characterized as the distinctive features of the elements in a set, and on the right of this symbol are further specifications of this set. Consider the following example and formalization:

(15)   *the two young dogs*

   '*dog – young* / 2 – THE'

The relation of stratification is also a progressive relation, which means that the semiotactic representation should be read from left to right: (((dog – young) / 2) – THE). Note that in this example it would not be correct to describe the relation between 'young dogs' and 'two' with a limitation relation because 'two' cannot be seen as a property of 'young dogs'. Instead, 'two' indicates the number of the set 'young dog'. In *the two young dogs* 'young' is a feature of 'dog', whereas '2' and 'THE' are features of the whole set 'young dog'. Since 'THE' provides information about the set of dogs as a whole, and not about individual members of this set, this information is given at the very end of the formula, and not before the meaning '2' (*'dog – young – THE / 2'). When the set number is **zero**, as in *no young dogs*, the relation is represented as: 'dog – young / PL – NO'.

   This order of the formula takes account of the way the construction is arranged from a semantic point of view. With respect to number, in English this is also visible in the form of the construction, since number is marked on the noun, whereas definiteness is expressed by a separate form. However, this feature is not taken into account in the representation of the construction. To illustrate this, we can refer to *high trees* when we provide the formula 'tree – high / PL', even though the noun expressing 'tree' is marked for number. If we were to follow the actual form of the construction, this would result in the notation 'tree / PL – high'. This representation is incorrect, however, since each individual instance of the set of trees is high and the feature 'high' does not pertain to the set of trees as a whole. One could also make a distinction between two different meanings for *the heavy boxes*, i.e. all boxes are heavy,

24   *Semiotactic Relations and Symbols*

which could be given the notation 'box – heavy / PL – THE', or the boxes taken together are heavy, which would be represented as 'box / PL – heavy – THE'. However, we argue that such a distinction is a matter of interpretation, which will not be taken into account here.

The same relation of stratification is found in other constructions and meanings, i.e. connecting the tense of the situation (which will be explained in Section 3.3), and for **singular** and **plural** markings, which are represented as '/ SING' and '/ PL', e.g.:

(16)   *the big dog*

'*dog – big* / SING – THE'

(17)   *the big dogs*

'*dog – big* / PL – THE'

In this case the plural marking is indicated because it is a meaningful element: there is an opposition between *the dog* and *the dogs*. This differs from *two young dogs* in (15), where the plural 'PL' is not placed in the notation because *two* already indicates more than one and 'two young dogs' is not opposed to 'two young dog'.

The analysis of a word being 'singular' or 'plural' is not always straightforward, especially in English, which has numerous uncountable nouns, such as water, rice, money, music, news, etc. These words are usually treated as singular and used with a verb in the singular form, e.g. *the water is hot* or *this is good news*, but they do not have a specifically singular or plural meaning. There are also nouns that may occur as countable nouns or as uncountable nouns (albeit with different meanings), such as *time* (*how many times* v. *we had a great time*), *room* (*this house has four rooms* v. *there is enough room for all of us*) and *light* (*there are two lights in the hallway* v. *there is not enough light to read*). Furthermore, the division between the two categories of nouns is not always clear-cut. For example, *water* is classified as an uncountable noun because it cannot be directly connected to a numeral and needs a quantity word for counting, i.e. *two glasses of water* instead of *two waters*; the same analysis is assumed to apply for *coffee*: *two cups of coffee*. However, in a restaurant it is not uncommon to hear someone ordering: '*four coffees, one mineral water, please*' (see also Section 13.6, example (159)). Other languages may have different structures or ways to distinguish between singular or plural (or make no distinction at all, as e.g. Japanese).

In this present study we have decided to leave aside the matter of countable and uncountable nouns and to concentrate on analysing many other constructions and showing the interrelated meanings of these constructions in the semiotactic representations. We therefore propose to use only the notation 'PL' when the plural meaning is indicated in the form and not to use 'SING' at all, with the understanding that unless a numeral or 'PL' is represented, the word can be taken to be non-plural (without differentiating whether this non-plural does or does not have a singular meaning), cf. the following examples:

(18)   *nice weather*

         '*weather* − *nice*'

(19)   *the old* **man**

         '*man* − *old* − THE'

(20)   *the old* **men**

         '*man* − *old* / PL − THE'

2.5   Gradation Relation

A gradation relation does not link a property to an entity but rather a property to the property of an entity, and it links only these two elements. The **gradation** relation is represented by the symbol '>' and can be illustrated with the following example:

(21)   *very big dog*

         '*dog* − *big* > *very*'

In this phrase we find a limitation relation between 'big' and 'dog', and a gradation relation between 'big' and 'very'. The representation for (21) indicates: 'a dog in which the feature big is present to a high degree', hence the term gradation. In this construction 'dog' and 'very' are not convergent, but 'big > very' as a whole is convergent with 'dog'. As such, it is the abstraction of 'big' (bigness) that is modified. Although the sentence parts that are connected with this relation are placed on the same line, the property connected with '>' is only convergent with the modifier, not with the entity itself. This representation should be read as (dog − (big > very)). The gradation relation '>' is **regressive**, which means that in the formula the splitting into ICs is done from right to left: 'x − y > z' is first split into the ICs 'y > z' and 'x', and secondly 'y > z' is split into 'y' and 'z'.

In the next example the relation between the meanings of the **adverb** *terribly* and the adjective *cold* is gradation, because 'terribly' pertains to the coldness,

26   Semiotactic Relations and Symbols

which is not the carrier, but a property of the entity 'weather'. (Note that in the semiotactic notations adverbs are represented by their basic (adjective) form).

(22)   *terribly cold weather*

$'weather - cold > terrible'$

A more complicated example is:

(23)   *not particularly well constructed plot*

$'plot - constructed > good > particular > $ NON$'$

The IC structure (splitting from right to left) is: (*plot* – (*constructed* > (*good* > (*particular* > NON)))). The semantic core of this construction is expressed by *plot*, which is modified by *not particularly well constructed*. Within this constituent *not particularly well* modifies *constructed*. As such, the meanings 'well', 'particularly' and 'not' do not modify 'plot', but rather modify 'constructed', which is a property of 'plot' (i.e. they are instances of gradation), whereas 'constructed' modifies plot directly (i.e. it is an instance of limitation). (For negation, see Chapter 7.)

The gradation relation is also used to connect adverbs and adjuncts that further specify an action or event, such as location (e.g. *he walked here* or *the cat sat in the tree*), time (e.g. *yesterday, now*) and negation, and to connect conjunctions (e.g. *when, if*). In short, we use gradation for all instances of modification or specification that do not involve modification in terms of creating a subset. A special use of the gradation relation is with coordinatives (*and, or*), as will be discussed in Section 4.3.

2.5.1   Reversed Gradation
Gradation is indicated by 'x > y' (where x is gradated by y). In some cases we will use the reverse order and write 'x < y' (where y is gradated by x). This symbol for reversed gradation is used for connecting elements that express coordination (see Section 4.3). Furthermore, it can be used to show changes in word order (see Chapter 17).

2.5.2   Temporal Gradation
For constructions such as *I like my tea cold* or *I like my fries salty* the notation for temporal gradation with the symbol '⊃' is used. In this construction an object is *liked* with the proviso that this is only the case if the object has a particular property (being cold or salty). This means that the

object of the action (and hence the action itself) has a conditional-temporal character: 'I like my tea *as long as/only if/when* it (the tea) is cold', i.e. the act of liking (drinking) tea applies only to tea when it is cold. The notation 'x ⊃ y' indicates that something ('x') is temporarily present (namely if 'y' applies).

(24) *I like my tea cold.*

$$'...[like_2] \; ; \; tea \supset cold...'^{7}$$

Note that temporal gradation differs from temporal limitation as in (*this was*) *granddad young* 'granddad ~ young' (see (7), Section 2.1.3), where 'granddad' is only presented at a time when he was young, implying that 'young' is a temporal property of the entity 'granddad'. In the case of temporal gradation, however, it is not the entity itself that is temporally modified (limited).

Another example of a construction with the relation of temporal gradation is the following Dutch sentence:

(25) *Hij is dronken gevaarlijk.*
      (lit. he is drunk dangerous)
      'He is dangerous when he is drunk.'

$$'...hij = gevaarlijk \supset dronken...'$$

The symbol for temporal gradation is also used for the semantics of the progressive form in English, as will be explained in Section 14.4.

---

[7] Three dots at the beginning and end of the representation indicate that the representation is incomplete, i.e. that not all the elements of the sentence that carry meaning are represented.

3 Nexus: Subject-Predicate Relation

The term **nexus** was introduced by Jespersen (1965 [1924]).[1] In the semiotactic representations the nexus relation, i.e. the relation between what is traditionally called 'subject' and 'predicate', is symbolized by '='. Ebeling (2006: 152) proposes that the terms subject and predicate should be avoided, and instead the terms **first nexus member** and **second nexus member** should be used. This symbol '=' indicates convergence between two elements. For example, in the case of *John is walking* there is a subject/first nexus member ('John') with the property (predicate/second nexus member) that he is walking. In the same vein, in the case of *the dress is black* we find a subject ('the dress'), which has the property 'black'. In addition to indicating convergence, '=' also expresses that the two convergent elements together yield a whole that is divergent with respect to each of the elements separately. Put differently, in the nexus relation 'x' and 'y' are convergent, but neither of them is convergent with 'x = y' as a whole. This is because the referent of 'x = y' is a situation (an event, a state of affairs) of which the convergence of 'x' and 'y' is a distinctive feature. This is what makes a construction such as *black dress* different from the corresponding nexus construction *the dress is black*. The latter construction not only attributes a property to an entity, but also has a more analytical structure, which has a temporal dimension.

The symbol 'Σ' is placed directly above the nexus symbol '=', indicating domination[2] over the nexus, and it represents the situation that is expressed by

---

[1] Jespersen (1965: 115–116) stated that the difference between a nexus and a junction (e.g. *the dog barks* v. *a barking dog*) is that in a junction the headword (primary word) and the modifier (secondary element) together form *one* denomination (a unit or single idea), whereas a nexus always contains two ideas that must necessarily remain separate: the secondary term adds something new to what has already been named.

[2] In addition to using the term 'domination' in the case of 'Σ', we also use this term to indicate that one valence dominates the other. As we will show, in the case of valences of verbs it is always the first valence ('subject', 'first nexus member') that dominates the other valences, whereas in the case of other valences, such as valences of prepositions, it is the entity (valence) that is the orientation point for the relation between the two entities (valences) that dominates the other (see Section 4.1).

the whole sentence, i.e. a piece of the world with a temporal dimension. This sigma symbol does not contribute any semantic content of its own, but is used as a frame to which are attached the semantic elements that apply to the situation as a whole, and cannot be said to apply to one of the individual semantic elements of the situation itself.[3] Examples are meanings that refer to the situation as a whole, such as meanings that concern the speech act, like tense or mood (which will be discussed in Section 3.3). Thus, a simple nexus (subject-predicate) model is represented as follows, where 'x' is the first nexus member, and 'y' the second nexus member:

$$'\Sigma \atop x = y'$$

There are also sentences that do not have a regular 'subject-predicate' nexus structure, which are semiotactically represented with the sigma 'Σ' for 'situation' but without the nexus symbol '=' (see examples in Section 3.2 and English gerund constructions in Section 14.3).

In addition, it should be noted that the nexus relation is also used for some constructions that do not have a temporal dimension of this kind. This is the case, for example, in the phrase *wide-brimmed hat*, where the referent of the nexus complex 'x = y' ('brim = wide') is a non-temporal entity. In the representation for such constructions, instead of 'Σ' the symbol 'X' is placed above the nexus symbol '=' (see Chapter 6 and Section 13.7).

3.1 Nexus Relation and the Verb 'Be'

In many instances the second nexus member is expressed by a verbal form, as in the case of a simple sentence like *the dog barks*, which is represented as follows:[4]

(26)   *The dog barks.*

$$'\Sigma \,/\, PR \atop dog - THE = bark'$$

Note that by convention we use the dictionary form to indicate the second nexus member (predicate), whereas Ebeling (2006: 153) uses the present participle form to represent the verbal predicate, although he admits that this

---

[3] Ebeling (1978: 281) writes, however, that 'Σ' stands for the features of a situation. In this book we will refrain from discussing the status of 'Σ' (but see van Helden 2017).

[4] 'PR' is the notation for present tense, which will be discussed in Section 3.3.

30   *Nexus: Subject-Predicate Relation*

is merely a convention because 'in the semantic formula only the lexical content of the verb' is represented.

We also use the same model for sentences with the copula 'be'. For these sentences, in the notation proposed by Ebeling (1978: 233) only the nominal part of the predicate is represented and the verb 'be' is left out, because apart from indicating the nominal predicate of the subject, the verb *be* does not add any lexical meaning. Put differently, the meaning of the copula 'be' equals '=' and can be left out of the representation. The semantic contribution of a copula 'be' can be further illustrated by the following examples, where the modified noun in (27) is compared with a nexus construction with a copula in (28):

(27)   *the big dog*

$'dog - big -$ THE$'$

(28)   *The dog is big.*

$'\Sigma\,/$ PR
$dog -$ THE $= big'$

A comparison of these two examples shows that their meanings are alike in one respect, but different in another: both examples indicate the existence of a big dog, but the difference between the two is that the feature of the situation is explicitly transmitted by (28) but not by (27). Furthermore, the meaning of (28) contains an element of tense, which is missing in (27). The semiotactic representation of (28) can be read as: 'the situation which consists of the fact that the dog is big'.

Note that for constructions with other meanings of *be*, i.e. 'exist' or 'be present/situated/located', the verb 'be' itself is represented in the semiotactic notations because of its added meaning, e.g.:

(29)   *There are cats everywhere.*[5]

$'\Sigma\,/$ PR $/$ THERE
$cat\,/$ PL $= be >$ *everywhere*$'$

(30)   *He is here.*

$'\Sigma\,/$ PR
$he = be >$ *here*$'$

We have argued that the copular verb 'be' should not be represented separately in the formalization. This does, however, complicate matters for languages where

---

[5] For the notation 'THERE' see Section 15.2.

3.1 Nexus Relation and the Verb 'Be'   31

there are different copular verbs that convey different meanings. In such cases, we would also like to indicate these differences in the formalization. An example is Spanish, which has two different copular verbs with the meaning 'be', i.e. *ser* and *estar*. According to Romeu (2015: 80): 'As *ser* denotes a single, unlinked state, it generally introduces inherent and permanent properties, unlike *estar*, which introduces non-permanent properties, as it represents a point linked to at least one other.' Jespersen (1965: 280) gives the following examples for *ser* and estar, which he analyses as expressing generic time and individual time respectively:

(31)   *Mi hermano es muy activo.*
        'My brother is very active.'

(32)   *Mi hermano está enfermo.*
        'My brother is ill.'

How might we represent the semantic difference proposed by Jespersen? Here we cannot convey the difference in meaning if in both cases the verbs are represented only by the symbol '='. One way of dealing with the difference in meaning is to indicate the specific characteristics of each copular verb with syntactic symbols, for example, to use the regular 'subject-predicate' notation for *ser* in (31), and to represent the temporal meaning of *estar* in (32) with the temporal limitation relation:[6]

(31')

$$'\Sigma / \mathrm{PR}$$
$$brother \downarrow = active > very$$
$$- I'$$

(32')

$$'\Sigma / \mathrm{PR}$$
$$brother \downarrow = X \sim ill$$
$$- I'$$

In (32) the message specifies that the brother is ill at a given time, thus the illness distinguishes a period of his life from other periods. This meaning is represented with the temporal limitation relation (cf. '*granddad ~ young*' in Section 2.1.3). The symbol 'X' is inserted to avoid a direct sequence of two symbols, namely '=' and '~' (each semiotactic relation should connect two different elements). An alternative notation would be to use Spanish instead of English as the metalanguage in the representations, and not omit the Spanish

---

[6] See also Ebeling (1978: 313).

32   *Nexus: Subject-Predicate Relation*

copular verbs, but represent them in the notations. We can then use the same notation for both constructions, i.e. connecting the verbs *ser* and *estar* with convergent limitation to the predicative:

(31'')

$$'\Sigma/PR$$
$$hermano \downarrow = ser - activo > mucho$$
$$- yo'$$

(32'')

$$'\Sigma/PR$$
$$hermano \downarrow = estar - enfermo$$
$$- yo'$$

This latter notation has the advantage that inserting the actual Spanish words in the representation (instead of an English translation) allows other possible nuances of meaning they might contain to be deduced. Furthermore, such a solution could also account for other instances in languages where we find different copular verbs that express 'be'.[7] However, these representations provided for Spanish could not be applied to languages where the different copular forms have meanings that have nothing to do with temporal or inherent properties. This can be exemplified by Russian, where 'be' is usually expressed by a null form in the present tense, in which case there is only a nominative predicate:

(33)   *On   student.*
he-NOM student-NOM
'He is a student.'

$$'\Sigma/PR$$
$$he = student'$$

However, in addition we find semantically similar but more bookish constructions with the verb 'be', i.e. *javljat'sja* (lit. 'appear' combined with the reflexive suffix *-sja*) with an instrumental predicate and *predstavljat' soboj* ('represent') with an accusative object:

(34)   *On   javljaetsja studentom.*
he-NOM appears-*sja* student-INSTR
'He is a student.' (cf. 'He serves as a student')

---

[7] For example, in Thai, which has a number of copulas, a similar difference can be found between the copular verbs *pen*, which can express 'attribution' or a 'temporal' property, and *khɯɯ,* which indicates a 'definition' (inherent property) (Iwasaki and Inkapiromu 2005: 221–223).

(35)   *On   predstavljaet soboj   studenta.*
         he-NOM represents himself-INSTR student-ACC
         'He is (represents) a student.'

According to Janda (1993: 175) the use of the instrumental in (34) is an instance of the attributive qualitative instrumental, where the instrumental denotes a general category to which the referent expressed by the subject belongs, as such serving as a label attached to the nominative. In example (35) the construction indicates that the referent expressed by the subject represents, by means of himself, a student (cf. Janda 1993: 148).

(34')

$$' \Sigma / PR$$
$$he = appear > [INSTR_1]$$
$$\qquad\qquad\quad [INSTR_2] \; ; \; student'$$

(35')

$$' \Sigma / PR$$
$$he = [represent_1] \qquad\qquad > [INSTR_1]$$
$$\quad [represent_2] \; ; \; student \quad | \quad [INSTR_2] \; ; \; himself'$$

Note that for the first example (34), we have argued that the construction is a monovalent construction, but in the second example (35) the construction is analysed as bivalent. The extent to which such solutions can also be applied to other languages with more than one copular 'be' would need additional research. For a further discussion of case meaning see Sections 4.2.1 and 4.2.2.

3.2   'Σ' without Nexus

We noted above that although most sentences with a nexus structure express a situation, and most sentences that express a situation contain a nexus structure, there are exceptions. To give an example, on the one hand we argue that the clausal gerund in English expresses a situation, with a temporal dimension, but the event expressed by the gerund does not evoke the idea of a subject.[8] Thus there is a situation but no nexus, because the first nexus member is lacking. On the other hand, we argue that in the case of some compounds (e.g. *wide-brimmed hat*) there is a nexus structure but the construction has no temporal dimension and therefore does not express a situation.

Besides sentences with a subject and a predicate, or sentences with a subjectless predicate (as in the Russian example (236)), we also find sentences

---

[8] The gerund is discussed in Section 14.3.

34   *Nexus: Subject-Predicate Relation*

where the predicate or another element, such as an object, is missing, i.e. so-called elliptical sentences (for a functional approach, see e.g. Culicover and Jackendoff 2005). In our model, such instances can be represented as occurrences of 'semantic doubling' (see example (79)). In addition to these elliptical cases, where the identity of the missing element can often be found in the context, we also find sentences without a regular nexus structure that do not have a clearly elliptical character, such as: *Nice!; Okay.; A mouse!.* (For a thorough analysis of such structures, see e.g. Stainton 2006.) These utterances can be seen as semantic and formal sentences, and they have their own intonational contour. Even though their interpretation is often highly contextual, they can be more or less conventionalized.

Within the model of Semiotactics the main question is whether these sentences should be seen as expressing a situation, i.e. something with a temporal dimension, or not.[9] One could argue that all these utterances have a predicate character and convey the idea of 'something being the case', and represent them with the 'Σ' symbol for situation, e.g.:

(36)   *A mouse!*

          'Σ / EXCL
          mouse – INDEF'

One could also argue, however, that in such sentences the idea of a situation is not expressed by the linguistic form itself but is an interpretation that is contextually given. According to this point of view, we can represent these utterances without a sigma symbol but with the addition of a final marker for the utterance, such as 'DECL', 'Q' or 'EXCL', which for this example would be:[10]

          '*mouse* – INDEF / EXCL'

Other examples of situations without a nexus are constructions where the verb conjugation is not in agreement with the subject. Let us compare:

(37)   *Three points are important.*

(38)   *Three points is enough.*

---

[9] Jespersen (1984: 80) discusses this problem of what he calls 'half-analyzable sentences': 'When a substantive stands alone, it is often impossible to decide whether it should be regarded as the subject or an object of an imaginary verb (. . .).' (e.g. a street vendor shouting 'Strawberries').

[10] See also Ebeling (2006: 150).

The first sentence (37) shows subject-verb agreement, and as such a regular nexus situation is represented:

(37')

'Σ / PR
point / 3 = *important*'

However, in the case of example (38) a different representation is made, based on the singular verb form 'is'. A 'Σ' symbol is inserted, dominating 'three points'; this situation as a whole is the first nexus member, thus representing the meaning: 'that/if there are three points, it is enough':

(38')

'Σ / PR
Σ = *enough*
point / 3'

3.3   Notations in the Top Layer

In the top layer of the representation we find the symbol 'Σ', indicating a situation. This layer can be used to represent several meanings expressed by the sentence that pertain to the situation as a whole, and not to individual semantic elements of the sentence. Most importantly, we find indications of tense and mood in this layer.[11] All these semantic particles are connected to the situation with the stratification relation. As we will discuss in various parts of this book, opinions may differ on whether the top layer should be used as pertaining to the situation as a whole for all meanings that express the speaker's attitude to the proposition (e.g. *hopefully, certainly, undoubtedly*). In this book we will reserve this layer for tense and mood (*pace* Ebeling 2006, who uses it for a much wider range of meanings).

The notation for the tense of a sentence is placed to the right of the symbol 'Σ', connected by the stratification symbol '/'. Present and past tense are given the notations 'PR' and 'PA' respectively. The tense of the sentence essentially locates the **narrated event** relative to some orientation point, often the

---

[11] Ebeling (1978) also represents aspect in Russian in the notation in this sigma layer. For reasons of simplicity we have chosen not to represent aspect in Russian in this book.

36 Nexus: Subject-Predicate Relation

moment of speech.[12] We take the view that this relation cannot be described in terms of modification (limitation) of a situation, because the indication of tense does not create the idea of a subset of the set of situations. Similarly, it is not possible to use the symbol for gradation, since tense cannot be seen as a further specification of a property of the event. Rather, the situation is stratified by being positioned relative to some orientation point, which means that the tense indication provides further information about the situation as a whole, represented by 'Σ'. An example is given in (39), where the **specimen set** is a situation 'Σ' and 'PR' is the specification of this set (i.e. it is in the present):

(39)   *He walks (quickly).*

$$'\Sigma\,/\,\mathrm{PR}$$
$$he = walk'$$

The relation of stratification is also used to indicate that the imperative mood is assigned to a situation. This is represented in the top layer, with the notation 'IMP'. In an imperative construction the subject is not linguistically expressed, but is distinctly implied as the person addressed, which is why this subject is represented in the notation by the symbol 'X' (see Section 4.4 for this symbol).

(40)   *Be quiet.*

$$'\Sigma\,/\,\mathrm{IMP}$$
$$\mathrm{X} = quiet'$$

(41)   *Come in.*

$$'\Sigma\,/\,\mathrm{IMP}$$
$$\mathrm{X} = come > in'$$

Ebeling (2006: 290) also uses the relation of stratification for the relation between 'Σ' and tense, but he proposes that the limitation relation should be used for connecting other meanings that are placed on the top layer after sigma and tense. He uses various abbreviations for semantic particles of different

---

[12] Ebeling (2006: 157–158) argues that tense can be described in terms of narrated events that can fill (part of) the narrated time. To give an example, in the case of *John worked* the narrated time is the whole period about which something is said (which may also contain moments when John stopped working), and which is filled with various events when John actually worked. As such, according to this theory of tense, a meaning like 'PR' deals with the number of times a situation that is conceptualized as a specimen occurs. Note that although we also use the symbol for stratification, we do not analyse tense in terms of the number of times an event occurs. Instead, we argue that in the case of tense, the concept of 'situation' is further specified.

moods in Dutch, such as 'DECL' (declarative), 'REAL' (realis), 'HYP' (hypothetic) and 'INC' (incomplete). Some of these semantic particles are language-specific. An example of the notation of semantic particles is the one for a Dutch present tense realis declarative sentence, which Ebeling formalizes as '...Σ / PR – REAL – DECL...'. The realis mood indicates that the situation is present at the time in which the speaker situates it, and 'DECL' points to the fact that, according to the speaker, the given projection is the correct one (out of a contextually determined set of alternative projections). In Ebeling's view, from the set of present tense situations, first the subset of 'REAL' situations is selected, and then from this set the subset of declarative situations is selected. This subset of a subset stratifies the situation as a whole ('...Σ / ((PR – REAL) – DECL)....'. However, in this book we have chosen to represent all the relations between the situation and the other meanings in the top layer with the symbol for stratification. In our view, the contribution of meanings like 'realis', 'declarative', 'exclamative' or 'interrogative' does not limit the set of the situation as a whole by creating a subset. Instead we argue that meanings indicated by the semantic particles further specify the meaning expressed by the entire situation, in the same way as 'PR' and 'PA'. From this it follows that the entire situation is regarded as one set that is further specified. To refer back to the example from Ebeling given above, we would write: '...Σ / PR / REAL / DECL...'

When several meanings are placed to the right of the sigma (e.g. 'past', 'interrogative', 'exclamative'), the order of the elements in the representation is relatively arbitrary, but as a convention we first give the symbols for tense followed by the other symbols. The symbols used in this book are: 'DECL' for 'declarative', indicating that the speaker believes the statement to be correct, 'Q' for questions, and 'EXCL' for exclamations.[13] To keep the notations as compact and uncluttered as possible, the abbreviation 'DECL' will not be used in the representations in this book, with the understanding that unless the notation contains 'Q' or 'EXCL', the sentence is considered to be declarative. In the following example we find that both 'PR' and 'EXCL' are connected by the stratification relation to the sigma symbol, which represents the situation:

(42)   *He walks (quickly)!*

    'Σ / PR / EXCL
    he = walk'

---

[13] We will not represent the notations for the semantic particles used by Ebeling (2006) for moods in Dutch, such as 'REAL', 'HYP', 'INC', etc.

38   *Nexus: Subject-Predicate Relation*

It may be that some languages make a formal distinction between the declarative and assertive mood, in which case this difference must also be represented. One might also question the extent to which a language like English has an exclamative mood, since there is no single linguistic form-meaning element that indicates an exclamative meaning. However, in this book we will use the term 'exclamative mood' for English to represent the exclamative meaning as in (42).

As will be explained in our discussions in Part II, there are constructions for which arguments exist for either placing a semantic element on the top layer next to the sigma sign 'Σ', or for placing it below this symbol. This is the case, for example, with modal verbs, as explained in Section 14.1. In such instances we propose as a convention that in case of doubt, or of two competing notations, we will place the semantic element below the sigma, *pace* Ebeling (2006: 172). As we will show, for example with respect to modal verbs, this approach makes it possible to follow the formal structure of the sentence as closely as possible in the formalization.

4 Valences

4.1 What Is Valence?

Some meanings cannot be described as a **projection** of one single entity because the distinctive features presuppose different and distinct carriers.[1] These meanings concern relations between different entities. Examples are constructions with a bivalent (transitive) verb, such as *read a book*, and prepositional phrases, such as *on the chair*. For instance, in (43) the semantic particle 'read' is a projection of two **complementary valences**, i.e. the **dominating** valence [reading] carried by John and the **dominated** valence [read] carried by book. Because the valences are part of the same complex meaning, their arrangement indicates that the combination contains not just a reader and something read, but a reader and something read by this very reader:

(43)   *John reads a book (every evening).*

The complementary valences are placed in one vertical column in the notation, with square brackets indicating that the different elements are part of the same meaning. The two valences are placed on different layers because they involve two different **direct participants** of the action. The first (dominating) valence is the subject/agent 'John', connected with the nexus relation symbol '=' to [reading], and the second valence (direct object) 'book' is connected to [read] with the relation symbol ';', which represents the dominated valence, resulting in the following notation:

(43')

$$'\Sigma\,/\,\text{PR}$$
$$John = [reading]$$
$$[read \quad]\;;\; book - \text{NONTHE}'$$

---

[1] Ebeling (1978: 2006) uses the term 'projection' as a theoretical construct of a mental representation in the case of referents or meanings. In the remainder of this book we will use this term in the same way.

40 *Valences*

There are currently three conventions for the notation of valences, the first of which is the representation given above in (43'). The second notation, also proposed by Ebeling (2006), is the following, where 'x' refers to *John* and 'y' to *book*:

(43'')

$$\begin{array}{l} \text{'}\Sigma/\text{PR} \\ John = [x; x\,\text{reads}\,y] \\ \qquad\quad [y; x\,\text{reads}\,y] \;;\; book - \text{NONTHE}' \end{array}$$

Geerdink-Verkoren (2009: 19) proposes a third notation, namely with the verb in the neutral (dictionary) form and number subscripts on the right marking the different valences, e.g. [$read_1$] for the first valence of 'read' and [$read_2$] for its second valence:

(43''')

$$\begin{array}{l} \text{'}\Sigma/\text{PR} \\ John = [read_1] \\ \qquad\quad [read_2] \;;\; book - \text{NONTHE}' \end{array}$$

This notation is more compact than the second notation, which would take up a lot of space for complex sentences (with more than one bivalent structure), and it allows the reader to focus more clearly on other issues under discussion. Furthermore, this third notation is more suited than the first for those who prefer to use the original languages in the representations, instead of using English as the metalanguage. This third notation is the one that will be used most frequently in this book.

Prepositions are also analysed as bivalent, since they presuppose two entities. In example (44) the preposition *in* directly connects the cat to the location 'the tree', which is represented by the relation symbol for limitation. The second valence of 'in' is connected to 'the tree' by the symbol ';' for dominated valence:

(44)   *The cat in the tree is grey.*

$$\begin{array}{l} \text{'}\Sigma/\text{PR} \\ cat - \text{THE} - [in_1] = grey \\ \qquad\qquad\quad [in_2] \;;\; tree - \text{THE}' \end{array}$$

Although in (45) the prepositional phrase also provides information about the entity 'cat', it does so indirectly by specifying where the event took place. In this case, 'in the tree' does not have a limiting relation with 'cat' or with 'sit', but is a further specification of the subject and predicate taken together, i.e.

4.1 What Is Valence?   41

'the cat sat'. Therefore, we see this as an instance of gradation. The same analysis is made for sentence (46) with the preposition *on*:

(45)   *The cat sat in the tree.*

$$'\Sigma/\text{PA}$$
$$cat - \text{THE} = sit > [in_1]$$
$$[in_2] \; ; \; tree - \text{THE}'$$

(46)   *The cat sits on the chair (every evening).*

$$'\Sigma/\text{PR}$$
$$cat - \text{THE} = sit > [on_1]$$
$$[on_2] \; ; \; chair - \text{THE}'$$

There are also prepositional phrases that have a direct limitation relation with a verb. This is the case with idiomatic expressions consisting of a verb and a dependent preposition, as in the following example, where the action 'she decided' did not take place on the car as a location, but rather the verb 'decide' is further modified/limited by 'on the blue car':

(47)   *She finally decided on the blue car.*

$$'\Sigma/\text{PA}$$
$$she = decide - [on_1] > final$$
$$[on_2] \; ; \; car - blue - \text{THE}'$$

Let us further discuss this issue by comparing the next two sentences; in the first example we find a gradation relation connecting the prepositional phrase to the verb, whereas in the second there is a limitation relation. These different relations show the difference in meaning. In (48) the prepositional phrase modifies 'subject + predicate', indicating that the event 'he waits' takes place on the platform as the location, which places the subject and his waiting in that location, as indicated by the gradation relation.

(48)   *He waits on the platform (every morning).*

$$'\Sigma/\text{PR}$$
$$he = wait > [on_1]$$
$$[on_2] \; ; \; platform - \text{THE}'$$

However, in (49) the prepositional phrase does not refer to the location; instead we find a combination of a verb and a dependent preposition (cf. example (47)). As such, in the notation the prepositional phrase is directly connected by the limitation relation to the verb, because 'wait' is further specified by/limited to 'for the train'.

42   *Valences*

(49)   *He waits for the train (every morning).*

$$
\begin{array}{l}
{}^{\prime}\Sigma\,/\,\text{PR}\\
he = wait - [for_1]\\
[for_2]\ ;\ train - \text{THE}'
\end{array}
$$

The distinction between entities and properties of entities is a very basic one in language. Because of the fundamental difference between entities and properties (or features) of entities, it is important to make a distinction between limitation and gradation.

4.2   How Many Valences?

With regard to the concept of valence, it is important to establish whether words have inherent valences or not. For instance, do we assume that some verbs are by definition intransitive (monovalent) and others monotransitive (bivalent), or even ditransitive (trivalent)? In this section we will analyse a number of arguments and example sentences to determine whether words have fixed valences or show variations in the number of valences depending on the situation and sentences in which they occur.

In the semiotactic representations for ditransitive constructions (also called 'double-object' constructions[2]) with three valences, as a convention we will always use the first valence for the subject, the second valence for the direct object and the third valence for the indirect object or another participant (as in e.g. '*x* considers *y z*', where '*z*' (the third valence) refers to the object complement, i.e. how something is considered). When there are only two valences (e.g. in English: *I helped **him**, I hindered **him**, I saw **him**, I praised **him***), we will indicate the non-subject valence as the second valence, regardless of whether it has the semantic properties of a direct or an indirect object. This is especially important for languages without case marking, where there are no clear criteria to determine what is a direct object and what is an indirect object.

For the discussion of ditransitive constructions, we also refer to Haspelmath (2015: 19–41), who writes that ditransitive constructions have a verb denoting the transfer of an entity (T) from an agent (A) to a recipient (R), and that while the A argument in a ditransitive construction is treated the same as the subject of a monotransitive construction, the behaviour of the two object arguments R and T is more variable, both within and across languages. He also states that: 'The most salient difference between languages with respect to ditransitive constructions

---

[2] For a discussion of double-object constructions, see also Hudson (1992).

4.2 How Many Valences? 43

concerns the alignment of the coding of the two object arguments, i.e. the question whether it is the R or the T of the ditransitive clause that is coded like the P of the monotransitive clause'. Such alignment patterns may be different for different constructions.

Apresjan (2009: 491–492) points out that lexemes such as predicates can be associated with a large of number of participants[3] ('actants' in his terminology), which are obligatorily or optionally expressed in language, and the formal expressions of which can each be dependent on the predicate. This can be illustrated with the English word *rent,* which can be associated with several participants, namely the person who rents, the thing that is rented, the person or institution from which something is rented, the period for which something is rented and the sum of money that it costs to rent something. These participants can all be expressed in language with conventionalized constructions, such as the following English example:

(50)   *The company rented the second floor for a whole year from the institute for just one hundred dollars a month.*

In this sentence the subject (first valence) 'the company' and the object of the verb (second valence) 'the second floor' are indicated by means of word order, whereas the other participants are indicated by prepositional phrases ('x for y', 'x from y'). In our model (*pace* Apresjan 2009), we make a distinction between valences of the verb (subject, direct object, indirect object) and other (so-called oblique) valences. In English, these latter valences are expressed by prepositional phrases, which themselves are seen as bivalent constructions. As such, we can provide the following formalization for this sentence:[4]

(50')

$$
\begin{aligned}
&'\ldots \Sigma/\mathrm{PA} \\
&company = [rent_1] \qquad\qquad\qquad > [for_1] \qquad\qquad\qquad > \mapsto^* \\
&\qquad\qquad [rent_2] \ ; \ floor - second \ \mid \ [for_2] \ ; \ year - whole \ \mid \\
&\mapsto [from_1] \qquad\qquad > [for_1] \\
&\qquad [from_2] \ ; \ insitute \ \mid \ [for_2] \ ; \ldots'
\end{aligned}
$$

The number and type of valences that are associated with a meaning, for example a verbal meaning, depends on the construction in which the meaning

---

* The symbol $\mapsto$ is the division sign for semiotactic notations which are too wide to fit the paper size.
[3] Note that we make a distinction between 'participants' involved in an event, and 'direct participants' as verb valences.
[4] The symbol 'l' in the representation above is a division sign to separate elements that are on the same line but have no syntactic relation.

44   *Valences*

is used. Goldberg (1995: 43) distinguishes between *participant roles* (inherently associated with the verb) and *argument roles* (induced by the construction). This can be illustrated with the much-cited example from Goldberg (1995: 9) with the verb *sneeze*, which is usually associated with just one (subject) valence, since it normally occurs in constructions with a subject and a predicate, like *John sneezed*. The same verb can, however, also occur in the 'caused-motion construction', as in: *He sneezed the napkin from the table*, in which case the construction itself requires the verb to have two valences. As such, if we proceed from the more frequent use, we can speak of a **valence addition.** Another example of valence addition is given by Ebeling (2006: 337), i.e. *Hij verfde de deur groen* 'He painted the door green', where the bivalent verb 'paint' gets three valences, 'he', 'door' and 'green'.

We can also find cases of **valence reduction.** For example, the verb *eat* is usually associated with more than one valence, and is often used in constructions where both the first valence (subject) and a second valence (direct object) are expressed, e.g.:

(51)   *He ate an apple.*

$$'\Sigma/\text{PA}$$
$$he = [eat_1]$$
$$[eat_2] \; ; \; apple - \text{NONTHE}'$$

But the same verb can also be used in sentences where the focus is on the process itself, and where the idea of something that is eaten is pushed to the background, for example:

(52)   *He ate the whole day.*

One could argue that in example (52) the verb is also bivalent because *eat* inherently requires the idea of something that is eaten. This would mean that the second valence is part of the syntactic representation, but the identity is contextually determined, which could be represented with an 'X':

(52')

$$'\Sigma/\text{PA}$$
$$he = [eat_1] > day - whole - \text{THE}$$
$$[eat_2] \; ; \; \text{X}'$$

However, in this sentence the idea of something that is eaten plays no part in the linguistic utterance. The identity of the second valence is not supplied in the form and consequently does not need to be included in the representation;

in this sentence the speaker's focus is entirely on the process of eating. Whether or not this is possible depends on the meaning of the verb. Note, for example, that whereas it is possible to focus on the process for the verb *eat*, this is much more difficult for a verb with a similar meaning like *devour*. We propose to represent a verb as bivalent only if the second valence (object) is linguistically expressed.[5] If this is not the case, the verb is considered to occur as a monovalent verb. The following syntactic description for example (52) is therefore proposed:

(52'')

$$'\Sigma\,/\,\text{PA}$$
$$he = eat > day - whole - \text{THE}'$$

There are other cases where the valence structure is not immediately obvious. Consider the **comparative**:

(53)   *He is older.*

The comparative *older* presupposes that the feature 'old' is compared with another entity ('older than X'). There are two ways in which one might represent the valence structure here. The first is to argue that the comparative is inherently bivalent. In that case, the representation for (53) would be the following, with 'X' as the symbol for the non-linguistically specified element:

(53')

$$'\Sigma\,/\,\text{PR}$$
$$he = old > [\text{COMP}_1]$$
$$[\text{COMP}_2]\ ;\ \text{X}'$$

When the second entity is expressed, as in (54), we would then, following the same reasoning, make a similar notation:

(54)   *He is older than me.*

(54')

$$'\Sigma\,/\,\text{PR}$$
$$he = old > [\text{COMP}_1]$$
$$[\text{COMP}_2]\ ;\ I'$$

---

[5] If the object is non-expressed but nevertheless an integral part of the mental projection, we can indicate this with an X as the second valence. This is the case, for example, with the Russian past tense perfective *napisal* (write-1/3SG-M-PF 'I/he wrote (it)'), which always presupposes some contextually given object.

46   *Valences*

However, a weakness in this notation is that the semantic contribution of *than* is not indicated; it is 'absorbed' in the meaning of the comparative. Thus the representation would not be applicable to languages that have two different comparatives, since both would be merged into the valence of the comparative meaning itself. This is the case, for example, in informal Dutch, where *als* is sometimes used instead of the regular conjunction *dan*: *hij is ouder dan/als ik* ('he is older than me'). By representing the actual conjunctions in the notation, their respective lexical meanings could be indicated.

We argue that all words that carry meaning should be represented in the notation. Otherwise the correspondence between the syntactic representation and the form-meaning structure of the sentence would not be straightforward. We therefore propose to present the comparative in the examples quoted above as monovalent, and when the second entity is linguistically expressed, the conjunction will be presented as the bivalent factor. As a result, the following representations are proposed for examples (53) and (54):

(53'')

$$'\Sigma / \text{PR}$$
$$he = old > \text{COMP}'$$

(54'')

$$'\Sigma / \text{PR}$$
$$he = old > \text{COMP} > [than_1]$$
$$[than_2] \; ; \; I'$$

This also enables us to make a distinction between occurrences with and without a conjunction, as in Russian, where the comparative can occur both with the conjunction *čem* (in (55)) and without a conjunction but with the second noun in the genitive, e.g. (56). The first Russian example with the conjunction is given a representation similar to the one proposed above for (54):

(55)   *On   byl starše čem ja.*
        he-NOM was older than I-NOM
        'He was older than me.'

$$'\Sigma / \text{PA}$$
$$on = staryj > \text{COMP} > [čem_1]$$
$$[čem_2] \; ; \; ja'$$

4.2 *How Many Valences?*   47

However, where the comparative is used without a conjunction, as in (56), it is
the use of the genitive form that adds the extra valence to the comparative.[6]

(56)   *On   byl   starše menja.*
        he-NOM was older I-GEN
        'He was older than me.'

            ˙Σ/PA
        on = staryj > COMP > [GEN$_1$]
                       [GEN$_2$] ; *ja*'

Valence reduction may also occur with trivalent (ditransitive) verbs, such as
the verb 'give', which in the English sentence (57) has three valences, referring
to three direct participants, namely someone who 'gives', something that is
'given' and someone who 'receives', e.g.:

(57)   *I gave John a book.*

        'Σ/PA
        I = [*give$_1$*]
             [*give$_2$*] ; *book* − NONTHE
             [*give$_3$*] ; *John*'

This verb, however, may also occur in a different construction, as in example
(58), where the recipient is not a direct participant in the action but is expressed
by a prepositional phrase. In this case there is valence reduction: there are only
two valences because there are two direct participants in the action, i.e. the
subject 'I' and the direct object 'book', and the prepositional phrase is indicated with a bivalent preposition:[7]

(58)   *I gave a book to John.*

        'Σ/PA
        I = [*give$_1$*]   > [*to$_1$*]
             [*give$_2$*] ; *book* − NONTHE | [*to$_2$*] ; *John*'

In Japanese it is not possible to make this distinction between two kinds of
constructions with verbs of giving. There are no prepositions in Japanese and
the postposition (dative particle) *ni*, which can also be used to express the same

---

[6] Because of the particular characteristics of the Russian genitive, which is used in a wider range
of occurrences and meanings than the genitive in other languages discussed in this work, we
have decided not to use the divergent limitation notation for the genitive here.
[7] *Pace* Ebeling (1978: 323), but similar to Ebeling (2006: 254).

48   *Valences*

meaning as the English preposition 'to' indicating direction, cannot be omitted in such constructions, the receiver is always marked by *ni*:[8]

(59)   *watashi ga   Jon   ni hon   o   ageru*
        I   NOM John to book ACC give-PR

        'I give (a) book to John.'

Therefore, for this Japanese example we propose a representation with the bivalent verb 'give' and an adjunct to connect 'John', similar to the representation above for example (58):

(59')

$$
\begin{array}{c}
\text{'}\Sigma / \text{PR} \\
watashi = [ageru_1] \qquad > [ni_1] \\
[ageru_2] \ ; \ hon \ \mid \ [ni_2] \ ; \ Jon\text{'}
\end{array}
$$

4.2.1   Valence and Case

In many languages, parts of speech such as nouns, pronouns or adjectives are marked for case, which expresses the grammatical function of that word. In a language like English the case system has largely been lost, but traces can still be seen in personal pronouns, where we find remnants of the nominative, accusative and genitive, with the nominative expressing the subject (*I see him*), the accusative expressing the object (*I see **him***), and the genitive expressing the possessor (*that book is **yours***). Other languages, such as Russian, have a much more developed case system. Russian has six cases (nominative, genitive, dative, accusative, instrumental, locative), and every noun, pronoun, adjective, participle and numeral is marked for case.

Cases can be seen as form-meaning elements, since each case has a form side and a meaning side. This can be illustrated with the Russian sentence *Ja čital knigu* (I-NOM read book-F-SG-ACC; 'I read/was reading a book'), where we find a nominative first person pronoun *ja*, expressing the subject, and a singular feminine noun marked for the accusative *-u*, which expresses the object. Note, however, that the principle of 'one form – one meaning' does not apply in a simple and straightforward way, as will be illustrated below with other examples from Russian.

First of all, in many languages, including Russian, functionally distinct cases can be identical in form. This can be exemplified by the ending *-u*

---

[8] The particle *ni* may express other meanings as well; for a discussion, see Geerdink-Verkoren (2009: 67–72).

4.2 How Many Valences? 49

mentioned above, which marks not only the accusative of a singular feminine noun (*kniga*), but also the dative of a singular masculine noun, for example *Ja dal knigu bratu* (I-NOM gave book-F-SG-ACC brother-M-SG-DAT; 'I gave that book to my brother'). Also note that within one paradigm different cases may be marked in the same way. To give one example, both the nominative and accusative of a masculine singular noun have no ending (or to put it differently, both end with a null form '-ø'). Because of this, the word *xleb* 'bread' can function as both the nominative and the accusative of 'bread', and its function is determined by the context in which it is used. Such instances of case syncretism do not, however, distort the functionality of the case system, since despite the identity in form, users of the Russian language can still determine the difference in function.

Second, cases usually have a variety of different functions rather than just one clearly delineated function per form. To give an example from Russian, in all three of the following sentences we find the instrumental, even though the function of the instrumental differs considerably:

(60)   *Ja   rezal xleb   nožom.*
       I-NOM cut   bread-ACC knife-INSTR
       'I was cutting the bread with a knife.'
       (knife-INSTR expresses an instrument)

(61)   *Xleb   režetsja Olegom.*
       bread-NOM cut-*sja* Oleg-INSTR
       'The bread is being cut by Oleg.'
       (Oleg-INSTR expresses an agent of a passive sentence)

(62)   *On   byl studentom.*
       he-NOM was student-INSTR
       'He was a student.'
       (student-INSTR expresses the predicate of a copular construction)

One may approach this question from different angles, either by postulating very abstract general meanings for each instrumental case (see e.g. Jakobson 1990 for Russian case meanings), or by postulating polysemous meanings for case (e.g. Janda 1993 for the instrumental case in Russian). Note, furthermore, that some of these uses clearly share properties with one another, and it is sometimes difficult to delineate distinctly different functions. This is pointed out by Janda (1993: 143), for example, who argues that the typical 'instrument' meaning and the 'passive agent' meaning should be seen as syntagmatic variants of the same instrument meaning (expressing a 'conduct'). This can

50   Valences

be illustrated with examples where the instrumental can be said to be either an agent or an instrument:

(63)   *Orkestr   gremit basami.*
        orchestra-NOM booms basses-INSTR
        'The orchestra is booming with basses.'

Third, the meaningfulness of cases depends on the type of context in which they are used. Consider, for example, the following sentences with the dative first person pronoun *mne* ('me'):

(64)   *On   dal **mne**   knigu.*
        he-NOM gave I-DAT book-ACC
        'He gave me a book.'

(65)   *On   pomogal **mne**.*
        he-NOM helped   I-DAT
        'He helped me.'

(66)   ***Mne**   ne ponjat'   ego.*
        I-DAT not understand-INF he-ACC
        'I cannot understand him'

(67)   *On   pošel ko   **mne**.*
        he-NOM came towards I-DAT
        'He walked towards me.'

A clear example of the dative can be found in ditransitive sentences with the verb 'give', where it expresses the third valence of the verb, which can be identified as the recipient of the action (see e.g. Goldberg 1995 for an analysis of English ditransitives). A similar meaning can be found in sentences with bivalent verbs such as 'help', where the dative marks the participant as the recipient of the help given by someone, or in constructions with an infinitive predicate, where the dative participant, marking the potential subject of the infinitive event, is construed as the recipient of the infinitive event brought about by an external force (see Fortuin 2000). Finally, there are also prepositions that govern the dative, such as *k(o)*. It is questionable whether the dative should be seen as a meaningful element here, since there is no typical 'dative' meaning in these instances (but see e.g. Jakobson for an analysis trying to link such uses to other dative meanings).

4.2.2   How to Represent Case?

In Semiotactics, case is represented in two different ways. Cases that mark direct participants of the action or event expressed by the verb are indicated by verb valences, as explained in Section 4.1. The participants that are not analysed as direct participants but as 'peripheral' participants (cf. Jakobson's 1990 notion of peripheral status, and Ebeling 2006: 254), which are expressed by the use of prepositions, postpositions or cases, are given a separate bivalent notation, as shown above in Section 4.2.

For a language like Russian, which has a case system, our approach means that the direct object (indicated by the accusative) and the indirect object (indicated by the dative) are formalized as verbal valences, as in example (68), where we find the ditransitive construction:

(68) *Ja   dal emu   knigu.*
      I-NOM gave he-DAT book-ACC
      'I gave him (a) book.'

$$'\Sigma^{\prime}\mathrm{PA}$$
$$I = [give_1]$$
$$\quad [give_2] \ ; \ book$$
$$\quad [give_3] \ ; \ he'$$

Other syntactic roles expressed by the dative and accusative are indicated as bivalent case meanings; for example, as in existential constructions where the dative expresses the experiencer of a situation (see Section 15.2). Similarly, the meanings of other cases, such as the genitive or the instrumental (as in example (69)), are indicated as bivalent meanings.

(69) *On   režet nožom.*
      he-NOM cuts knife-INSTR
      'He cuts with a knife.'

$$'\Sigma/\mathrm{PR}$$
$$he = cut > [\mathrm{INSTR}_1]$$
$$\quad\quad\quad [\mathrm{INSTR}_2] \ ; \ knife'$$

For bivalent verbs in Russian where the second valence is not indicated by the accusative but by the dative case, we represent the meaning expressed by the dative as a second verbal valence:

(70) *Ja   zvonil emu.*
      I-NOM called he-DAT
      'I called him.'

$$'\Sigma/\mathrm{PA}$$
$$I = [call_1]$$
$$\quad [call_2] \ ; \ he'$$

52   *Valences*

However, when there is a choice between different cases, each with a different meaning, we give two different representations. In the first notation (71') for the next sentence, the accusative is represented as the second valence of the verb 'wait', whereas in the second notation (71'') the genitive is represented as the bivalent element:[9]

(71)   *Ja   ždu avtobus/avtobusa.*
         I-NOM wait bus-ACC/GEN
         'I wait for the/a bus.'

(71')

$$'\Sigma\,/\,\mathrm{PR}$$
$$I = [wait_1]$$
$$[wait_2] \; ; \; bus'$$

(71'')

$$'\Sigma\,/\,\mathrm{PR}$$
$$I = wait - [\mathrm{GEN}_1]$$
$$[\mathrm{GEN}_2] \; ; \; bus'$$

It should be noted that our approach means that the actor of a passive sentence expressed by a (pro)noun in the instrumental is seen as a peripheral participant, and not as a direct participant. However, this latter analysis is given by Ebeling in his notation (1980: 370) for the following sentence:

(72)   *Xleb   režetsja Olegom.*
         bread-NOM cut-*sja* Oleg-INSTR
         'The bread is being cut by Oleg.'

(72')

$$'\Sigma\,/\,nonperf.\;\mathrm{PR}$$
$$bread = [y; x\;cuts\,y]$$
$$[x; x\;cuts\,y] \; ; \; Oleg'$$

According to this formalization, the meaning of the instrumental is not part of the representation as such, since the function of the instrumental is merely to express the first valence (actor) of the passive sentence (which is demoted from subject of the sentence to a dominated valence). Whether or not this is indicated by the instrumental case, or by a preposition as in the English *by*, is then considered irrelevant. In the formalization that we propose, we retain

---

[9] See also Section 4.1, examples (47) and (49), for the notation of prepositions with a limitation relation.

the semantic contribution of the instrumental in order to emphasize that the semantics of the instrumental is a relevant part of the meaning of the sentence (cf. Janda's analysis of the instrumental given above):

(72'')

$$'\Sigma / PR$$
$$bread = [being\ cut_2] > [INSTR_1]$$
$$[INSTR_2]\ ;\ Oleg'$$

The association between the instrument (Oleg) and the semantic role of actor is due to the meaning of the instrumental, which construes Oleg as the conduit for the action. Note, however, that the semantic role of actor is not seen as part of the valence structure of the verb. See also Sections 12.2 and 14.5 for our analysis of passive constructions.

4.3   A Special Type of Valence: Coordination

The conjunctions *and* and *or* are bivalent, since their meanings presuppose by definition two entities that are conjoined. Even though they combine two separate entities, they are represented as one unit because together they create one complex, as in the following example:

(73)   *John and Tom are friends.*

To make semiotactic representations for instances of coordination proved to be rather complicated, as will be evident from the different notations given below. The first option would be to assume that the regular notation for a bivalent structure could apply, which would yield the following representation, with the use of the limitation symbol indicating that the entity 'John' is further limited or modified by bivalent 'and':

(73')

$$'\Sigma / PR$$
$$John - [and_1] = friend / PL$$
$$[and_2]\ ;\ Tom'$$

However, in the case of coordination it is not possible to use the relation of limitation, since it cannot be argued that in (73) 'John' is limited by 'and Tom'; or to put it differently, we cannot say that the set of 'John' is further specified in terms of the subset 'John and Tom' (which would mean that we first think of the set containing John, and then from this set we select the subset where John co-occurs with Tom).

54   *Valences*

The second notation, proposed by Ebeling (2006: 288), is a three-layered representation, which for this example would be:

(73'')

$$'\Sigma / PR$$
$$[x; x \text{ is } y \text{ and } z] = friend / \text{PL}$$
$$[y; x \text{ is } y \text{ and } z] \; ; \; John$$
$$[z; x \text{ is } y \text{ and } z] \; ; \; Tom'$$

In this representation the first valence 'x' is intended to refer to the conjoined unit 'John and Tom', and the two other valences to John ('y') and Tom ('z') separately. This representation captures the fact that coordinative *and* presents two separate entities as functioning as one syntactic unit. However, a weakness of this representation is that the first valence is not linked to any other element in the notation. As a rule, all elements, x, y and z, should be linked to the element to which they refer, e.g.: *the cat in the tree is grey* (already quoted above as example (44)), where 'cat' ('x') is linked to the first valence of 'in', and 'tree' ('y') to the second valence of 'in':

(44')

$$'\Sigma / PR$$
$$cat - \text{THE} - [x; x \text{ is IN } y] = grey$$
$$[y; x \text{ is IN } y] \; ; \; tree - \text{THE}'$$

This participant 'x' is lacking in the representation (73'') above.

Now that we have rejected two options for representing coordination, namely using the limitation relation and representing three valences, we will move on to a third possible notation. This is to use the gradation relation for representing coordination. Note that gradation, as discussed in Section 2.5, often refers to the property of a property (such as 'big > very' in *a very big dog*). In the case of *John and Tom,* however, neither 'John' nor 'Tom' expresses a property of something, but what this phrase has in common with *very big dog* is that we find a relation of modification or specification that does not involve selecting a subset of a set of entities. It should therefore be noted that coordinatives are unique in that they exemplify gradation in contexts where the meaning of an entity is further specified (modified).

Thus, in the third notation of example (73), the limitation relation with the symbol '–' in (73') above is replaced by the gradation symbol '>' to connect the coordinative elements, which yields the following representation:

4.3 A Special Type of Valence: Coordination   55

(73''')

$$'\Sigma/\text{PR}$$
$$John > [and_1] = friend/\text{PL}$$
$$[and_2] \; ; \; Tom'$$

However, we argue that this representation (73''') too is incorrect: in this case, because the representation shows divergence, not coordination. John is presented as the first nexus member and subject of the nominal predicate, with Tom as the 'dominated valence', as indicated by the symbol ';'. This representation would not reflect the fact that Tom also functions as a subject.

Ultimately, we have opted for the representation for coordination introduced by Geerdink-Verkoren (2009: 96), i.e. placing the two entities on one line (since together they function as one unit) with a double gradation relation connecting them: the first entity 'John' is connected by the gradation symbol to the coordinative 'and', indicating that John is modified (gradated) by the fact that he is with Tom; the second entity 'Tom' is connected to the coordinative 'and' by the reversed gradation symbol, indicating (from right to left) that Tom is modified (gradated) by the fact that he is with John:

(73'''')

$$'\Sigma/\text{PR}$$
$$John > and < Tom = friend/\text{PL}'$$

That the conjoined entities of two words connected by a coordinative do not form one single entity is evident in the following example:

(74)   *I saw John and Paul there. (Paul in the morning and John in the afternoon.)*

This sentence clearly shows that Paul and John are understood as two separate entities. However, Paul and John are conjoined because together they constitute the direct object of *see* (cf. *I saw them there*). This can be visualized by using the same notation for the coordinative as proposed above in (73'''') for this example (74):

$$'\Sigma/\text{PA}$$
$$I = [see_1] > there$$
$$[see_2] \; ; \; John > and < Paul'$$

The coordinative conjunction *or* is represented by the same notation, e.g.:

(75)   *Is she a singer or an actress?*

$$'\Sigma/\text{PR}/\text{Q}$$
$$she = singer - \text{NONTHE} > or < actress - \text{NONTHE}'$$

56 *Valences*

4.4 Non-Specified Element 'X'

It may be necessary to insert the symbol 'X' for an element that is indispensable for the coherence of the construction but is intrinsically only specified by the syntactic context. The element 'X' in itself does not correlate with any semantic element and is only included in the notation to indicate semantic relations of other elements. The symbol 'X' has no other semantic value than the one it acquires by its position in the representation.

For instance, for the imperative (see Section 3.3), where the subject is not mentioned, the symbol 'X' is inserted in the notation as the first nexus member, referring to the hearer (the person addressed). Other examples are given below of contexts where this element 'X' is used, such as in sentence (76) to indicate the subject of the infinitive. The infinitive itself expresses an 'event type'. In contrast to events expressed by finite verbs, the infinitive does not refer to an individual instantiation of an event but rather to a type. Event types can be seen as abstractions from individual occurrences of situations that are grouped together on the basis of similarity. Because of the type character of the infinitive, it does not express tense, person or number. However, since it is a situation, it does evoke the thought of a subject or agent of the predicate (if the verb is personal). The identity of the infinitive subject is therefore given in the context and not expressed by the infinitive itself. (For a further discussion of infinitives with or without *to*, see Section 14.2.)

(76)   *I want to walk.*

$$
\begin{array}{l}
{}'\Sigma/\,PR \\
I = want > [to_1] \\
\qquad\quad [to_2]\;;\;\Sigma \\
\qquad\qquad\quad X = walk'
\end{array}
$$

Other examples with an element 'X' are elliptical constructions, as in the following example, where the meaning 'accurate' is linguistically expressed only once and for the second semantic meaning is represented by 'X', to indicate the intended meaning 'is this accurate or not accurate'. (For negation, see Chapter 7.)

(77)   *Is this accurate or not?*

$$
\begin{array}{l}
{}'\Sigma/\,PR/\,Q \\
this = accurate > or < X > NON'
\end{array}
$$

The conjunction *if* basically connects two elements, but in example (78), an instance of subordination, one of the elements, i.e. the first element (which is its first valence), is not linguistically expressed (cf. *I would love to do it myself, if only I could!*). It could be argued that the non-linguistically expressed element, which in this case is the main clause, does not need to be represented because it is not present in the form. On the other hand, one could also argue that, since there is a condition, semantically there must be another element that connects to the condition expressed by the subordinate clause. This element, the unexpressed main clause, can be represented by the symbol 'X'. This analysis would result in the following representation, where 'X' is connected to the first valence of 'if' and the second valence of 'if' is the subordinate clause 'I could':

(78) *If only I could!*

$$
\begin{array}{l}
{}'X > [\mathit{if}_1] > \mathit{only} \\
\quad [\mathit{if}_2] \; ; \; \Sigma/\mathrm{PA} \\
\qquad I = \mathit{can}{}'
\end{array}
$$

In the next sentence (79), there is ellipsis compared with the original sentence: *I believe that this party can win the next election and will win the next election.* For this case of **semantic doubling**, i.e. ellipsis of a sentence part, which as a result appears only once in the form but is semantically present twice, we can show the **coreference** by using one and the same superscript on (the right side of) the substitute symbol 'X' and on the sentence part to which it refers, which in this example is the situation 'win the next election'.

(79) *I believe that this party can, and will, win the next election.*[10]

$$
\begin{array}{l}
{}'\Sigma/\mathrm{PR} \\
I = \mathit{believe} > [\mathit{that}_1] \\
\qquad\qquad\quad [\mathit{that}_2] \; ; \; \mapsto \\
\qquad\qquad \mapsto \Sigma/\mathrm{PR} \\
\mathit{party} - \mathit{this} = [\mathit{can}_1] > \mathit{and} < [\mathit{will}_1] \\
\qquad\qquad\quad [\mathit{can}_2] \; ; \; \mathrm{X}^1 \quad | \quad [\mathit{will}_2] \; ; \; \Sigma^1 \\
\qquad\qquad\qquad\qquad\qquad\qquad \mathrm{X} = [\mathit{win}_1] \\
\qquad\qquad\qquad\qquad\qquad\qquad\quad [\mathit{win}_2] \; ; \; \mathit{election} - \mathit{next} - \mathrm{THE}{}'
\end{array}
$$

4.5 Quasi-Divergence

As a rule, in the semiotactic representations convergence is indicated by placing the convergent elements on the same horizontal line. However, in some constructions the same entity is projected twice in the semantic complex,

---

[10] The conjunction *that* is analysed in Section 4.6; the verbs *can* and *will* are discussed in Section 14.1.

58 *Valences*

in two different roles. In such cases, placing the meanings on the same line (as stipulated for convergent elements) is not possible. This special kind of convergence is called **quasi-divergence**, because although the elements are convergent, they appear on different layers in the representation. An example was given in (76) above with an infinitive (*I want to walk*), where 'I' is the subject of the matrix clause but also the subject of the infinitive. Since 'I' only appears once in the linguistic form, it cannot be placed twice in the semiotactic representation, therefore an 'X' is inserted. The coreference between 'I' and 'X' can be indicated by (letter) superscripts on the left, thus showing that the subject of 'walk' is the same person who 'wants':

(76')

$$\begin{array}{l} {}^{\prime}\Sigma / \text{PR} \\ {}^{a}I = want > [to_1] \\ \qquad\qquad [to_2] \; ; \; \Sigma \\ \qquad\qquad\qquad {}^{a}X = walk' \end{array}$$

In the example above we have discussed a construction with quasi-divergence that involves an infinitive. In English, quasi-divergence is a typical feature of the infinitive and can be explained in terms of the meaning of the infinitive. The infinitive expresses an event abstracted away from a specific subject, the identity of which can only be established by coreference with another participant in the sentence in which the infinitive occurs. In the same vein, it follows from the infinitive's type character that other valences of the infinitive are also established by coreference, such as the second valence (direct object). In the following example, we find two kinds of coreference:

(80)   *I have nothing to say.*

In the semiotactic representation for this sentence, we show that 'nothing' is the second valence of the verb 'have'. The infinitive situation 'to say' further modifies 'nothing', as represented by the limitation relation. There is coreference between the subject of the matrix verb 'I' and the unexpressed subject 'X' of the infinitive verb 'say', which may be represented with superscripts:

(80')

$$\begin{array}{l} {}^{\prime}\Sigma / \text{PR} \\ {}^{a}I = [have_1] \\ \qquad [have_2] \; ; \; nothing - [to_1] \\ \qquad\qquad\qquad\qquad [to_2] \; ; \; \Sigma \\ \qquad\qquad\qquad\qquad\qquad {}^{a}X = say' \end{array}$$

4.5 Quasi-Divergence 59

At the same time, 'nothing' refers to the non-expressed second valence of the verb 'say'. This coreference between 'nothing' and the second valence of 'say' is also an instance of quasi-divergence, which can be demonstrated by using the following representation, where this non-linguistically expressed second valence of the infinitive is represented by 'X' and connected by superscripts to 'nothing', which is the object of the main verb:

(80'')

$$
\begin{array}{l}
\text{'}\Sigma/\text{PR} \\
{}^{a}I = [have_1] \\
\quad [have_2] \; ; \; {}^{b}nothing - [to_1] \\
\quad\quad\quad\quad\quad [to_2] \; ; \; \Sigma \\
\quad\quad\quad\quad\quad\quad {}^{a}X = [say_1] \\
\quad\quad\quad\quad\quad\quad\quad [say_2] \; ; \; {}^{b}X'
\end{array}
$$

However, there are other examples where a coreference of this kind is not so evident and placing superscripts would require further knowledge, context or interpretation, as in example sentence (81) with the trivalent verb 'consider', where the implication could be that I consider 'to dine here' a treat for myself, but it could also express the meaning that it is considered a treat for other (or all) people, in which case 'X' is not convergent with 'I':

(81)   *I consider it a treat to dine here.*[11]

$$
\begin{array}{l}
\text{'}\Sigma/\text{PR} \\
I = [consider_1] \\
\quad [consider_2] \; ; \; it \quad\quad\quad\quad - \; [to_1] \\
\quad [consider_3] \; ; \; treat - \text{NONTHE} \quad | \quad [to_2] \; ; \; \Sigma \\
\quad\quad\quad\quad\quad\quad\quad\quad\quad\quad\quad X = dine > here'
\end{array}
$$

Although the judgement on whether or not there is convergence between two elements is evident and unambiguous in many constructions, as in example (76), there are also cases where this analysis is less straightforward and would require further knowledge or interpretation (as in (81)). We have therefore decided not to use these superscript notations in this book, unless we specifically wish to point out a coreference between two meanings in a particular construction.

---

[11] The infinitive situation 'to dine here' is represented as a modifying clause with 'it' as the headword. For a discussion of such embedded infinitive situations, see Section 14.2.

60   *Valences*

4.6   Other Examples of Valence

Besides verbs and prepositions, there are other elements in language that can have multiple valences, such as conjunctions and relative pronouns. **Conjunctions** are inherently bivalent because they relate one situation to another. In the following sentences the coordinative conjunctions *and* and *but* connect two sentences and are linked with the gradation and reversed gradation symbols in the same way as already explained for the coordinatives (Section 4.3):

(82)   *John shouted and everybody waved.*

$$'\Sigma/PA \quad > and < \quad \Sigma/PA$$
$$John = shout \quad | \quad everybody = wave'$$

(83)   *We went to his house but he wasn't there.*

$$'\Sigma/PA \qquad\qquad > but < \quad \Sigma/PA$$
$$we = go > [to_1] \qquad\qquad | \quad he = be > there > NON$$
$$[to_2] \; ; \; house \downarrow$$
$$- he'$$

A **conjunction** may also refer to a subordinate relation, as in (84), where *when* points to a moment in time at which the situation in the subordinate clause takes place, after which another situation will take place, which is expressed in the main clause.

(84)   *When he leaves, I will leave too.*

$$'\Sigma/PR \qquad\qquad > [when_1]$$
$$I = [will_1] > too \quad | \quad [when_2] \; ; \; \Sigma/PR$$
$$[will_2] \; ; \; \Sigma \qquad | \qquad\qquad he = leave$$
$$X = leave'$$

In this case, the first valence of 'when' connects to the meaning of the main clause (which as such is put first in the notation) and the second valence to the meaning of the subordinate clause.[12] Note that here we link the meaning expressed by the *when* clause at the top level of the sigma. An argument in favour of this representation is that 'when' provides information about the situation as a whole, including tense. This differs from the meanings such as 'tomorrow', which we represent below the sigma, as a further specification of

---

[12] An alternative representation of this sentence is given in Chapter 17; for a discussion of the verb *will*, see Section 14.1.

the subject plus predicate, and also differs from complement clauses with *that*, where the *that* clause provides new information about the meaning expressed by the matrix verb (see e.g. example (89)). Alternatively, one might also argue that since the *when* clause is a subordinate clause, it should be represented below the sigma as a further specification of the predicate, which falls within the domain of the situation of the main clause. However, in the absence of clear evidence favouring either of the two analyses, we will keep to our current representation.

A construction with two clauses may also be made without a conjunction, as in the next example, where the conditional meaning is implied by inversion:[13]

(85)   *Had I known, I would have told you.*

$$
\begin{array}{ll}
\text{'}\Sigma\,/\,\text{PA} & > \;\; [\text{COND}_1] \\
I = [\text{will}_1] & | \;\;\; [\text{COND}_2]\; ; \;\Sigma\,/\,\text{PA} \\
\quad [\text{will}_2]\; ; \;\Sigma & | \qquad\qquad I = [\text{have}_1] \\
\qquad X = [\text{have}_1] & | \qquad\qquad\quad [\text{have}_2]\; ; \; know > \text{PF} \\
\qquad\quad [\text{have}_2]\; ; \;[\text{tell}_1] > \text{PF} & \\
\qquad\qquad [\text{tell}_2]\; ; \; you\text{'} &
\end{array}
$$

The syntactic structure of this sentence (85) is rather complex at first sight and merits some extra explanation. It can be deconstructed by first establishing that in the semiotactic representation we find the structure of the main clause on the left and the structure of the subordinate clause on the right. The situation of the main clause is connected with the gradation relation to the first valence of the condition, whereas the subordinate clause, which expresses the condition under which the information in the main clause would occur, is linked to the second valence of the bivalent conditional structure. This means that the situation expressed in the main clause can be seen as convergent with the condition, whereas the situation expressed by the subordinate clause is convergent with the second valence of the conditional structure. Note that the conditional expressed by the inversion construction with 'have' is represented with 'COND'. In a complete description of the syntax of English, this meaning should be supplemented with a semantic description of this type of conditional, and how it differs from conditional sentences with *if* (see e.g. (78)).

Relative pronouns are bivalent because they link a headword to a sub-clause, indicating that the antecedent has two roles. In the following sentence 'the man' is the one who 'is John' as well as the one who 'owns the bar':

---

[13] Past participles are discussed in Section 14.5.

62   *Valences*

(86)   *The man who owns the bar is John.*

$$'\Sigma/\text{PR}$$
$$man - \text{THE} - [who_1] = John$$
$$\Sigma/\text{PR}$$
$$[who_2] = [own_1]$$
$$[own_2] \; ; \; bar - \text{THE}'$$

This syntactic representation can be read as follows. We find the phrase 'the man' ('*man* – THE'), which equals 'John' (indicated by '= John'). Since these elements are convergent, they are placed on the same horizontal line (below the sigma symbol and present tense notation). At the same time, 'the man' is further modified (limited '–') by 'who owns the bar'. The relative pronoun 'who' is bivalent: the first valence is convergent with 'the man', and the second valence is the subject (first nexus member) of 'own the bar'. Since 'who owns the bar' is a nexus with a time frame, an upper layer is added with the symbol 'Σ' for 'situation', followed by the (present) tense of that situation.

Relative clauses may have a restrictive reading or an appositive reading. When the relative clause is not restrictive, in spoken language this is indicated by an interruption in intonation before the relative pronoun and, if necessary, a second interruption after the clause (in written language this is commonly indicated by commas). For example (86) above, a restrictive meaning has been represented. However, this sentence may also occur with an appositive reading, for which a different representation can be made, namely with the symbol '⊢' for apposition[14] (cf. Ebeling 2006: 303):

(87)   *The man, who owns the bar, is John.*

$$'\Sigma/\text{PR}$$
$$man - \text{THE} \vdash [who_1] = John$$
$$\Sigma/\text{PR}$$
$$[who_2] = [own_1]$$
$$[own_2] \; ; \; bar - \text{THE}'$$

One word may occur with different functions and meanings, and as such must also be analysed differently, depending on its relation with the other elements in the sentence. For example, 'that' can be used as a relative pronoun or as a conjunction. If we compare (88) and (89), we find that in the first example 'that' is a relative pronoun, which modifies (limits) the headword and is connected by the limitation relation to the noun it modifies, which is 'book':

---

[14] For appositions, see also Chapter 9.

4.6 Other Examples of Valence   63

(88)   *The book that you gave me is very interesting.*

$$
\begin{array}{l}
\quad\quad\quad\quad '\Sigma\,/\,PR \\
book - \text{THE} - [that_1] = interesting > very \\
\quad\quad\quad\quad [that_2] \;\; ; \;\; \Sigma\,/\,PA \\
\quad\quad\quad\quad\quad\quad you = [give_1] \\
\quad\quad\quad\quad\quad\quad\quad [give_2] \;\; ; \;\; I'
\end{array}
$$

However, the conjunction 'that' in (89) has a different function and relation to the element to which it connects, namely adding extra information to the 'subject + predicate', i.e. it connects the content clause of the matrix verb 'tell'. This is therefore represented with the relation of gradation, i.e.:

(89)   *He told me that it was very interesting.*

$$
\begin{array}{l}
'\Sigma\,/\,PA \\
he = [tell_1] \quad\quad > [that_1] \\
\quad [tell_2] \;\; ; \; I \;|\;\; [that_2] \;\; ; \;\; \Sigma\,/\,PA \\
\quad\quad\quad\quad\quad\quad\quad it = interesting > very'
\end{array}
$$

If we compare the example above with the next example, we find that in (89) 'I' is represented as the second valence of the matrix verb, because there is no direct object here, whereas in (90), without the conjunction 'that', 'I' is linked to the third verb valence, because the second situation, which expresses the content of what was told, is analysed as the direct object, and as such is represented as the second valence of 'tell':[15]

(90)   *He told me it was very interesting.*

$$
\begin{array}{l}
'\Sigma\,/\,PA \\
he = [tell_1 \\
\quad [tell_2 \;\; ; \quad\quad\quad \Sigma\,/\,PA \\
\quad [tell_3 \;\; ; \; I \;\;|\;\; it = interesting > very'
\end{array}
$$

There are also relative clauses without relative pronouns; in the semiotactic representations for such constructions, the relative clauses are linked directly to their antecedents by the divergent limitation relation. Examples of different kinds of relative clauses are analysed in Section 16.2.

---

[15] See also Section 4.2 for a discussion of valences.

5 Set Expression 'SE'

Language is full of expressions with a complex meaning that is not identical to the sum of the meanings of their separate parts. In some cases an expression has an idiomatic meaning even though the syntactic structure is still transparent. The question is whether one should represent the internal syntactic structure of these idiomatic expressions or opt for the notation 'SE' for **set expression**. We argue that the differences but also the similarities in meaning of these phrases can be adequately illustrated by representing the different syntactic structures of the constructions. This is also the case for metaphorical expressions, such as *lone wolf*, which is used to refer to someone (e.g. a terrorist) who prefers to act alone, but for which a regular semiotactic representation can be given, i.e. 'lone' modifies (limits) 'wolf':

(91)   *a lone wolf*

'*wolf* − *lone* − NONTHE'

In other expressions, the relation between the different parts is less transparent. This is the case, for example, in the expression *right away* (meaning: 'without delay'), which can be regarded as an expression that is probably processed by language users as one block, where *away* has no distinct, separate, independent semantic contribution (in contrast to similar expressions like *right now*). For such expressions we can use the abbreviation 'SE' (for set expression) and place the expression between curly brackets, without indicating the relation between the separate parts:

(92)   *right away*

'SE{*right away*}'

Consider also, for example, the Dutch expression *hij nam de benen*, which has the literal meaning: 'he took the legs', but the idiomatic meaning: 'he ran away/fled'. Even though for many speakers the idea of running will probably be associated with the word *benen* ('legs'), which may also be recognized as the object of *nemen* ('take'), language users probably do not project the idea of 'taking' and 'legs' when they hear this expression. This can be seen as a motivation not to provide an internal syntactic structure for the predicate *de benen nemen*, and instead to regard it as one semantic unit. An English example is: *hold your tongue,* which has the idiomatic meaning 'don't speak', and although the literal meaning 'take hold of your tongue' is not plausible, the tongue certainly plays a part in the act of speaking, and 'stop the tongue from moving' would be a plausible literal meaning. There are also set expressions that may have both a literal and an idiomatic interpretation, in which case the choice of representing one meaning or the other would be based on interpretation, as in: *I was just pulling your leg,* for example. All things considered, we have decided to semiotactically represent the syntactic structure of idiomatic (or possibly idiomatic) structures unless there is no syntactic structure that adequately represents their semantic contents.

In the case of compounds (see Section 2.2.1), which may have an idiomatic character in terms of their internal structure, we have also chosen to represent the internal structure. As such, the compounds *blackbird* and *frisdrank* ('soft drink') are represented as convergent compounds, and compared with their counterparts, which consist of a regular adjective-noun construction, *a black bird* and *een frisse drank* ('a refreshing drink') respectively.[1]

---

[1] Ebeling (1978: 122) discusses other examples, such as *gooseberry* and *raincoat*, analysing the first of these as a set expression but not the second.

6 Nexus Relation as Entity (Bahuvrihi)

In the instances of nexus discussed so far, the referent was a situation, a piece of the world with a temporal dimension. However, there are also syntactic means that lead to a nexus relation but do not have this additional effect of evoking a temporal dimension. In these 'Bahuvrihi'[1] constructions, the nexus complex has an entity rather than a situation as its referent. It consists of two convergent elements that stand in a nexus relation to each other and together constitute an entity. This entity as a whole is what modifies the headword, not its separate parts (Ebeling 2006: 197), and it is represented with the symbol 'X' (instead of 'Σ'), e.g.:

(93)　　*a wide-brimmed hat*　　　(a hat with the feature that the brim is wide)

　　　　'*hat* −　X　− NONTHE
　　　　　brim = *wide*'

(94)　　*a bald-headed man*　　　(a man with the feature that the head is bald)

　　　　'*man* −　X　− NONTHE
　　　　　head = *bald*'

Other Bahuvrihi constructions will be discussed in Section 13.7.

---

[1] The term *Bahuvrihi* comes from Sanskrit grammar and has the meaning 'having much rice', denoting a rich man. We follow Ebeling (1978) in using this term more broadly to refer to instances of nexus without situation.

7 Negation

Negation is indicated by the notation 'NON'. In order to represent negation, two important questions need to be answered. First, is the negation related to the negated element by a relation of stratification '/' or gradation '>'? And second, does the negation pertain to the situation as a whole (which is expressed by the sentence or clause), or does it pertain to an element within this sentence or clause?

With respect to the first question, we argue that negation involves a relation of gradation and not stratification. The stratification relation is not suitable (even though it is typically used with quantitative elements) because negation is not a matter of countability (of something occurring zero times), but of something not occurring/existing at all. We consider the relation of gradation more appropriate, since in the meaning of most occurrences of gradation something can be presented to a highest ('completely'), higher or lower degree, and the lowest degree can reach the point of absolute zero, when the feature is no longer present, e.g.:

(95) *not a big dog*

'*dog − big −* NONTHE $>$ NON'

(96) *not very kind*

'*kind* $>$ *very* $>$ NON'

When the negation is within a word (part of the word), expressing an opposite meaning compared with the original word, the notation 'CCNTR' is used instead; the difference between them is defined as:

- 'NON' = 'a feature that is not there/is absent'
- 'CONTR' = 'a feature of which the contrary is present'

(97) *unkind*

'*kind* $>$ CONTR'

68   *Negation*

This can be negated into:

(98)   *not unkind*

'*kind* > CONTR > NON'

The second question, which arises when analysing negation in a nexus, is whether the negation is taken to refer to one (or more) element(s) within this situation or to the situation as a whole. The first option, i.e. the analysis of negation referring directly to the negated element, will be given the same representation as the examples above. However, if one assumes the second analysis to be correct, the negation should be represented in the top layer of the representation, after the sigma and tense. An argument supporting this view is that when the predicate is negated, this indicates that the speaker wishes to convey the meaning that the whole situation is not taking place (or did not take place). According to this reasoning, for the next example:

(99)   *Peter is not kind.*

the following representation could be given:

(99')
$$'\Sigma / PR > NON$$
$$Peter = kind'$$

This representation conveys the meaning that the situation 'Peter is kind' does not exist. In other words, Peter is (inherently) not a kind man. However, on the basis of the assumption that this sentence renders the meaning that the situation 'Peter is not kind' exists, another representation could be made, i.e.:

(99'')
$$'\Sigma / PR$$
$$Peter = kind > NON'$$

When we extend this example by adding other elements, e.g. *Peter was not kind to me yesterday (but today he was)*, we get the idea that it depends on the time or circumstances whether Peter is kind or not. Furthermore, in the syntactic representation, the time element ('yesterday') is also placed below the sigma layer, indicating that it is part of the situation.[1] Thus it does not seem feasible to assume that the speaker's intention is to convey specifically the meaning that the entire situation 'Peter was kind yesterday' does not exist (and

---

[1] This is a different notation for *yesterday* from the one proposed by Ebeling, as discussed in Chapter 17.

Negation 69

that conversely the situation 'he was kind today' does exist). What is most probably expressed is the intended meaning that the entire situation is: 'Peter was not kind to me yesterday', which is represented as follows:

(100)   *Peter was not kind to me yesterday.*

$$\Sigma / PA$$
$$Peter = kind \ > NON > [to_1] \ > yesterday$$
$$[to_2] \ ; \ I'$$

We can give another example: *Peter is not working now (because it's lunch-time)*, where the implication could be that the negation refers to the whole situation, namely the speaker states that the situation 'Peter is working' does not exist. On the other hand, it seems much more likely that the intended meaning is that Peter has just stopped working for a moment.

However, the view on how the negation in a nexus situation is taken to affect the meaning, namely whether it is at a predicate level or concerns the entire situation, is often a matter of interpretation. In some languages the distinction between a negation that connects only to the predicate and a negation indicating the whole situation is easier to determine. In Japanese, for example, sentences with an affirmative verb form and a negated verb form within one predicate occur regularly, which leaves representation of the nega-tion within the situation as the only option. On the other hand, when the finite polite verb form (indicating politeness towards the person addressed) in Japanese is negated, the negation is considered to belong to the speech situation and is therefore represented on the top layer after the sigma. Such instances of negation in Japanese will be discussed in Section 16.3.

Taking all these arguments into consideration, we argue that in most cases we can treat negation in a nexus in the same way as negation in phrases, namely by assuming that it only refers to the part of the sentence that is being negated, rather than to the whole situation it is in, unless there are specific indications in form or meaning to suggest otherwise.

8 The Auxiliary Verb 'Do'

In English the auxiliary verb *do* is used for constructing negation ('NON'), questions ('Q') and emphasis ('EMPH'), and for carrying the tense of the situation. As such, unlike the main verb *do*, this auxiliary is used only grammatically and seems to have lost its lexical meaning. One could therefore argue that, since only elements that carry meaning are represented in the notations, this auxiliary 'do' should be left out of the representations, and only the grammatical elements that it indicates should be represented. Following this reasoning, two different representations would be made for, on the one hand, the main (bivalent) verb 'do', as in example (101), and on the other hand, the auxiliary, as in (102), (103) and (104):[1]

(101)   *She does her homework every night.*

(101')

$$
\begin{array}{l}
{}'\Sigma\,/\,\mathrm{PR} \\
she = [do_1] > night - every \\
\quad\ [do_2] \ ; \ homework \downarrow \\
\qquad\qquad\qquad - she'
\end{array}
$$

(102)   *He didn't come.*

(102')

$$
\begin{array}{l}
{}'\Sigma\,/\,\mathrm{PA} \\
he = come > \mathrm{NON}'
\end{array}
$$

(103)   *Did he come?*

(103')

$$
\begin{array}{l}
{}'\Sigma\,/\,\mathrm{PA}\,/\,\mathrm{Q} \\
he = come'
\end{array}
$$

(104)   *He did come.*

---

[1] Cf. Ebeling (1978: 372).

(104')

$$'\Sigma / PA / EMPH$$
$$he = come'$$

These formalizations clearly indicate the difference between *do* expressing lexical meaning and *do* as a grammatical element with a semantically bleached meaning. However, even in the latter case it is the auxiliary verb *do* that carries the tense and number markings of the entire sentence (the second verb is an infinitive), and as such the verb 'do' establishes its place in the predicate by its relation with the first nexus member. These properties of the sentence's formal structure are left out in the formalizations above for examples (102), (103) and (104). Furthermore, because 'do' is absent from the formalization, we cannot show, for example, that in the formal structure of the sentence (102) the verb *do* is negated, not the infinitive. This also means that it is difficult to provide an adequate formalization for sentences such as: *that censorship does not and will not take place in libraries,* where the use of *do* is syntactically-intonationally linked to the use of *will* in the language structure (DOES not and WILL not INF). In view of all these arguments, we propose to represent the auxiliary verb 'do' in the same way as the main verb, i.e. as the bivalent predicate, with the situation of the infinitive verb as its second valence. Since *do* can be considered to be polysemous, one could argue that the different meanings of *do* should also be indicated in the syntactic representations. Within the model of Semiotactics this can be done by using number subscripts on the left side of the meaning element, for example $_1$do (regular 'do'), $_2$do ('do' occurring with questions), $_3$dc ('do' occurring with negation) and $_4$do ('do' indicating emphasis). However, in the case of the non-lexical meaning of *do*, 'do' only indicates the concept of a verbal meaning in its most abstract sense, including person and time. Therefore, we have decided to represent the lexical meaning of 'do' as '$_1$do' and all the grammatical meanings as '$_2$do':

(101'')

$$'\Sigma / PR$$
$$she = \left[{}_1do_1\right] > night - every$$
$$\left[{}_1do_2\right] \ ; \ homework \downarrow$$
$$- she'$$

(102'')

$$'\Sigma / PA$$
$$he = \left[{}_2do_1\right] > NON$$
$$\left[{}_2do_2\right] \ ; \ \Sigma$$
$$X = come'$$

72 *The Auxiliary Verb 'Do'*

(103'')

$$'\Sigma/\text{PA}/\text{Q}$$
$$he = \begin{bmatrix} {}_2do_1 \end{bmatrix}$$
$$\begin{bmatrix} {}_2do_2 \end{bmatrix} \; ; \; \Sigma$$
$$X = come'$$

(104'')

$$'\Sigma/\text{PA}/\text{EMPH}$$
$$he = \begin{bmatrix} {}_2do_1 \end{bmatrix}$$
$$\begin{bmatrix} {}_2do_2 \end{bmatrix} \; ; \; \Sigma$$
$$X = come'$$

One could argue that as a result of the decision to place the verb 'do' in the representation, the notation of 'Q' and 'EMPH' are no longer necessary; however, since interrogative and emphatic meanings may also be expressed by intonation or punctuation marks, e.g. *did he come?* v. *he came?* or *he did come* v. *he came!*, we propose to maintain the representation of the constructional meaning of these semantic particles.[2] Moreover, this enables us to account for the occurrences of the auxiliary verb 'do' ('$_2$do') when there is no other verb in the construction, as e.g. in instances of so-called 'VP-ellipsis': (*Did he come?*) *He did.* Such cases can now be represented with 'do' in the formalization, without any semantic particle notations except for the (past) tense:[3]

He did.

$$'\Sigma/\text{PA}$$
$$he = {}_2do'$$

---

[2] See also Ebeling (1978: 242).

[3] This construction could be analysed as a case of semantic doubling (see Section 4.4) and thus be represented with an 'X' as the second valence of 'do'. However, we prefer the analysis of valence reduction (as discussed in Section 4.2) because in our view the non-linguistically expressed element to which this sentence refers back is not part of its semantic-syntactic structure but rather belongs to interpretation.

9 *Appositions*

One syntactic sentence may contain separate elements called appositions. According to Jespersen (1984: 13), the difference between a junction and an apposition is that in the former there is a closer connection, and in the latter a looser coordination, which is often indicated by a slight pause and by intonation. In the semiotactic analysis, the elements that are 'set aside' by apposition are part cf the syntactic sentence but have no specific syntactic relation to other elements in it, apart from unspecified convergence. Apposition is indicated by the symbol '⊢', e.g.:

(105)   *The cantata, by Bach, was beautiful.*

$$'\Sigma/PA$$
$$cantata - \text{THE} \vdash [by_1] = beautiful$$
$$[by_2] \; ; \; Bach'$$

In the following example we find two appositions:

(106)   *I met Lawrence, the novelist, not the Colonel.*

$$'\Sigma/PA$$
$$I = [meet_1]$$
$$[meet_2] \; ; \; Lawrence \vdash novelist - \text{THE} \vdash colonel - \text{THE} > \text{NON}'$$

10 *Formal and Syntactic Sentences*

A group of words form one **formal sentence** when they have an uninterrupted intonational contour. A formal sentence is the largest syntactic unit and may consist of several syntactic sentences. A **syntactic sentence**, on the other hand, consists of a word (or group of words) held together by syntactic relations.

In the case of example (106) above in the previous section, the appositional element (*the novelist*) is related to another element of the sentence (*Lawrence*) by unspecified convergence and as such is part of the syntactic sentence. This kind of syntactic relation is absent in the case of an **extraposition**, where a word (or group of words) is placed outside a syntactic sentence. Ebeling (1978: 28) makes a distinction between example (107), which he analyses as one formal sentence consisting of two syntactic (semantic) sentences, and example (108), consisting of two formal sentences. In the representation for the first example, the two syntactic sentences are not linked to each other by a syntactic relation, therefore the relation symbol '::' for 'syntactic sentence boundary' is used between them. This representation also indicates that, although the two syntactic sentences connected by '::' are placed on the same horizontal line, they are not convergent:

(107) *No, you can't!*

$$'no :: \Sigma / PR / EXCL$$
$$you = can > NON'$$

In the next example (108), the two parts of the message unit have an interrupted intonational contour, and are analysed as two different formal sentences, which is represented as two separate unconnected situations:

(108) *He bought it. For his nephew.*

$$'\Sigma / PA \qquad | \quad '\Sigma$$
$$he = [buy_1] \qquad | \quad X > [for_1]$$
$$[buy_2] \; ; \; it' \; | \qquad [for_2] \; ; \; nephew \downarrow$$
$$- he'$$

74

Formal and Syntactic Sentences   75

However, the distinction between formal and syntactic sentences is not always easy to determine. Ebeling (2006: 126) writes that the borders of a formal sentence are determined by the intonation pattern, but the same argument could be made for extrapositions. Furthermore, the problem when analysing written sentences is that such a pattern cannot be found, unless intonation is somehow indicated in the text.

A more complicated example of a formal sentence consisting of two syntactic sentences is (109), where the first extrapositional phrase can be regarded as the topic or introduction of the situation that follows, and the relative clause is connected to 'the man' by the bivalent relative pronoun 'who':

(109)   *The man who is coming there, do you know his name?*

$$
\begin{aligned}
&'man - \text{THE} - [who_1] &&:: &&\mapsto \\
&\qquad\qquad\qquad \Sigma/\text{PR} && | \\
&\qquad\qquad [who_2] = come > \text{PROGR} > there \mid \\
&\mapsto \quad \Sigma/\text{PR}/\text{Q} \\
&you = \big[{_2}do_1\big] \\
&\qquad \big[{_2}do_2\big] \; ; \; \Sigma \\
&\qquad\qquad X = [know_1] \\
&\qquad\qquad\quad [know_2] \; ; \; name \downarrow \\
&\qquad\qquad\qquad\qquad\quad - he'
\end{aligned}
$$

The syntactic sentence that is set apart by extraposition does not need to appear at the beginning of the sentence, as is demonstrated by example (110) with a vocative in the middle of the formal sentence, which in this case consists of three syntactic sentences:

(110)   *I am really leaving, John, you can't stop me now.*[1]

$$
\begin{aligned}
&'\Sigma/\text{PR} \quad :: \quad John \quad :: \quad \Sigma/\text{PR} \\
&I = leave > \text{PROGR} > real \mid you = [can_1] > \text{NON} \\
&\qquad\qquad\qquad\qquad\qquad [can_2] \; ; \; \Sigma \\
&\qquad\qquad\qquad\qquad\qquad\quad X = [stop_1] > new \\
&\qquad\qquad\qquad\qquad\qquad\qquad [stop_2] \; ; \; I'
\end{aligned}
$$

We have discussed the influence of intonation or punctuation marks on the semiotactic analysis. But what about the information structure as expressed by word order? Word order can also be a meaningful linguistic sign and as such should be accounted for in the linguistic representations. This issue will be discussed in Chapter 17.

---

[1] For the notation 'PROGR', see Section 14.4.

11 *Abstraction*

It should be noted that in language we also find forms expressing properties of people or things that are conceptualized as entities. Examples are *redness, beauty* (related to *red* and *beautiful*), *hunger, hatred* (related to *hungry* and [*he*] *hates* [*him*]) and *a shooting* (related to [*he*] *shot* [*him*]). Such examples are treated as instances of the syntactic operation of abstraction. As Ebeling (1978: 187) argues, abstraction is a phenomenon midway between semantics and syntax because it presupposes a property and a carrier of this property, but at the same time conceptualizes the property as an entity. Ebeling treats such abstractions as the outcome of a syntactic rule and formalizes them with angle brackets (e.g. *redness* is indicated as <red>). In this book, however, we do not indicate abstraction in this way, and treat abstractions as regular meanings, without indicating the relation to the related property in the formalization.

12 *The Basic Principles of the Formalization*

12.1 Universal Syntactic Relations

The symbols and notations used and discussed in this book consist of a rather limited set of symbols indicating a limited set of syntactic relations. How do we know that the universal syntactic relations discussed here are sufficient to describe all constructions from all languages in the world? Is it possible, for example, that a deeper study of other languages will reveal syntactic relations that cannot be represented with the symbols we have introduced here? Or should it be possible to predict the number and types of universal syntactic relations on the basis of the axioms and fundamental principles of the theory?

The relations that we discuss in this book are based on a close empirical analysis of a number of well-known languages from different language families (e.g. English, Dutch and Russian from Indo-European, and Japanese), and have proven to be applicable to various languages. At the same time, the relations also reflect fundamental ways in which humans can deal with linguistic structures. As we mentioned in Section 1.2, many of the relations we posit can very well be explained with reference to the principle of economy that operates in language (see e.g. Bartsch (1998) for the process of concept formation, Zipf (1949) for the principle of 'least effort', and Haspelmath (2008) and Croft (2003) for frequency effects in the case of language universals). To give an example, even though we can perceive things and their properties (e.g. 'red rose') conceptually as one phenomenon, it would not be economical to have a separate word for each thing that also expresses a property of that thing in such a way that, for example, 'red rose', 'small rose', 'withered rose', etc. would be indicated with separate words. Similarly, it would not be economical to have a separate word for each thing or person that realizes an event ('the man is walking', 'the man is sitting', etc.), or for each complex act ('reading a book', 'eating an apple', etc.). From the perspective of an economical but communicatively suitable linguistic structure, it therefore makes sense to have separate words that point to (i) things and

78   *The Basic Principles of the Formalization*

persons, (ii) properties of things and persons, and (iii) events. This conceptual splitting is the direct origin of universal syntactic relations such as 'limitation', 'valence' and 'nexus structure'. Other syntactic universals may have another communicative basis. This is the case, for example, with the notion of 'apposition', where some linguistic information is 'set aside' but is still part of the sentence. The existence of this type of relation may be explained with reference to its semantic-pragmatic properties, such as the speaker's need to convey a secondary or partly separate message, providing extra speaker-oriented information. Since humans will have more or less similar communicative needs, and the process of concept formation and formation of the linguistic structure works in a similar way in all languages, we can expect to find the same syntactic relations cross-linguistically. In our view, however, there is no a priori reason why there should or could not be more relations and hence more symbols than we have posited here. In some cases it might be necessary to introduce an extra symbol, but in other cases it might be avoidable. We will illustrate this with three symbols for syntactic relations used by Ebeling (1978), which we do not support.

The first symbol concerns the linguistic phenomenon of reciprocal constructions, such as the English *each other* or Russian reciprocal constructions with the suffix *-sja*, which can have either a reflexive or reciprocal meaning:

(111)   *Oni   celujutsja.* (Russian)
         they-NOM kiss-*sja*
         'They are kissing each other.' (English)

Reciprocal constructions are represented in Ebeling (1978: 200) by the syntactic symbols '&' and '$^+$', e.g. *They are kissing each other:*

$$'\Sigma / PR$$
$$they = [kissing]^+ \,\&\, [kissed\,]^+$$
$$[kissed\,]^+ \quad [kissing]^{+\,'}$$

In this representation '&' indicates 'and/or' and also the splitting of a semantic particle (i.e. the whole group of four elements constitutes one semantic particle), while the symbol '$^+$' placed after two identically defined meanings indicates that these meanings have one shared formal correlate. As such, the notation (with valences on two different horizontal lines) indicates that the persons involved act both as agent and as patient. A possible objection to this notation is that the inherent reciprocal semantics of *each other* is formalized in terms of syntactic relations for which two new syntactic symbols are introduced. This is not the solution we prefer, since our goal is not to introduce any

12.1 Universal Syntactic Relations   79

new symbols unless it is absolutely clear that a particular construction cannot be adequately analysed and represented using the basic set of syntactic relations presented here. Furthermore, the formalization treats the verb 'kiss' as a bivalent verb, where the reciprocal form functions as a second valence of the verb. This notation is perhaps appropriate for the English *each other*, but does not seem justified for reciprocal forms, such as the Russian ('reflexive') *-sja*, which do not function as verb valences (note, for example, that *-sja* is a suffix and not a pronoun).

In Ebeling (2006: 374) the two syntactic symbols '&' and '$^+$' are no longer used and instead a new notation is proposed, i.e. with the abbreviation 'MUT' for 'mutually':

$$' \ldots they = [x, y; x \, kisses \, y] \; > \text{MUT} \ldots '$$

In this notation, '$[x, y; x \, \text{R} \, y]$' indicates the set of one or more ordered pairs '$x \, \text{R} \, y$' (R indicates the relation between 'x' and 'y'). The notation 'MUT' indicates the reciprocal semantics of forms like *each other*, i.e. 'a property of a set of pairs $x \, \text{R} \, y$ that is characterized by the fact that each element of each pair (...) is a part of two different pairs, of one pair in the role of x and of the other in the role of y.' Similar to the earlier formalization from 1978, the verb 'kiss' is represented as a bivalent verb, but in this case the two valences are placed on the same horizontal line to indicate that syntactically there is only one participant (the subject 'they') and no second valence (direct object).

The reciprocal meaning is analysed by Ebeling as further specifying the complex verbal meaning. In our view, this formalization is more suitable than the earlier one because it requires fewer syntactic symbols and follows more directly the form of the construction (the semantic contribution of forms like *each other* can largely be equated with 'MUT'). However, it remains rather counterintuitive that the verb is represented as a bivalent verb with only one participant. We therefore prefer to represent the meaning of the English *each other* with a bivalent verb, where the second valence is non-specified and the reciprocal meaning gradates the non-expressed valence:

$$\begin{aligned} &' \Sigma \, / \, \text{PR} \\ they = &[kiss_1] \\ &[kiss_2] \; ; \; X \; > \text{MUT}' \end{aligned}$$

Note that the relation R need not be a verb; for example, in the case of a possessive phrase like *each other's arms* we can represent 'each other' by modifying (limiting) 'arms' with 'MUT' (or alternatively, with the form itself:

80   *The Basic Principles of the Formalization*

'each other'), using the non-specified element 'X' and the symbol for divergent limitation:

$$'arm \downarrow / \text{PL}$$
$$- X > \text{MUT}'$$

In other languages, with different structures, a different notation may have to be construed. For example, for the Russian sentence (111) quoted above, where the reciprocal meaning is expressed by a (reflexive) suffix, it seems better to treat the verb as monovalent:

(111')

$$'\Sigma / \text{PR}$$
$$they = kiss > \text{MUT}'$$

The second symbol that we will discuss here concerns constructions indicating part of a whole, such as the English *two of us*. Ebeling (1978: 400) uses the symbol for 'part versus whole' (indicated by '÷') to represent this construction:

(112)   *two of us*

(112')

$$'2 \downarrow$$
$$\div we'$$

This formalization indicates that the two people are part of a larger group of people that constitute 'we' (in contrast to *the two of us*, where 'we' consists of two members). In our view, however, it is not necessary to use this symbol, because the meaning of 'part versus whole' can be described by means of the semantic contribution of *of*:

(112'')

$$'2 - [of_1]$$
$$[of_2] \, ; \, we'$$

It is entirely possible, however, that there are languages where the idea of 'part versus whole' is not expressed by a separate form, and where a construction like *we two* must be interpreted as 'two of us'. Perhaps such a language is the Austronesian (Oceanic) language Avava, in which we find constructions like the following, where 'one' is part of the whole 'they':

(113)   *ier sapm* (Crowley 2006: 39)
         3PL one
         'one of them'

12.1 Universal Syntactic Relations   81

One could argue, however, that this construction can be represented by using the symbol for limitation, indicating that 'one' is a subset of 'they':

(113')

> ' *they* ↓
>   − *one*'

Note furthermore that the same construction can also be used to indicate the number of members comprising the whole set:

(114)   *kopɾı*   *iru* (Crowley 2006: 40)
        1PL.EXCL two
        'the two of us'

This suggests that the idea of 'part versus whole' is indeed an interpretation of a more abstract meaning, which can be described in terms of divergent limitation. Consequently, the introduction of a new symbol can be avoided.

The third universal syntactic relation we would like to discuss is the relation symbol '+' for 'container'. Ebeling (1978: 258) uses this relation for constructions like the English *a cup of tea*, Georgian *pinʲani čaj* (lit. *cup tea*; 'cup of tea') or Dutch *kop thee* (lit. *cup tea*), where we find a container and something contained (the universal syntactic relation 'container' is indicated here as '...cup + tea...'). Ebeling (2006: 189), however, rejects this relation symbol, because it is often left to interpretation whether the notion of 'container' is involved, or whether the construction is used to refer to both the container and its content (or something in-between); for example:

(115)   *Ik dronk een kop thee.*
        'I drank a cup (of) tea.' (the content and not the cup is meant)

(116)   *Hij gaf me een kop thee.*
        'He gave me a cup (of) tea.' (both the content and the cup are meant)

Furthermore, the use of metonymic expressions like *this cup was tasty* (Dutch *dit kopje was lekker*) clearly shows that there is a close relation between container and contained. Since universal syntactic relations must be discrete, they cannot apply to such instances. In addition to this argumentation, it is also questionable whether the idea of 'container' itself is always discrete.

82   *The Basic Principles of the Formalization*

Let us have a closer look at Dutch constructions with the structure [noun + noun], also called 'binominals',[1] such as *een kom soep* (lit. *a bowl soup*; 'a bowl of soup') or *een druppel bloed* (lit. *a drop blood*; 'a drop of blood'), where the first noun expresses a quantity and the meaning of the second noun modifies the first. In the first example, the first noun refers to a container (the bowl *contains* soup) but this is not the case in the second example. Here one can say that the drop consists of blood, or that the drop is formed by the blood. Similarly, we find collective nouns that occur as the first part of a binominal construction, e.g. *een kudde schapen* 'a flock of sheep', where the flock consists of sheep. All these instances indicate a particular kind of quantity, although there are also examples with a different kind of relation between the nouns, e.g. *een reep chocola* 'a bar of chocolate', where the first noun may also be taken to refer to the shape, in addition to indicating a quantity. However the data may be analysed, it is clear that the binominal construction is polysemous and does not always express a container, at least not in the literal sense. It would therefore be incorrect to postulate a universal syntactic relation 'container' for this construction. The question then remaining is how such constructions should be analysed. Ebeling (2006: 277) proposes that the abbreviation 'CNT' for 'container' should be used to represent instances of such a construction when it actually expresses a container. On this basis, we could make the following representation:

(117)   *kop thee*
         'cup (of) tea'

         $'kop - [x; x\,is\,\text{CNT}\,y]$
         $[y; x\,is\,\text{CNT}\,y]$; *thee*'

A consequence of this approach is that for each different interpretation ('x contains y', 'x is formed by y', etc.) a new abbreviation for a **constructional meaning** would have to be introduced, which for the next example could be:

(118)   *druppel bloed*
         'drop (of) blood'

         $'drop - [x; x\,is\,\text{FORMED}\,by\,y]$
         $[y; x\,is\,\text{FORMED}\,by\,y]$; *blood*'

Alternatively, a thorough semantic analysis of the construction could reveal the systematics of the restrictions on the possible interpretations of the relation

---

[1] See also Broekhuis and Keizer (2012).

12.2 Formalization and Form-Meaning Elements   83

between 'x' and 'y', and perhaps a more adequate abstract definition of 'container'. Note, for example, that the use of the Dutch construction is more restricted than the corresponding English one, probably due to the absence of a form like *of*. In English, the corresponding construction with *of* can also be used to indicate that the entity expressed by the first noun is made of the material expressed by the second (e.g. *cane of wood*), but this is not always possible in Dutch: **stok hout* (lit. *cane wood*).

In our current approach to Semiotactics we describe constructions at a relatively abstract level. In the case of the Dutch construction under discussion one could therefore argue that at an abstract level the construction itself is compositional, since its interpretation can be based on the compositional parts and their syntactic relation (i.e. the meaning of the second noun *modifies* the meaning of the first). Such an abstract approach does, however, neglect some 'lower level' semantic features of constructions, such as the ones described by scholars working in Construction Grammar or Cognitive Linguistics. In a more fine-grained, deeper semantic analysis such lower level features are an inherent part of the linguistic analysis and could also be made part of the semiotactic formalization.

12.2 Formalization and Form-Meaning Elements

Another important theoretical issue is the extent to which form-meaning elements should be represented in the formalization. A guiding principle of the theory is that form-meaning elements and their interrelations are formalized only if they contribute meaning. In some cases this requires making a judgement as to whether a form contributes meaning or not. To give an example, in English the infinitive is usually introduced by the form *to* and there is a limited set of constructions where the infinitive occurs without *to* (e.g. with modal predicates such as *can*). One could therefore treat *to* as a fully grammaticalized element, which adds no meaning other than indicating an infinitive verb. According to this view, the absence or presence of *to* can be seen as a grammatical automatism that is fully predictable on the basis of the other meanings in the construction, and therefore it should not be represented as a separate element in the formalization. We will argue, however, that the existence of minimal pairs (with a *to*-infinitive and a bare infinitive) makes it necessary to indicate the semantic contribution of *to* (see Section 14.2).

As a general rule, we have opted to represent form-meaning elements whenever possible. It should be noted, however, that there are different views on this issue. For example, with regard to the representation of form-meaning

84   *The Basic Principles of the Formalization*

elements, Ebeling (1978) presents a model that goes much further in abstracting away from some language-specific features than Ebeling (2006). Examples are instances where there is a logical subject of a passive construction that is expressed with a *by* phrase in English, and Dutch pseudo-passive constructions with intransitive verbs and a *door* phrase.[2] In such cases, Ebeling (1978) does not provide a separate representation for 'by' or 'door' respectively, but rather a representation that expresses the semantic contribution of these forms by means of syntactic symbols.[3] For the English passive construction, the following representation is given by Ebeling (1978: 267):

(119)   *The man was bitten by the dog.*

(119')

$$' \ldots \Sigma$$
$$man = [bitten]$$
$$dog = [bite \quad] \ldots '$$

This same structure could be represented by our notation:

(119'')

$$' \ldots \Sigma$$
$$man = [bite_2]$$
$$dog = [bite_1] \ldots '$$

This formalization correctly indicates that the subject is convergent with the idea of 'bitten' (represented by 'bite$_2$') rather than with the idea of 'bite' (represented by 'bite$_1$'). Our view is that the formalization with two nexus constructions (indicated by '=') does not accord with the structure of the passive construction, which expresses only one nexus. Nevertheless, following the argument that it is not meaningful through which preposition or case the agent in a passive clause is expressed, since the speaker has no choice but to use the dedicated marker for this (e.g. the *by* phrase in English), there is another possible representation, i.e.:

(119''')

$$'\Sigma / PA$$
$$man - THE = [bite_2]$$
$$[bite_1] ; dog - THE'$$

---

[2] See Ebeling (1978: 267, 273 and 291, 429).
[3] See also Section 4.2.2 for Russian constructions, where the actor has an instrumental case marking.

12.3 Meaning, Interpretation, Polysemy and Formalization   85

However, as we will explain in Section 14.5, we argue that the representation should follow the formal structure of the construction more closely, resulting in the following representation:[4]

(119'''')

$$'\Sigma / PA$$
$$man - THE = [bite_2] > [by_1] > PF$$
$$[by_2] \; ; \; dog - THE'$$

In our view, the use of a prepositional phrase expressing an oblique agent (instead of a regular agent expressed by the nominative subject) is meaningful, and therefore a form-meaning element such as 'by' does in fact add a meaning that cannot be captured by the mere use of syntactic symbols. Ebeling (2006: 447) proposes a notation similar to (119'''') for the agent of passive constructions, namely by representing the bivalent structure of *door* in the notation. As such, our work is much closer in spirit to Ebeling (2006) than to Ebeling (1978).

12.3   Meaning, Interpretation, Polysemy and Formalization

As the preceding sections have made clear, a guiding principle in Semiotactics is that meaning should be kept apart from interpretation as much as possible, and the semiotactic formalization deals with meaning rather than interpretation. The semiotactic analysis therefore does not deal with the actual mental 'picture' of linguistic utterances or with referents and truth conditions, but with information that is directly associated with form-meaning elements and the relations between these meanings. This can be illustrated with an example we mentioned earlier, which involves distributive versus collective interpretations:

(120)   *Two men are carrying three tables.*
'The two men together are carrying the three tables.'
'One man is carrying one table, and the other man is carrying two tables.'
'Each of the men is carrying three tables.' (so in total 6 tables are carried)

The construction is such that each of these interpretations is possible, but the semantics is the same for all these interpretations, thus the same formalization can be given:[5]

(120')

$$'\Sigma / PR$$
$$man / 2 = [carry_1] > PROGR$$
$$[carry_2] \; ; \; table / 3'$$

---

[4] For the abbreviation 'PF', see Section 14.5.
[5] For the notation 'PROGR', see Section 14.4.

86   *The Basic Principles of the Formalization*

Whether or not an interpretation is allowed is language-dependent and also depends on the existence of oppositional forms (cf. Ebeling 1978: 106–107 for Russian versus English, and Gil 1992 for an analysis of distributive-collective expressions across languages). At the same time, we have argued that in some cases the boundary between meaning and interpretation is more difficult to determine, as in the case of the binominal constructions in Dutch that we discussed above in Section 12.1. In such cases the construction can be analysed at various levels of abstraction (see also Fortuin 2000).

As we noted earlier, in language some forms are associated with several interrelated meanings; i.e. they are polysemous. This can be illustrated with the form *run*, which can be used in sentences like *I **run** every morning*; *She was weeping and her nose was **running***. We analyse the verb 'run' in these constructions as being polysemous, and as such it is not necessary to indicate in the formalization what the basic non-metaphoric meaning of the word is. In other cases, however, the question of whether the meaning of a form should be seen as polysemous or whether it is necessary to indicate the different meanings by using different formalizations is more difficult to answer. This can be illustrated with the following sentences containing the verb *write* or its Dutch equivalent *schrijven*:

(121)   *This pen writes smoothly.* (English)

(122)   *Deze pen schrijft prettig.* (Dutch)

This use differs from the more basic use of the verb, as in *John **writes** with a pen*, with a human subject, an inanimate object and an instrument indicated by the *with* phrase. In this construction the instrument of the act of writing (the pen) is conceptualized as the first participant (subject). We therefore find the metonymic relation 'instrument – subject/first participant'. The construction itself expresses that the subject has such properties that it lends itself well to realizing the action expressed by the verb. In Dutch a construction of this kind is more widely used than in English, and it also occurs with verbs where the relation between the original (basic) meaning of the verb and the 'coerced' meaning is less clearly that of 'instrument – subject'; for example, *dat bed **ligt** lekker* 'that bed is comfortable to lie in', (lit. that bed lies comfortably), where we find the relation 'location as instrument – subject'. The construction also shows similarities to the **middle passive** construction, where the meaning of the verb presupposes a human being and the subject causes the event to be realized by this human being, e.g. *the fruit peels easily*. Such constructions differ from those in (121) and (122), because the subject of the sentence is the direct object of the transitive alternative.

12.3 Meaning, Interpretation, Polysemy and Formalization 87

Ebeling (2006: 350–351), in his discussion of the Dutch example (122), proposes that the construction should be represented as:

(122')

$$pen - deze = {}^{a}\text{X} \downarrow \begin{array}{c} {}'\Sigma / \text{PR} \\ \\ - \Sigma \\ {}^{b}\text{X} = schrijven > prettig > \text{EXP}' \end{array}$$

This representation with two 'X' symbols and a second sigma situation can be read as follows: the symbol '^{a}X' represents the predicative, which is the property attributed to *pen*, whereas the second symbol '^{b}X' indicates a non-linguistically expressed agent/subject of the verb *schrijven* 'write'. The situation of writing is connected to the property '^{a}X' with the divergent limitation relation.[6] This entire representation expresses the meaning: 'this pen has the property that someone writes smoothly (with it)'. Even though this formalization correctly expresses the meaning of the construction, it diverges quite considerably from the actual form-meaning structure. Note, for example, that the formalization presents a second situation, although this is not part of the form-meaning structure of the construction. Furthermore, two instances of 'X' are represented, but these Xs are not coreferent with other meanings in the notation. Because our guiding principle is that we try to follow the form-meaning elements in the construction as closely as possible, we propose the regular nexus notation for the examples quoted here; e.g. for (122) this would be:

(122'')

$$pen - deze = schrijven > prettig \begin{array}{c} {}'\Sigma / \text{PR} \\ \\ {}' \end{array}$$

Such a formalization should, however, be accompanied by a semantic analysis of the meaning of the construction, so that it becomes clear how a verb like *write* (or *peel*) can be coerced into another related meaning due to the influence of the construction in which it occurs. As such, as argued in Section 12.1 with respect to the binominal construction in Dutch, we leave open the possibility

---

[6] Ebeling (2006: 350) additionally indicates in his formalization that the writing is *experienced* as *prettig* ('smoothly') by introducing the abbreviation 'EXP', which stands for experienced. This meaning element is a typical non-compositional constructional meaning, which does not have a one-to-one correspondence with a form element in the construction. We refrain from further discussion of this element.

88 *The Basic Principles of the Formalization*

that a more fine-grained (less abstract) analysis of the construction could also be represented.

To summarize, the most important rules to which we have tried to adhere in this work are:

a) a consistent use of the syntactic symbols, which also means that we try to avoid introducing new syntactic symbols as long as possible;

b) to follow the form-meaning elements as strictly as possible in the formalization;

c) if the use of a form-meaning element is predicted by the construction or context, not to represent this meaning in the formalization (e.g. in the case of plural marking with numbers);

d) to try to avoid introducing extra semantic abbreviations (for semantic particles) that do not correlate directly or indirectly with a form element; and

e) to take into account that the formalization deals with semantics and syntax, not with interpretation.

PART II   Application of the Theory

In the second part of this book we will analyse and formalize a large number of examples, starting with some basic constructions in English and other European languages, notably Dutch, French, German and Russian. The purpose of this part of the book is to illustrate how fruitfully the semiotactic approach can be applied to a wide array of languages and constructions across languages.[1] First we analyse noun modifications (Chapter 13), followed by various verb constructions, such as modals, infinitives, gerunds, progressive forms and past participles (Chapter 14). Then a more complicated issue, i.e. impersonal constructions, will be tackled in Chapter 15. Next, in Chapter 16, we examine other constructions, specifically in non-European languages. Finally, Chapter 17 is devoted to the difficult question of information structure (including word order) and how Semiotactics might deal with it.

---

[1] As such, these analyses are not intended to be exhaustive.

13 *Noun Modifications*

13.1 Compound and Equipollent Junctions

The two elements related by compounding constitute one unit, whereas the combination of an adjective and a noun has a more analytical structure. The headword of the compound is placed first in the semiotactic notation and is connected to the second part by the symbol for compounding '∪'. The relation between the parts may be convergent, as in the adjective-noun combination in example (123), or divergent, as in the noun-noun combination in (124):

(123) *blueberries*

$\qquad$ '*berry* ∪ *blue* / PL'

(124) *a bookshop*

$\qquad$ '*shop* ↓ −NONTHE
$\qquad\quad$ ∪ *book*'

However, there are similar constructions that are not analysed as compounds, but as having an equipollent relation. The equipollent relation symbol '·' was introduced in the first chapter for the notation of words of equal status, such as names. We propose to use the same relation of equipollence for constructions consisting of descriptive names and titles, where we do in fact find some kind of modification relation. Such constructions are often treated as instances of a 'modifier-head' construction, where the first noun modifies the second (cf. Matthews 1996: 240; Ebeling 2006: 127). When we apply this analysis to example (125) *King Edward*, the inferred meaning would be that 'King' limits the set indicated by 'Edward'. However, it can also be argued that in such constructions the first noun expresses an entity and the second noun further specifies which kind of entity is meant (e.g. the king named Edward). Although both analyses are equally possible, we have decided to follow Jespersen (1984: 11), who makes the distinction between equipollent relations

91

92 *Noun Modifications*

and compound relations on the basis of their word order. When a descriptive name is placed before a proper name, the relation is analysed as being equipollent (as in (125) and (126)), and with the opposite word order the word group is classified as a compound, as in (127).

(125)   *King Edward*

          '*King • Edward*'

(126)   *the River Thames*

          '*River • Thames* – THE'

(127)   *The Amazon river*

          '*river ∪ Amazon* – THE'

The difference between the representations for examples (126) and (127) is that in the first *Thames* is seen as a further specification of river, whereas in (127) river is added to Amazon to distinguish it from another entity (e.g. as opposed to the Amazon rainforest). Because these instances conform to the normal word order pattern of compounds, we follow Jespersen's analysis here, even though such cases show that the boundaries between a relation of 'compounding' and the category of 'equipollence' are to some extent arbitrary. Compare also the next two examples with a compound and an equipollent structure:

(128)   *the Crown Inn*

          '*inn ∪ Crown* – THE'

(129)   *Captain Smith*

          '*Captain • Smith*'

13.2   Adjectives and Adverbs

As explained in the first chapter, the relation between the meanings of a noun and an adjective is represented as a limitation relation, creating a subset. For instance, in the following example (130) a subset of 'men' is created.

(130)   *bright young men*

          '*man – young – bright* / PL'

13.2 Adjectives and Adverbs   93

In the same way, in the following example the French adjective *sec* 'dry' has a limitation relation with *été* 'summer'. However, the syntactic relation of the adverb *terriblement* 'terribly' is a different one: it does not directly modify *été*, but is a modifier of the adjective *sec*. This relation is represented with the gradation symbol '>'.

(131) *un été   terriblement sec*
       a   summer terribly   dry
       'a terribly dry summer'

       '*été* − sec > *terrible* − NONTHE'

Each of the following two phrases contains the adjective *burning*, which is polysemous. This adjective may refer to two different meanings, i.e. literally 'something that burns' and the second meaning 'hot to a very high degree'. Since these two different meanings lead to different syntactic constituents, they are given different notations. In example (132) only the second meaning is expressed, i.e. 'burning' modifies 'hot' not 'soup', which is represented by the gradation relation, indicating that 'hot > burning' as a whole modifies 'soup'. But in the second example the other interpretation, i.e. 'burning' directly modifies 'wood' (thus a limitation relation), is also possible:[1]

(132) *burning hot soup*

       '*soup* − hot > *burning*'

(133) *burning hot wood*

(133') '*wood* − hot > *burning*'   (wood is hot to a very high degree)

(133'') '*wood* − hot − *burning*'   (wood is burning and hot)

The difference between convergent and divergent limitation can also be found when the following examples are compared: there is a convergent limitation relation between 'society' and 'cooperative' in (134), whereas in (135) the limitation relation is divergent rather than convergent, because prices are not 'cooperative' but have the price level of a cooperative.

---

[1] Although Ebeling (1978: 188) proposes the notation for 'abstraction' for derived nouns such as 'paleness', 'redness', 'the shooting', etc., he does not use this notation for adjectives such as 'burning'. We propose not to use the notation for 'abstraction' at all in this book, but rather to represent such words as lexical units.

94 *Noun Modifications*

(134)   *cooperative society*

'*society — cooperative*'

(135)   *cooperative prices*

'*price* ↓ / PL
— *cooperative*'

Some adverbs can also occur in a noun-modifying function. In the following instances *then* and *here* function as regular indicators of limitation:[2]

(136)   *the then government*

'*government* ↓ — THE
— *then*'

(137)   *the man here*

'*man* — THE ↓
— *here*'

When the headword of an adjective-noun construction is not mentioned, a symbol 'X' is inserted into the semiotactic representations to connect the modifier, as in the following example from German:

(138)   *ein schwarzes Pferd und vier weisse*
'one black   horse and four white (ones)'

'*pferd — schwarz* / 1 > *und* < X — *weiss* / 4'

13.3   Genitival Adjuncts

The genitive is represented in the notation as an instance of limitation, and more specifically divergent limitation, because the separate elements refer to different entities, e.g.:

(139)   *John's hat*

'*hat* ↓
— *John*'

---

[2] Note that the difference in word order between examples (136) and (137) is reflected in their notations.

13.3 Genitival Adjuncts   95

(140)   *his poor mother's heart*

'*heart* ↓
        − *mother* − *poor* ↓
                        − *he*'

The genitive most commonly expresses possession but may express other related meanings as well, such as 'product' ('made by'), as in the next example (with the equipollent symbol '•' in the name):

(141)   *William Shakespeare's plays*

'*play* ↓ ⋮ PL
        − *William • Shakespeare*'

There are occurrences where the headword of a genitive adjunct construction is not mentioned, and in such cases the symbol 'X' is inserted, cf.:

(142)   *the butcher's shop*

'*shop* ↓ −THE
        − *butcher*'

(143)   *the butcher's*

'X ↓ −THE
        − *butcher*'

(144)   *This hat is mine.*

          'Σ / PR
hat − *this* = X ↓
                − *I*'

In the following sentence, where poems are being compared, there are two genitives without a headword, which is why two 'X' symbols are inserted:

(145)   *Shelley's are better than Keats's.*

            'Σ / PR
X ↓ / PL = *good* > COMP > [*than*₁]
    − *Snelley* | [*than*₂] ; X ↓ / PL
                                          − *Keats*'

96 *Noun Modifications*

13.4 Genitival Compounds

The following examples quoted by Jespersen (1984: 17) contain two kinds of genitives, namely the regular genitives indicated by *his,* and two other structures, both expressed by 's, which are not analysed as genitival adjuncts, but are represented as genitival compounds because they express a category rather than a genitive relation. In (146) the uniform is not owned (or made) by a captain, but is a kind of uniform of someone else ('his'), and in (147) it is not the heart of the mother that is being described, but rather 'mother's' is a qualification of 'her' own heart, which differs from example (140) *his poor mother's heart,* analysed above.

(146)   *his new captain's uniform*

'*uniform* ↓   − *new* ↓
    ∪ *captain* | − *he*'

(147)   *her warm mother's heart*

'*heart* ↓   − *warm* ↓
    ∪ *mother* | − *she*'

The next example (148) is also represented with a divergent compounding relation. Compared with example (141) with the genitive (*William Shakespeare's plays*), which expresses 'owned/made by', this example expresses a different meaning, namely a special kind of play. Therefore, a different representation is made, i.e.:

(148)   *a typical William Shakespeare play*

'*play* ↓ − *typical* − NONTHE
    ∪ *William · Shakespeare*'

13.5 Prepositional Phrases

Prepositional phrases can be used to modify or limit the information expressed by a noun. The preposition is inherently associated with two participants, i.e. it is bivalent.

This can be illustrated with the following examples:

(149)   *a man of honour*

'*man* − NONTHE − $[of_1]$
                $[of_2]$; *honour*'

13.6 Numerals and Quantities   97

(150)   *secretary to the premier*

$'secretary - [to_1]$
$[to_2] \; ; \; premier - \text{THE}'$

(151)   *the man in the moon*

$'man - \text{THE} - [in_1]$
$[in_2] \; ; \; moon - \text{THE}'$

(152)   *the faces of the girls*

$'face/\text{PL} - \text{THE} - [of_1]$
$[of_2] \; ; \; girl/\text{PL} - \text{THE}'$

In the example phrase (153) we find a combination of the genitive form and a prepositional phrase with *of*:

(153)   *the King of England's castles*

(153')

$'castle \downarrow /\text{PL} - \text{THE}$
$- king - [of_1]$
$[of_2] \; ; \; England'$

Note that whereas for genitival adjuncts the definite or indefinite article is always taken to modify the adjunct as a whole, for prepositional phrases with *of* there may be two possible analyses. For example, in this phrase (153), one could argue that the definite article should be regarded not as a modification of 'castles' (as indicated in the notation above), but as a modification of 'King of England', which would yield the following alternative representation:

(153'')

$'castle \downarrow /\text{PL}$
$- king - \text{THE} - [of_1]$
$[of_2] \; ; \; England'$

13.6   Numerals and Quantities

In Section 2.4 the stratification relation for indicating set numbers was briefly explained. In this section more complex examples with numbers and quantities will be discussed. There are words that cannot be counted directly and need another word in between to connect to the numeral, e.g. *glasses* and *wood*:

98   *Noun Modifications*

(154)   *three pairs of reading glasses*[3]

$'pair - [of_1] / 3$
$[of_2] \; ; glasses \downarrow$
$\cup reading'$

(155)   *four pieces of wood*

$'piece - [of_1] / 4$
$[of_2] \; ; wood'$

In the following Dutch examples, we find three different phrases about *rode wijn* 'red wine'. In the first example (156), *wijn* is in the singular and *glazen*, the Dutch plural form of the container *glas*, refers to the numeral, which is represented with a stratification relation. The relation between the container[4] and its contents is represented as a divergent limitation relation, whereas between 'wine' and 'red' there is a convergent limitation relation.

(156)   *twee glazen rode wijn*
'two glasses (of) red wine'

$'glas \downarrow / 2$
$- wijn - rood'$

However, in Dutch *wijn* (singular) may also occur without a container, as in (157), which can be someone's order in a restaurant. In such cases the symbol 'X' is inserted to connect to the numeral, since the container (glasses or bottles) is not mentioned and the noun *wijn* itself is not in the plural form and therefore cannot connect directly to the number:

(157)   *twee rode wijn*
(lit. two red wine)

$'X \downarrow / 2$
$- wijn - rood'$

In (158), however, *wijnen* is the plural form, so it can connect directly to the numeral and as such expresses a different meaning than the examples above, namely: two different kinds of red wine (for example on a wine list).

---

[3] In this example 'glasses' is used as a plural noun (not the plural of 'glass') and as such it does not have a singular form, therefore we have decided not to use the notation 'PL' in the representation (see also Section 2.4).

[4] The notation 'CNT' for container proposed by Ebeling (2006: 277) is not used here, as explained in Section 1.2.

13.6 Numerals and Quantities   99

(158)   *twee rode wijnen*
        'two red wines'

        '*wijn − rood / 2*'

In English when ordering drinks without mentioning a container (cups/glasses/bottles), the plural is most commonly used, e.g.:

(159)   '*Four coffees, two beers, one mineral water!*' he called to the barman.

        '*... coffee / 4* ⊢ *beer / 2* ⊢ *water* ∪ *mineral / 1 ...*'[7]

A Dutch speaker would place the same order with the nouns in the singular form, which is why these nouns cannot directly connect to the numerals and the symbol 'X' is inserted three times in the representation:

(160)   '*Vier koffie, twee bier, één mineraalwater*'

        '$\dots X \downarrow / 4 \quad \vdash X \downarrow / 2 \quad \vdash X \downarrow / 1$
        $\quad - koffie \mid \quad - bier \mid \quad - water \cup mineraal \dots$'

Quantifiers, such as *much, many, few, some, several, all, numerous*, etc., denote a non-countable quantity. They refer to a group as a whole, expressing a collective quantity, not separate sets. Therefore, they are represented in the notations connected with the relation symbol for limitation rather than stratification.

(161)   *I'm bringing some friends with me.*

        'Σ / PR
        $I = [bring_1] > PROGR \qquad > [with_1]$
        $\qquad [bring_2] \; ; \; friend / PL - some \mid [with_2] \; ; \; I$'

(162)   *We don't have much time.*

        'Σ / PR
        $we = [_2do_1] > NON$
        $\qquad [_2do_2] \; ; \; \Sigma$
        $\qquad\qquad X = [have_1]$
        $\qquad\qquad\quad [have_2] \; ; \; time - much$'

---

[5] One could argue that 'mineral water' should be analysed as a divergent compound. The criterion is whether there are two entities (e.g. wheelchair), or one entity with a property. In the English thesaurus 'mineral' is listed as a noun, but also as an adjective: 'of or denoting a mineral' (with example: mineral ingredients). For Dutch, in the van Dale Dictionary we find: 'minerale olie', mineraal = adjective. Hence we have chosen the representation for 'convergent compounding'.

100   *Noun Modifications*

(163)   *Every cloud has a silver lining.*

$$
\begin{array}{l}
\quad\quad\quad\quad \text{'}\Sigma\,/\,\text{PR} \\
cloud - every = [have_1] \\
\quad\quad\quad\quad [have_2] \; ; \; lining - silver - \text{NONTHE'}
\end{array}
$$

However, there are other quantifiers, such as 'each' (Dutch: *elk*), that do not refer to a collective quantity of a group but to individual units within a group, thus creating separate sets. This semantic difference between 'every' (indicating a collective group) and 'each' (indicating individual units) leads to different notations. Since 'each' indicates a division into separate sets, it is represented in the notations with the stratification relation.

(164)   *Each day is different.*

$$
\begin{array}{l}
\quad\quad\text{'}\Sigma\,/\,\text{PR} \\
day\,/\,each = different'
\end{array}
$$

(165)   *Elke doos woog zes kilo.*
'Each box weighed six kilos.'

$$
\begin{array}{l}
\quad\quad\quad\text{'}\Sigma\,/\,\text{PA} \\
doos\,/\,elk = [wegen_1] \\
\quad\quad\quad\quad [wegen_2] \; ; \; kilo\,/\,6'
\end{array}
$$

13.7   Bahuvrihi and Other Nominal Constructions

There are nominal constructions that cannot be represented with a convergent or divergent limitation relation, such the next examples (166) and (167) below, where we find the compounds *blue-eyed* and *good-natured*. These words are compounds consisting of two convergent elements that together constitute one entity, and this entity as a whole is the modifier of the headword. For instance, in (166) the girl is not 'blue' but her eyes are. We need to postulate an extra notation to represent the relation between these words, and for this the notation 'nexus relation as entity' (introduced in Chapter 6) is used.

(166)   *The blue-eyed girl had red hair.*

$$
\begin{array}{l}
\quad\quad\quad\quad\text{'}\Sigma\,/\,\text{PA} \\
girl - \;\; X \; - \text{THE} = [have_1] \\
\quad\;\; eye = blue \quad | \;\; [have_2] \; ; \; hair - red'
\end{array}
$$

In these examples the entity construed by the two convergent elements is a modifier to a headword. This can be found in (167), where the headword 'man'

13.7 Bahuvrihi and Other Nominal Constructions   101

is further modified by the non-specified entity 'X', which dominates the convergent meanings 'nature' and 'good', the two parts of the nexus relation 'nature = good'. The whole expression can be paraphrased as 'He was a man (of the type): (his) nature is good'.

(167)   *He was a good-natured man.*

> 'Σ/PA
> *he* = *man* –   X   – NONTHE
>   *nature* = *good*'

There is another construction for which Ebeling (2006: 197) proposes to use the same notation, i.e. for Dutch compounds such as *een kaalkop*[5] 'a baldy; a bald-headed man'. He compares (168), which has a modifier-head construction, with (169), where there is a Bahuvrihi compound that does not refer to a particular kind of head but to a person:

(168)   *een kaalhoofdige man*
        'a bald-headed man'

> '*man* – X – NONTHE
>   *hoofd* = *kaal*'

(169)   *een kaa'kop*
        'a baldy' (lit. a baldhead)

> 'X – NONTHE
> *kop* = *kaal*'

The only difference between these two representations is that in (168) 'man' is further modified by the entity 'X', which dominates the nexus, and in (169) the headword 'man' is absent and 'X' functions as the headword.

Similar constructions are also found in English. They are called Bahuvrihi compounds by Huddleston and Pullum (2016: 1651), who give examples such as *redhead, skinhead, egghead, birdbrain, lazybones, butterfingers,* which denote an entity that is characterized by having the property indicated, e.g. *a redhead* is a person who has red hair. The difference between such compounds and compounds like *blackbird* and *frisdrank* (analysed in Section 2.2.1) is that in those cases the compound noun is a special type of the noun that is one of the elements, namely a kind

---

[6] Dutch *kop* is an informal word for *hoofd* 'head'.

102 *Noun Modifications*

of *bird* and a kind of *drank* ('drink') respectively. In the case of a Bahuvrih compound, however, the compound as a whole refers to a different entity or rather a person. In most cases there is a metonymic part-whole relationship between a body part and the person with this body part. For example in (170) 'redhead' is not referring to a kind of head but to a person. If we follow Ebeling's reasoning, for this example we should give the same notation as for (169) above:

(170)   *She is a redhead.*

(170')

$$
\begin{array}{l}
{}^{\prime}\Sigma / \text{PR} \\
she = \quad \text{X} - \text{NONTHE} \\
\quad head = red'
\end{array}
$$

The question is, however, whether this analysis can be sustained. First of all, according to this analysis we find a nexus relation here, whereas it is debatable whether *redhead* (or Dutch *kaalkop*, for that matter) really expresses a meaning where 'head' signals the idea of an entity ('head') and 'red' separately expresses a property that is attributed to the head. Instead, we argue that the meaning of *redhead* has a closer resemblance to the meaning of any other compound without a nexus structure. This is further underlined by the fact that not all the Bahuvrihi compounds listed above (as quoted from Huddleston and Pullum) can be represented this way. For example, for the compound *egghead* the representation of a nexus relation 'head = egg' is incorrect, and the same holds for *birdbrain*. Finally, also note that if we were to follow the analysis in terms of a nexus relation for Bahuvrihi compounds, we would have to provide a different kind of representation for the alternative literal interpretation, where the speaker is actually referring to a 'head' when speaking of a *redhead*. In this case, the notation with the symbol 'X' and a nexus would not be possible and instead a notation without a nexus would have to be given. In our view, therefore, the notation of a nexus relation as an entity 'X' is appropriate only for noun-modifying compounds such as *blue-eyed* and *bald-headed*, as analysed above, but not for the representation of Bahuvrihi compounds.

The question remains, then: how do we represent such compounds? Jespersen (1984: 117) represents the Bahuvrihi compound *blackshirt* (= one wearing a black shirt) as: '2(21)1^{0}', in which 2 is a secondary (modifier), 1 is a primary (headword) and 1^{0} is a 'latent, not expressed' primary (i.e. 'X' in our terminology). In other words, a non-expressed person (1^{0} or X) is

13.7 Bahuvrihi and Other Nominal Constructions 103

modified by the compound *blackshirt* as a whole, which in turn consists of two parts: 'black' and 'shirt'. Jespersen's notation '21' suggests that this is an adjective-noun relation,[7] which means that the following representation could be made for (170):

(170'')

$$\text{'}\Sigma\,/\,\text{PR}$$
$$she = X \downarrow -\text{NONTHE}$$
$$- head - red\text{'}$$

Even though we agree with Jespersen that it is correct to represent such Bahuvrihi compounds without a nexus relation, his analysis does not take account of the compound character of *redhead*. This word functions syntactically as a unit where, for example, the adjective cannot be further modified (**a very redhead*). Therefore, we propose to represent this as a compounding relation, resulting in the following representations for *redhead* and *blackshirt*:

(170''')

$$\text{'}\Sigma\,/\,\text{PR}$$
$$she = X \downarrow -\text{NONTHE}$$
$$- head \cup red\text{'}$$

(171)   *He is a blackshirt.*

$$\text{'}\Sigma\,/\,\text{PR}$$
$$he = X \downarrow -\text{NONTHE}$$
$$- shirt \cup black\text{'}$$

The question that presents itself now is why it is necessary to indicate that such Bahuvrihi compounds refer to a person ('X') that is not linguistically expressed. One could argue that such a complicated notation is uncalled for, since we do not indicate metonymy in other instances, such as in the case of individual words like *The whites were descendants of the European settlers* ('...white / PL – THE...'). However, an important argument in favour of assuming that there is reference to a person in the case of Bahuvrihi compounds is the occurrence of compounds such as *lazybones* and *butterfingers*, which have a plural marking on the noun, but can occur with a singular indefinite article: *He is a lazybones/butterfingers*. In such cases the

---

[7] Jespersen's notation for adjective-noun, e.g. *black shirt*, is: 21.

104   *Noun Modifications*

occurrence of the singular indefinite article *a* can be explained by postulating a non-expressed element 'X', which refers to a singular person. In the cases where compounds such as *redhead* are used to express their basic meaning, i.e. not referring to a person but, for example, to an actual kind of 'head' (unlikely though it may be), then no 'X' should be represented, but only the compound itself: '*head* $\cup$ *red*–NONTHE'.

14 *Verb Constructions*

14.1 Modal Verbs

In English and various other European languages modal verbs are often distinguished as a class on the basis of their syntactic and semantic properties. Their functions can generally be related to a scale ranging from possibility, assumption, likelihood, probability, necessity to certainty. Examples are the English verbs *must, may/might, can/could, will/would,* and *shall/should*. Unlike other verbs, these auxiliaries have no -s form for the third person singular and can be directly negated (without the auxiliary *do*). This category of verbs proved to be difficult to analyse, because they can occur not only expressing epistemic modality, but may have other meanings as well. The epistemic meaning of a modal verb in a sentence does not have a direct relation with the meaning of another element in the sentence, but rather expresses the opinion/attitude of the speaker to his/her utterance as a whole. In other words, these verbs can be considered to belong in the domain of the speech act and as such their meanings would not be part of the situation expressed by the sentence.

So the question is: how should we represent such modal verbs in the semiotactic notations? Let us make an attempt to answer this question by analysing a few example sentences. For instance, in the next example (172) *must* expresses epistemic modality, referring to an assumption of the speaker. One could argue that, since this epistemic meaning of *must* refers to the entire situation expressed by the sentence, it should be placed on the top layer in the syntactic representation of this sentence, after the sigma symbol:

(172)   *He must be home (because the lights are on).*

(172')

>   'Σ *I must* / PR
>   *he = be > home*'

106   *Verb Constructions*

However, the problem with this representation is that although it does indeed reflect the meaning of the verb, it does not take account of its form (grammar/syntactics), namely the fact that *must* carries the tense marking of the sentence and has a direct relation with the first nexus member (the subject or agent), which requires it to be placed as the second nexus member in the situation (the other verb in the construction, the existential verb 'be', is an infinitive).

Note, for example, that if we were to follow this analysis for modal verbs, we would have to analyse the following Dutch sentence with modal *kunnen* 'can' as a sentence without a nexus (subject-predicate) structure:

(173)   *(Kan het dat Daan thuis is?)* ***Ja dat kan.***
          '(Could it be that Daan is home?) Yes it could (be).'
          (lit. can it that Daan home is? yes that can)

(173')

$$'ja :: \Sigma / \text{KUNNEN} / \text{PR}$$
$$dat'$$

This is a rather counterintuitive analysis. We prefer to give the following representation with a regular nexus for this example:

(173'')

$$'ja :: \Sigma / \text{PR}$$
$$dat = kunnen'$$

Moreover, modal verbs such as Dutch *kunnen* 'can' and English *must* may have other meanings as well, as in (174), where *must* expresses a necessity or (175), where 'must not' expresses a prohibition. In these cases, the meaning of 'must' refers directly to the subject of the sentence and is analysed as a bivalent verb, with the infinitive situation as its second valence.[1]

(174)   *You must eat something (or you'll die).*

$$'\Sigma / \text{PR}$$
$$you = [must_1]$$
$$[must_2] ; \Sigma$$
$$X = [eat_1]$$
$$[eat_2] ; something'$$

---

[1] Constructions with infinitive situations are discussed in Section 14.2.

14.1 Modal Verbs 107

(175)   *Jenny, you must not play in the street!*

$$'Jenny :: \Sigma / PR / EXCL$$
$$you = [must_1] > NON$$
$$[must_2] \; ; \; \Sigma$$
$$X = play > [in_1]$$
$$[in_2] \; ; \; street - THE'$$

A possible approach would be to argue that modal verbs like *must* are polysemous and that depending on the type of 'must' (which could be indicated by the left-subscript notation for polysemous meanings (e.g. '$_1$must', '$_2$must', etc.)) it should be represented either next to the sigma symbol or below the sigma. This would indeed be an approach to modal verbs that could show the difference in meaning in the syntactic representation. However, all the occurrences of *must* are the same in form (i.e. finite form of predicate, followed by an infinitive) and there is not always a clear-cut boundary between the differences in meaning. The different meanings are not always easy to establish without interpretation, context or previous knowledge; for example: *Could you do it?* may be meant to ask about either the possibility or the ability of someone to do something.

All things considered, we have decided to use one representation for all occurrences of modal verbs, i.e. as a regular bivalent verb within the sigma situation (cf. Ebeling, 2006: 411–414), which results in the following representation for (172):[2]

(172'')   *He must be home.*

$$'\Sigma / PR$$
$$he = [must_1]$$
$$[must_2] \; ; \; \Sigma$$
$$X = be > home'$$

A strong argument in favour of this approach is that we can now clearly indicate that the infinitive situation is the second valence of the modal verb, something that cannot be represented if we place 'must' next to the sigma symbol.

---

[2] Ebeling (1978: 474) treats a similar issue under the heading 'analogous patterning'. He discusses the Russian equivalents of the English X *wants to* Y and X *will* Y. Even though one could argue that in the syntactic representation the future tense would have to be represented next to the sigma sign, this would lead to the undesirable consequence that two similar formal structures are paired with completely different syntactic patterns. Ebeling therefore proposes that the semantic contribution of the finite verb (in the case of both 'want' and 'will') should be represented below the sigma sign. We agree with his reasoning.

108   *Verb Constructions*

For the Dutch modal verb *moeten*, expressing an assumption of the speaker, the same analysis can be made:

(176)   *Piet moet   rijk zijn.*
Piet must-3SG-PR rich be-INF
'Piet must be rich.'

$$'\Sigma\,/\,PR$$
$$Piet = [moeten_1]$$
$$[moeten_2]\ ;\ \Sigma$$
$$X = rijk'$$

The representations for the other modal verbs are made on the basis of the same arguments, as demonstrated by the following examples with, respectively: 'may' (permission); 'can' (impossibility), 'can' (ability); 'shall' (suggestion), 'shall' (promise); 'will' (prediction) and 'will' (voluntary action).

(177)   *Johnny, you may leave the table (when you have finished your dinner).*

$$'Johnny :: \Sigma\,/\,PR$$
$$you = [may_1]$$
$$[may_2]\ ;\ \Sigma$$
$$X = [leave_1]$$
$$[leave_2]\ ;\ table - THE'$$

(178)   *He can't come.*

$$'\Sigma\,/\,PR$$
$$he = [can_1] > NON$$
$$[can_2]\ ;\ \Sigma$$
$$X = come'$$

(179)   *He can play the piano.*

$$'\Sigma\,/\,PR$$
$$he = [can_1]$$
$$[can_2]\ ;\ \Sigma$$
$$X = [play_1]$$
$$[play_2]\ ;\ piano - THE'$$

(180)   *Shall I help you?*

$$'\Sigma\,/\,PR\,/\,Q$$
$$I = [shall_1]$$
$$[shall_2]\ ;\ \Sigma$$
$$X = [help_1]$$
$$[help_2]\ ;\ you'$$

14.2 Infinitive Constructions   109

(181)   *I shall make the travel arrangements for you.*

$$'\Sigma\,/\,PR$$
$$I = [shall_1]$$
$$[shall_2]\ ;\ \Sigma$$
$$X = [make_1] \qquad\qquad\qquad\qquad > [for\ ]$$
$$[make_2]\ ;\ arrangement \downarrow /\,PL - THE \mid [for_2]\ ;\ you$$
$$\cup\,travel'$$

(182)   *John Smith will be the next President.*

$$'\Sigma\,/\,PR$$
$$John \cdot Smith = [will_1]$$
$$[will_2]\ ;\ \Sigma$$
$$X = president - next - THE'$$

(183)   *Will you help me move this heavy table?*

$$'\Sigma\,/\,PR\,/\,Q$$
$$you = [will_1]$$
$$[will_2]\ ;\ \Sigma$$
$$X = [help_1]$$
$$[help_2]\ ;\qquad\qquad \Sigma$$
$$[help_3]\ ;\ I \mid X = [move_1]$$
$$[move_2]\ ;\ table - heavy - this'$$

14.2   Infinitive Constructions

As already explained in Section 4.4, the infinitive situation is an event type and does not express tense, person or number. In the semiotactic representations, the infinitive is presented as a separate situation, which is indicated by the symbol 'Σ' but without a tense marking. Because the infinitive expresses an event it is associated with a subject, but the identity of the subject is provided by the construction in which the infinitive is used. The subject of the infinitive most commonly refers to the same subject as the one in the main situation (e.g. *I want to eat*), but it can also refer or to another participant (e.g. *I let them eat*). If no coreference can be established, the identity of the subject often remains generic ('people in general'), as in: *to see is to believe*. Since the subject of the infinitive is not present in the form, it is represented by the symbol 'X'.

In English grammar, a distinction is made between 'bare infinitive' and 'to-infinitive' (also called 'full infinitive'). The *to*-infinitive is more commonly used, whereas the bare infinitive is mainly used after modal verbs

110   *Verb Constructions*

and auxiliaries. The question that presents itself is: should we represent the two infinitives in the same way or do we consider the two constructions to be semantically different? In other words, is the use of *to* a convention in English that can be fully predicted on the basis of the construction in which it occurs, or does *to* add meaning and therefore it should be separately represented in the infinitive constructions in which it occurs?

Before answering this question, let us first analyse a few examples with bare infinitives (i.e. infinitives without *to*). In the first sentence, the infinitive situation is presented as the second valence of the matrix verb 'can':

(184)   *Can you help me?*

$$
\begin{aligned}
&\quad\ '\Sigma\,/\,\mathrm{PR}\,/\,\mathrm{Q} \\
&you = [can_1] \\
&\qquad\quad [can_2] \ ; \ \Sigma \\
&\qquad\qquad\quad X = [help_1] \\
&\qquad\qquad\qquad\quad [help_2] \ ; \ I'
\end{aligned}
$$

A more complicated example with a bare infinitive is the following sentence, where the infinitive occurs with a perception verb (*see*) and an 'accusative' pronoun (*him*):

(185)   *We saw him run.*

The situation expressed by the bare infinitive coincides with the situation expressed by the perception verb (cf. *we saw him while he was running*).

In the literature three different analyses are given for this type of construction:

- (a)   the infinitive is the object (second valence) of the perception verb, and the accusative *him* expresses the subject of the infinitive
- (b)   this a trivalent use of the verb *see* (valences: subject, object and infinitive)
- (c)   this is a bivalent use of the verb *see* (valences: subject, object), and the infinitive must be seen as a further modification of the second valence

First, Jespersen (1984: 43) analyses this construction as: 'S-V-O(S$_2$I)' (subject-verb-object(subject$_2$-infinitive)), indicating that the entire combination 'him run' is analysed as the object of the matrix verb 'see', with 'he' as the subject of the infinitive. Based on this analysis, the following semiotactic representation is made for this sentence:

14.2 Infinitive Constructions   111

(185')

$$
\begin{aligned}
&\quad\;\, '\Sigma\,/\,\text{PA}\\
&we = [see_1]\\
&\qquad\quad [see_2] \; ; \; \Sigma\\
&\qquad\qquad\quad he = run'
\end{aligned}
$$

However, the fact that 'he' is in the accusative case has led to a different analysis in other sources, i.e. that 'he' is the object of the matrix verb (e.g. Kroeger 2004: 1097). In some syntactic frameworks, this construction is called a 'subject-to-object raising' construction, which is said to be 'transformed' from the sentence: *we saw that he was running*. This term 'subject-to-object raising' indicates that the subject 'he' of the situation in the content clause introduced by 'that' becomes the object of the matrix verb in the construction with the infinitive.

Whether one accepts this idea of 'raising-to-object' or not, it is indeed possible to treat the accusative form as the actual object (or second valence) of the main verb. If we do so, there are two possible analyses for the infinitive in the syntactic representation. One possibility is the notation given below as (185''), where we find that the verb *see* has three valences: the first valence is 'we', the second valence is the embedded infinitive situation 'run' and the third valence is 'he'. The non-linguistically expressed subject of the infinitive is represented by 'X', which is coreferent with the entity 'he':

(185'')

$$
\begin{aligned}
&\quad\;\, '\Sigma\,/\,\text{PA}\\
&we = [see_1]\\
&\qquad\quad [see_2] \; ; \qquad\qquad\quad \Sigma\\
&\qquad\quad [see_3] \; ; \; {}^{a}he \quad | \quad {}^{a}X = run'
\end{aligned}
$$

Note that since *see* normally functions as a bivalent verb, this would be a case of 'valence addition', where the bivalent verb is coerced into a trivalent verb because of the construction in which it occurs.

Alternatively, we could consider the infinitive situation to be an 'object complement' (see Leech, Cruickshank and Ivanič 2001: 331) or 'a grammatical adjunct' to the object (Sweet 1913: §124), as quoted by Jespersen (1965: 117) in his discussion on 'accusative + infinitive' constructions.[3] Following Sweet's analysis we represent the matrix verb 'see' with only two valences, and the infinitive situation is connected to the object 'he' by the divergent

---

[3] Since Jespersen's view is that the entire infinitive nexus is the object, he does not agree with Sweet.

112   *Verb Constructions*

limitation relation in the same way as the other instances of modification (adjuncts, relative clauses, etc.) discussed in previous sections.

(185''')

$$\begin{array}{l} '\Sigma\,/\,\mathrm{PA} \\ we = [see_1] \\ \quad\ [see_2] \;;\; he \downarrow \\ \qquad\qquad -\Sigma \\ \qquad\ X = run' \end{array}$$

This last representation (185''') is the one we prefer, arguing that the object *him* and the act of his running are not two separate participants to the act of seeing (e.g. 'I saw him', and 'I saw someone running'), but together they fill the second valence of 'see'.

Now we will return to the matter of the *to*-infinitives. From a semiotactic point of view, there are three choices for the representation of *to*-infinitives, depending on how the semantic contribution of *to* in these infinitive constructions is analysed. In other words, does 'to' still retain (part of) its original meaning of the prepositional use indicating a direction towards something, or has it lost this meaning and now become a purely grammatical element devoid of meaning?

We will discuss the three possible analyses here, with arguments from different sources.

1) *To* is analysed as a grammatical element, adding no additional meaning to the construction other than what is already implied by the other elements in this construction.

Tallerman (1998: 68) writes: 'This *to* is an infinitive marker, not to be confused with the entirely different *to* which is a preposition'. It follows from this analysis of *to* as a purely grammatical element without any separate meaning that it has no place in the semiotactic representations, since only elements that have meaning are represented. Consequently, for the next example (186), a representation is made without 'to' and with the infinitive situation as the second valence of the main verb:

(186)   *He agreed to help me.*

(186')

$$\begin{array}{l} '\Sigma\,/\,\mathrm{PA} \\ he = [agree_1] \\ \quad\ [agree_2] \;;\; \Sigma \\ \qquad\qquad X = [help_1] \\ \qquad\qquad\qquad [help_2] \;;\; I' \end{array}$$

14.2 Infinitive Constructions 113

According to this analysis, the verb *agree* is a bivalent verb with the infinitive situation as the direct object (in contrast to sentences where *agree* occurs without an element that expresses what is agreed upon, such as: *yes, I totally agree*). Note that this also means that for sentences where *agree* occurs with a preposition (*he agrees with me; they have agreed on a sale price*), we will have to argue that *agree* has turned into a monovalent verb because of the prepositional phrase. A similar phenomenon can be found in the case of other verbs, such as the difference between trivalent 'give' and bivalent 'give' when combined with a *to*-phrase: *he gave me the book* v. *he gave the book to me*.

A weakness of this first option (i.e. not to represent 'to') is that in some contexts *to* does in fact add meaning, for example in a sentence where there seems to be a purposive meaning: *he went to fetch a beer*.[4] Furthermore, the potential meaninglessness of 'to' is contradicted by the occurrence of minimal pairs, such as the following two sentences from Duffley (1992: 14), who gives these examples to illustrate that 'the hypothesis of meaningless variants must be ruled out once and for all: the two constructions do not mean the same thing':

(187)   *I saw him be impolite.*

(188)   *I saw him to be impolite.*

Sentence (187) is an instance of the same construction as in (185) above, where the event expressed by the infinitive coincides with the event expressed by the perception verb. This differs from (188), which could be paraphrased as 'I got to know him as someone impolite'.

2)   We could also argue that there are infinitive constructions where 'to' does express meaning and therefore, following the principle 'one form – one meaning', we should represent all occurrences of *to*.

This analysis seems appropriate particularly because making a distinction between different occurrences of *to*-infinitives would require further interpretation or contextual knowledge. Furthermore, this analysis could also account for the occurrences of minimal pairs as given above, for which two different semiotactic notations are needed to distinguish their different meanings. As a

---

[4] Another possible argument in favour of *to* being meaningful is that it occurs without verb form in the case of VP-ellipsis (e.g. *Yes, I want to*). In this case *to* explicitly signals the idea of a non-formally expressed verb. As such, we could represent the non-expressed second valence of *to* with an X ('...[to$_2$] ; X').

114   Verb Constructions

result of the decision to represent 'to', we can propose the following representation for example (186) above, with only one valence for the verb *agree* and with *to* connecting to 'subject + predicate' with the gradation relation in the same way as already explained for prepositions in Section 4.1:

(186'')

$$
\begin{aligned}
&\;'\Sigma/\text{PA}\\
he = agree &> [to_1]\\
&\;[to_2] \;;\; \Sigma\\
&\quad\quad X = [help_1]\\
&\quad\quad\quad\;\; [help_2] \;;\; I'
\end{aligned}
$$

In this case one would have to argue that the semantic contribution of *to* is rather abstract and can be equated with notions such as futurity (Wierzbicka 1988: 188) or the possibility of movement from a 'before-position' to an end-point (Duffley 1992: 16–17).

A weakness of this analysis appears to be that although one could argue that *to* has meaning in some constructions, there are also constructions where a meaning is quite difficult to assume, for example in sentences where the infinitive occurs as the subject of the sentence:

(189)   *To resist is futile.*

If we argue that *to* has meaning here, it has to be represented in the semiotactic notation. Since both valences of 'to' should be filled (otherwise an 'empty' valence would remain), we would have to insert an 'X' to connect to its first valence:

(189')

$$
\begin{aligned}
&\quad\quad\;'\Sigma/\text{PR}\\
X &> [to_1] = futile\\
&\;[to_2] \;;\; \Sigma\\
&\quad\quad X = resist'
\end{aligned}
$$

However, besides the difficulty of determining the meaning of 'to', there is another problem with this notation, namely the fact that it is difficult to determine what the referent of 'X' is in this case.

3) The third possible analysis is to make a distinction in representing different occurrences of *to*-infinitives, based on the view that in some infinitive constructions *to* is considered to have retained (part of) its original meaning as a preposition, whereas in other constructions this is not the case.

14.2 Infinitive Constructions   115

Jespersen (1940: 154–155) states that *to*, which originally had its ordinary meaning before an infinitive as a preposition of direction, still preserves this meaning in some combinations, but has lost it in others, where it has become a 'mere "empty" grammatical appendix to the infinitive'. He also argues that the use of *to* with a prepositional meaning is especially frequent with infinitives of 'purpose' (e.g. *he came to see you*), 'direction' (e.g. *I hastened to accept*) and 'result' (*he opened his eyes to find a stranger in the room*). Jespersen further gives examples of infinitives where the usual meaning of the preposition *to* is still 'distinctly felt': *he went to fetch his hat; he was led (inclined) to believe*, or is more or less 'vaguely present': *ready to believe; anxious to believe*. Leech et al. (2001: 533) make another distinction, i.e. between *to* used to form 'prepositional verbs' and 'phrasal-prepositional verbs' (such as *add to, belong to, look forward to*), *to* following adjectives in 'adjective patterns' and *to* as an 'infinitive marker'.

After considering the various arguments, we have decided to reject option 1 (i.e. never represent *to* when it is an infinitive marker) and option 2 (always represent *to*) for the semiotactic analyses. Instead we prefer the third option, i.e. the view that a distinction should be made between infinitives with a 'mere grammatical' *to* and infinitives with *to* expressing a particular meaning. Now the question remains: how to make this distinction and based on what criteria? The distinction can be made on the basis of the meaning, as suggested by Jespersen, or we can take account of the function and meaning of the elements to which the *to*-infinitives connect, as suggested in the above-cited work of Leech et al. In this light, we also refer to the following classification made by Jespersen (1965: 100), who writes that infinitives, according to circumstances, may belong to each of the three ranks,[5] and in some positions they require in English 'to':

1. infinitives as 'primary' (e.g. *to see is to believe; to resist is futile*)
2. infinitives as 'secondary' (adjuncts, e.g. *in times to come; the correct thing to do*)
3. infinitives as 'tertiary' (subjuncts, e.g. *he came here to see you; he is inclined to welcome a stranger*)

Jespersen's first category consists of what we propose to call 'independent infinitive situations', where 'to' does not connect to any other element in the

---

[5] Jespersen (1965: 96) classifies words into three 'ranks': the chief word ('primary') is defined (qualified, modified) by another word ('secondary'), which in its turn may be defined by a third word ('tertiary').

116   *Verb Constructions*

sentence. Jespersen's second and third categories will be taken together here, both being called 'dependent infinitive situations' and represented in the same way. We will analyse a few examples of these two kinds of infinitive situations, starting with the first category, the independent infinitive situations. For these cases we have decided not to represent 'to', since it is difficult to determine any added meaning and also this construction is grammatical in that it only occurs with 'to', and not with a bare infinitive. As a result, we now propose the following representation for sentence (189) above (*to resist is futile*):

(189'')

$$'\Sigma / PR$$
$$\Sigma = futile$$
$$X = resist'$$

In the same vein, 'to' is not represented in sentences with two independent infinitive situations, e.g.:

(190)   *To see is to believe.*

$$'\Sigma / PR$$
$$\Sigma \quad = \quad \Sigma$$
$$X = see \mid X = believe'$$

For the dependent infinitive situations, a different analysis is made. The first example is a construction with the motion verb *going to*, where the verb has a monovalent meaning and the element *to* a purposive-like meaning. In the representation for such constructions, 'to' is represented as the bivalent element that connects the infinitive situation to the 'subject + predicate' of the main situation with the gradation relation, as also used for prepositions:

(191)   *I am going to entrust you with a secret.*

$$'\Sigma / PR$$
$$I = go > PROGR > [to_1]$$
$$[to_2] \; ; \; \Sigma$$
$$X = [entrust_1] \qquad > [with_1]$$
$$[entrust_2] \; ; \; you \mid [with_2] \; ; \; secret - \text{NONTHE}'$$

However, a different notation must be made for similar constructions in Dutch or Russian, where there is no element like the English *to* (Dutch has an element *te*, which is used in other constructions but not in this next example, whereas Russian has no such element at all).

14.2 Infinitive Constructions 117

(192) *Ik ga lunchen.*
       I go have lunch-INF
       'I am going to have lunch.'

In this case there is no element to connect the matrix verb to the infinitive situation. We argue that in this Dutch sentence the verb *gaan* ('go') is not used as a motion verb but expresses a different meaning, i.e. a literal or metaphorical movement directed towards the future event that is expressed by the infinitive, which is represented as follows, with *gaan* as a bivalent verb. The Russian example (193), also without a 'to' element, would be given a similar representation.

(192')
$$'\Sigma / PR$$
$$ik = [gaar_1]$$
$$\quad [gaar_2] \; ; \; \Sigma$$
$$\qquad\qquad X = lunchen'$$

(193) *Ja   idu obedat'.*
       I-NOM go have.lunch-INF
       'I am going to have lunch.'

The *to*-infinitive is not always used in direct combination with a verb, but is also combined with other words, such as adjectives, adverbs and nouns, e.g.: *he is ready to go; he works hard to earn money; this is the game to watch; this question is difficult to answer; it is time to go.* In such constructions the infinitive situation has the function of modifying the headword. Therefore, in the notation the infinitive situation is represented as the second valence of 'to', with the first valence of 'to' connecting to a noun with convergent limitation, as in (194), or to an adjective with the gradation relation, as in (195):

(194) *This is the game to watch.*

$$'\Sigma / PR$$
$$this = game - THE - [to_1]$$
$$\qquad\qquad\qquad [to_2] \; ; \; \Sigma$$
$$\qquad\qquad\qquad\qquad X = watch'$$

(195) *This question is difficult to answer.*

$$'\Sigma / PR$$
$$question - this = difficult > [to_1]$$
$$\qquad\qquad\qquad\qquad [to_2] \; ; \; \Sigma$$
$$\qquad\qquad\qquad\qquad\qquad X = answer'$$

Having decided to represent 'to' in the dependent *to*-infinitive constructions, we can now give different semiotactic representations for the two 'minimal

118   *Verb Constructions*

pairs' quoted above from Duffley as (187) and (188) and repeated here. In the first example (196) the bare infinitive is analysed as an adjunct to 'he', which is the direct object of the matrix verb 'see'. The infinitive is represented with the divergent limitation relation, because it further specifies (limits) what is expressed by 'he'.

(196)   *I saw him be impolite.*

$$
\begin{aligned}
&'\Sigma / PA \\
I = &[see_1] \\
&[see_2] \; ; \; he \downarrow \\
&\qquad\quad - \Sigma \\
&\qquad\quad X = impolite'
\end{aligned}
$$

For the next example with the *to*-infinitive, we make a different analysis. Jespersen (1940: 157–158) writes that after *see* and *hear* the *to*-infinitive may be used when these verbs do not denote the immediate sense-perception, but rather 'an inference' or 'a logical conclusion'. We propose the following representation for this construction: the infinitive situation is the second valence of 'to' and the first valence of 'to' is connected to the 'subject + predicate' by the gradation relation. Thus the meaning is expressed that I concluded about him that he was impolite.

(197)   *I saw him **to** be impolite.*

$$
\begin{aligned}
&'\Sigma / PA \\
I = &[see_1] \qquad > [to_1] \\
&[see_2] \; ; \; he \mid \; [to_2] \; ; \; \Sigma \\
&\qquad\qquad\qquad\quad X = impolite'
\end{aligned}
$$

Another example of a pair of bare infinitive v. full infinitive sentences is given by Huddleston and Pullum (2016: 1244), who write that with *help* some speakers restrict the bare infinitival to cases of relatively direct assistance, comparing the meaning of (198), where *he* actually did some of the work, with (199), where *he* enabled *me* to do it myself:

(198)   *He helped me finish on time (by doing the bibliography for me).*

$$
\begin{aligned}
&'\Sigma / PA \\
he = &[help_1] \\
&[help_2] \; ; \; I \downarrow \\
&\qquad\quad - \Sigma \\
&\qquad\quad X = finish > [on_1] \\
&\qquad\qquad\qquad\qquad [on_2] \; ; \; time'
\end{aligned}
$$

14.2 *Infinitive Constructions* 119

(199)   *He helped me to finish on time (by taking the children away for the week-end).*

$$
\begin{aligned}
&\text{'}\Sigma\,/\,\text{PA}\\
&he = [help_1] \qquad > [to_1]\\
&\qquad [help_2]\; ;\; I \;\mid\; [to_2]\; ;\; \Sigma\\
&\qquad\qquad\qquad\qquad X = finish > [on_1]\\
&\qquad\qquad\qquad\qquad\qquad\quad [on_2]\; ;\; time\text{'}
\end{aligned}
$$

However, Huddleston and Pullum also remark that it is questionable how widely shared such judgements are: many speakers would allow a bare infinitival in (199) no less than in (198), and there is certainly no clear-cut distinction between direct and indirect help.

Besides differences in meaning between bare infinitive and *to*-infinitive, we may also find different meanings for one *to*-infinitive construction. For example, the following sentence (200) (quoted from the lyrics of a song) could be interpreted with two meanings, namely: 'I need that you change my life' and: 'I need you so that I can change my life'.

(200)   *I need you to change my life.*

These two possible meanings have only one form, there is only one construction, and therefore we could make just one representation for this sentence, leaving the difference to interpretation. However, we could also show the differences in meaning in the notation, i.e. by the use of superscripts. For the first meaning, as illustrated by (200'), the superscripts indicate coreference between 'you' and the subject ('X') of the infinitive:

(200')

$$
\begin{aligned}
&\text{'}\Sigma\,/\,\text{PR}\\
&I = [need_1] \qquad\qquad > [to_1]\\
&\qquad [need_2]\; ;\; {}^{a}you \;\mid\; [to_2]\; ;\; \Sigma\\
&\qquad\qquad\qquad\qquad\quad {}^{a}X = [change_1]\\
&\qquad\qquad\qquad\qquad\qquad\quad [change_2]\; ;\; life \downarrow\\
&\qquad\qquad\qquad\qquad\qquad\qquad\qquad - I\text{'}
\end{aligned}
$$

Note that another possible option for representing this meaning, i.e. to analyse 'need' as monovalent and represent 'you' as the subject of the infinitive, is not the analysis advocated here, as discussed above for example (185). To represent the second meaning, placing superscripts on 'I' and 'X', as represented below, indicates the coreference between 'I' and the subject of 'change':

120   *Verb Constructions*

(200'')

$$
\begin{array}{l}
'\Sigma / PR \\
{}^a I = [need_1] \qquad > [to_1] \\
\quad [need_2] \; ; \; you \; | \; [to_2] \; ; \; \Sigma \\
\qquad\qquad\qquad\qquad {}^a X = [change_1] \\
\qquad\qquad\qquad\qquad\quad [change_2] \; ; \; life \downarrow \\
\qquad\qquad\qquad\qquad\qquad\qquad - I'
\end{array}
$$

We have discussed here only a few of the many arguments written about the function and meaning of *to*-infinitives. In our view, a more extensive and detailed discussion of this subject would be needed in order to find the correct semantic-syntactic analysis for *to* as an infinitive marker. However, such an extensive study would not be appropriate for this present book. It may well be that owing to an ongoing process of grammaticalization the data themselves are fuzzy, and there are no discrete boundaries between meaningful and non-meaningful uses of *to*. For now, on the basis of the arguments presented above, we have decided to represent the infinitive marker *to* in all its occurrences, except in those where the infinitive functions as an independent nexus situation.

14.3   Gerund Constructions

The gerund form may function as a noun (e.g. *feeling, meeting*), an adjective (e.g. *surprising, following*) or a verb. In this section, only the verb form will be discussed. A gerund verb is represented in the semiotactic notations as a separate situation with the symbol 'Σ' because it has the temporal dimension of a verb (expressing a duration in time), although there is no tense marking. However, unlike the representation for the infinitive, the gerund is not given a subject notation 'X', because the act expressed by the verb is considered to be impersonal, focusing more on the action that is taking place than on the agent performing the action. We compare the infinitive construction with the gerund construction by analysing the following two examples:

(201)   *I like to walk.*

$$
\begin{array}{l}
'\Sigma / PR \\
I = like > [to_1] \\
\quad [to_2] \; ; \; \Sigma \\
\qquad X = walk'
\end{array}
$$

In (201) the subject of the sentence is necessarily coreferent with the subject of the infinitive. As such, there is a clear idea of an infinitive subject. This differs from (202), where the idea of a subject is contextually given (I like other people walking; I like walking myself, etc.) and is therefore not an inherent

14.3 Gerund Constructions 121

part of the gerund's meaning. Consequently, in the representation for the gerund situation, there is no first nexus member, and hence no nexus symbol '='; only the predicate is represented below the sigma symbol 'Σ'. Furthermore, contrary to the infinitive situation in (201), which is connected by bivalent 'to', the gerund situation is represented as the second valence of the matrix verb 'like':

(202)   *I like walking.*

$$
\begin{array}{l}
\text{'Σ/PR} \\
I = [like_1] \\
\quad [like_2] \; ; \; Σ \\
\qquad\qquad walk'
\end{array}
$$

Other examples with gerunds are:

(203)   *He avoided talking to her.*

$$
\begin{array}{l}
\text{'Σ/PA} \\
he = [avoid_1] \\
\quad [avoid_2] \; ; \; Σ \\
\qquad\qquad talk \; > \; [to_1] \\
\qquad\qquad\qquad\quad [to_2] \; ; \; she'
\end{array}
$$

(204)   *I remember going to the beach every summer as a child.*

$$
\begin{array}{l}
\text{'Σ/PR} \\
I = [remember_1] \\
\quad [remember_2] \; ; \; Σ \\
\qquad\qquad go > [to_1] > summer - every > \mapsto \\
\qquad\qquad\qquad\quad [to_2] \; ; \; beach - \text{THE} \quad | \\
\mapsto [as_1] \\
[as_2] \; ; \; child - \text{NONTHE}'
\end{array}
$$

The gerund may also occur in a more complex construction, which resembles the 'subject-to-object raising' construction discussed in the previous section for the infinitive. For example, the sentence: *I remember that he came back early* can be rephrased as:

(205)   *I remember **him** coming back early.*

For this sentence, we propose an analysis similar to the one given for the construction with a bare infinitive (see examples (185) and (187)). i.e. that the matrix verb 'remember' has two valences: the subject 'I' and the direct object 'he', which is further modified by the gerund situation 'coming back early'. This modification is represented by the divergent limitation relation:

122   *Verb Constructions*

(205')

$$
\begin{aligned}
&\ '\Sigma/\text{PR} \\
&I = [remember_1] \\
&\quad\ [remember_2] \ ; \ he \downarrow \\
&\qquad\qquad\qquad\qquad -\ \Sigma \\
&\qquad\qquad\qquad come > back > early'
\end{aligned}
$$

An alternative construction for this example sentence is with a possessive pronoun instead of the accusative, i.e.:

(206)   *I remember **his** coming back early.*

In this case, the analysis of 'he' as the direct object of the main verb is not acceptable because of the possessive case marking. Furthermore, the notation of 'he' as the subject of the embedded situation would not be consistent with our decision not to represent a subject in gerund situations. A different representation is therefore proposed. In the semiotactic notations in this book, possessive pronouns are connected to the element they modify with the divergent limitation relation (e.g. (4) *my book*), which we propose to be the correct notation here, too. Thus 'his' modifies the action expressed by the gerund verb, which is represented as follows:

(206')

$$
\begin{aligned}
&\ '\Sigma/\text{PR} \\
&I = [remember_1] \\
&\quad\ [remember_2] \ ; \ \Sigma \\
&\qquad\qquad\quad come > back > early \downarrow \\
&\qquad\qquad\qquad\qquad\quad -\ he'
\end{aligned}
$$

In general, the gerund construction seems to focus more on the overlap between the event expressed by the gerund and another reference point, whereas the *to*-infinitive has a more future-oriented meaning (cf. *I am happy doing that*; *I am happy to do that*).

14.4   Progressive Form Constructions

The *-ing* form of a verb is also used in active progressive constructions, where it is combined with other verbs as one complex predicate, as in:

(207)   *She left crying.*

In such constructions the verb in the progressive is analysed as part of the main predicate, because the two actions have the same agent and happen at

14.4 Progressive Form Constructions 123

the same time, and as such they are represented in one and the same situation. The verb that is inflected for tense and number is put first in the notation. The relation for temporal gradation is proposed to connect the two verbs, because it indicates that an action or event takes place during a certain length of time. For instance, in (207) the past tense marking is carried by the verb 'leave', which is put first in the representation, connected by the temporal gradation relation to the gerund verb 'cry', thus expressing: 'she left while she cried':

(207')

$'\Sigma / PA$
she = leave ⊃ cry'

The same analysis is made for the next example:

(208)   *He woke up screaming.*

$'\Sigma / PA$
he = wake > up ⊃ scream'

When the other verb in the combination with the progressive form is the verb 'be', as in (209), this construction could be given a representation similar to the one made for example (207) above, with the verb *be* analysed as a non-copular verb. As such, in the representation, the verb 'be', which carries the tense marking of the sentence, is put first, connected by the temporal gradation relation to the gerund verb 'walk', thus expressing the meaning: 'he is present while he walks':

(209)   *He is walking.*

(209') $'\Sigma / FR$
he = be ⊃ walk'

However, the analysis of this construction depends on how the verb 'be' is interpreted. We argue that 'be' in such progressive constructions is not an independent verb but a copula, and should be represented in the same way as proposed by Ebeling (2006: 382) for Dutch present participles, with 'PROGR' indicating: 'a property that has a temporal development':

(209'') $'\Sigma / PR$
he = walk > PROGR'

124   *Verb Constructions*

Another example is:

(210)   *He is living in London.*

$$'\Sigma\,/\,PR$$
$$he = live > PROGR > [in_1]$$
$$[in_2] \; ; \; London'$$

14.5   Constructions with a Past Participle

Past participles in English occur in many different combinations and constructions. The past participle is a non-finite verb form used in various constructions, such as the perfect (e.g. *I have finally **arrived***) or passive constructions (e.g. *I was **given** an award*). Past participles may also occur as noun or verb modifications, functioning as adjectives or adverbs (e.g. *the **fallen** angel*). In this section, however, only the verbal functions of past participles will be analysed.

14.5.1   *'Be' + Past Participle*

In this construction the past participle indicates the result of a completed action or event. The past participle in English is given the notation 'PF' for 'perfective', which in this construction indicates a new or resulting state of an event (process, action, etc.). (Cf. Ebeling 2006: 392.)

(211)   *His appetite was gone.*

$$'\Sigma\,/\,PA$$
$$appetite \downarrow \; = go > PF$$
$$- he'$$

However, when the subject of the copula 'be' is not also the subject of the participle verb, as in a passive construction, for example, a different analysis is made. For the purpose of analysing passive constructions, we will first discuss the following example:

(212)   *John was attacked by Peter yesterday.*

In line with the notation for the previous example (211), this sentence could be represented as follows:

(212')

$$'\Sigma\,/\,PA$$
$$John = attack > [by_1] > PF > yesterday$$
$$[by_2] \; ; \; Peter'$$

14.5 Constructions with a Past Participle   125

However, although 'attacked' in the phrase *John was attacked* is indeed a past participle, which can be said to have a 'perfective' meaning, (212') is not the correct representation for this example because, unlike 'appetite' in (211), 'John' is not the subject of the past participle verb but the direct object, the undergoer, of 'attack'. Therefore, the notation of 'John' as the first valence of the predicate 'attack' is not correct and another representation must be made. In order to find the correct notation, we will first analyse the active sentence:

(213)   *Peter attacked John yesterday.*

$$\begin{array}{l} '\Sigma\,/\,\text{PA} \\ Peter = [attack_1] > yesterday \\ [attack_2] \; ; \; John' \end{array}$$

Or with the same analysis, but using Ebeling's notation, we can show that the first valence 'Peter' is represented by x and the second valence 'John' by y:

(213')

$$\begin{array}{l} '\Sigma\,/\,\text{PA} \\ Peter = [x; x\,\text{attacks}\,y] > yesterday \\ [y; x\,\text{attacks}\,y] \; ; \; John' \end{array}$$

If we now compare this active sentence with the passive construction in (212), we find that in the passive construction 'John', the subject of the (copula) verb 'be', is also the direct object (= second valence 'y') of the past participle verb 'attack'. We therefore propose that in the passive sentence the predicate is not the first but the second valence of 'attack'. The subject/agent of 'attack' is Peter, but he is linguistically expressed by a prepositional phrase and as such is not a direct participant or valence of the verb. As in the case of active sentences with a past participle, the notation 'PF' is also used in the notations for such passive constructions, because the past participle can be analysed as having the same perfective-like meaning here.[6] This analysis results in the following representation for (212):

---

[6] One could argue that because the second valence [y; x attacks y] is indicated, the representation of the perfective character of the past participle becomes more or less unnecessary. However, the notation of [y; x attacks y] without 'PF' could be interpreted as a process where someone ('John') is being attacked. For this reason we will retain the representation of 'PF' in the formula. For some passive sentences, however, it is questionable whether the participle actually has a perfective-like meaning, for example in *He is hated by everyone*. This only shows that in English (or Dutch, French or German) 'perfective' is a constructional meaning, which can be triggered by a past participle in some contexts or with some verbs, but is not an inherent part of the semantics of the past participle.

126   *Verb Constructions*

(212'')

$$'\Sigma\,/\,\text{PA}$$
$$John = [y; x\,\text{attacks}\,y] > [by_1] > \text{PF} > yesterday$$
$$[by_2] \; ; \; Peter'$$

which may be represented in our notation as:

(212''')

$$'\Sigma\,/\,\text{PA}$$
$$John = [attack_2] > [by_1] > \text{PF} > yesterday$$
$$[by_2] \; ; \; Peter'$$

In the same way, we can compare the following two examples with an active and a passive construction respectively:

(214)   *He does no harm.*

$$'\Sigma\,/\,\text{PR}$$
$$he = [x; x_1\,\text{does}\,y]$$
$$[y; x_1\,\text{does}\,y] \; ; \; harm\,/\,\text{NO}'$$

(215)   *No harm is done.*

$$'\Sigma\,/\,\text{PR}$$
$$harm\,/\,\text{NO} = [y; x_1\,\text{does}\,y] > \text{PF}'$$

Or, with the same analysis but our alternative notation:

$$'\Sigma\,/\,\text{PR}$$
$$harm\,/\,\text{NO} = [_1do_2] > \text{PF}'$$

Other examples are:

(216)   *I was asked to leave.*

$$'\Sigma\,/\,\text{PA}$$
$$I = [ask_2] > [to_1] > \text{PF}$$
$$[to_2] \; ; \; \Sigma$$
$$X = leave'$$

(217)   *These chairs were made by my uncle.*

$$'\Sigma\,/\,\text{PA}$$
$$chair - this\,/\,\text{PL} = [make_2] > [by_1] > \text{PF}$$
$$[by_2] \; ; \; uncle\!\downarrow$$
$$- I'$$

(218)   *La tarte est faite par Anne.*

14.5 Constructions with a Past Participle   127

'The pie was made by Anne.' (lit. The pie is made by Anne.)[7]

$$'\Sigma/\text{PR}$$
$$tarte - \text{THE} = [faire_2] > [par_1] > \text{PF}$$
$$[par_2] \; ; \; Anne'$$

In the notation for the English example (219), two situations are represented. The second situation is based on the presence of the verb 'be'. The subject 'Tommy' in the main situation with the predicate 'deserve', is the direct object (the undergoer) of the verb 'hate' in the second situation, represented by the symbol 'X' and connected to the second valence of the verb 'hate'. Although commonly the verb *deserve* occurs as a bivalent verb (e.g. *he deserves high praise*), in this construction it is analysed as a monovalent verb, which is a valence reduction due to the presence of 'to'.

(219)   *Tommy deserved not to be hated.*

$$'\Sigma/\text{PA}$$
$$Tommy = deserve > [to_1]$$
$$[to_2] \; ; \; \Sigma$$
$$\text{X} = [hate_2] > \text{PF} > \text{NON}'$$

14.5.2   *'Have' + Past Participle*
This construction is called a perfect and also indicates a completed action or event. However, a different analysis is made, compared with the construction discussed in the previous section with the monovalent verb *be*. The auxiliary verb *have* is analysed as a bivalent verb with the meaning: 'to possess' and what is possessed here is a past experience. One could argue that the meaning of the perfect (which is a constructional meaning expressed by 'have + past participle') should be formalized by placing 'PF' next to the symbol for 'situation', on a par with the formalization for tense (cf. Ebeling's 1978 indication of verbal aspect in Russian next to the sigma). However, in our view, unlike tense and verbal aspect in Slavic, the perfect in English (and French or Dutch) is expressed by a separate verb, which one can argue still maintains part of its original possessive meaning. As such, we propose to formalize 'have' as a regular verb with a valence structure and its own possessive meaning and tense or mood marking, and to indicate the perfect aspect with the combination of both the verb *have* and the past participle.

---

[7] Because the aspectual (and tense) systems of French and English are not identical, the literal meaning of this sentence is different from the English translation. It would appear that in French (and Dutch: *Deze taart is gemaakt door Anne*) the focus is on the resultative state, which is still valid at the moment of speech, whereas in English the focus is on the realization of the event in the past.

128   *Verb Constructions*

In example (220) the subject of 'have' ('he') is also the subject of the past participle verb 'walk'. Therefore, in the representations for 'have + past participle', the second valence of 'have' is the first valence of the past participle verb 'walk', which is given the notation 'PF' for perfective.[8]

(220)   *He has walked.*

$$'\Sigma / PR$$
$$he = [have_1]$$
$$[have_2] \; ; \; walk > \mathrm{PF}'$$

When the past participle verb is bivalent and the second valence is linguistically expressed, the construction is represented as follows:

(221)   *She has written various articles.*

$$'\Sigma / PR$$
$$she = [have_1]$$
$$[have_2] \; ; \; [write_1] > \mathrm{PF}$$
$$[write_2] \; ; \; article / \mathrm{PL} - various'$$

(222)   *He has sold the books.*

$$'\Sigma / PR$$
$$he = [have_1]$$
$$[have_2] \; ; \; [sell_1] > \mathrm{PF}$$
$$[sell_2] \; ; \; book / \mathrm{PL} - \mathrm{THE}'$$

(223)   *J'ai   vu   le   château.*
'I have seen the castle.'

$$'\Sigma / PR$$
$$je = [avoir_1]$$
$$[avoir_2] \; ; \; [voir_1] > \mathrm{PF}$$
$$[voir_2] \; ; \; château - \mathrm{THE}'$$

In the following example sentence, a second nexus is proposed on the basis of the verb *be*. In this second situation, the verb 'be' has the same subject as 'have' in the main situation (which we have indicated by superscripts), but this subject is the 'affected/undergoer' (i.e. direct object or second valence) of the past participle verb:

---

[8] *Pace* Ebeling (2006: 404), who also represents *hebben* ('have') in Dutch as a bivalent verb but indicates the participle verb as the predicate of a second embedded situation. In other words, he analyses the past participle as a clause.

14.5 Constructions with a Past Participle 129

(224)   *We have been invited to a party.*

$$'\Sigma / \text{PR}$$
$$^a we = [have_1]$$
$$[have_2] \; ; \; \Sigma / \text{PF}$$
$$^a\text{X} = [invite_2] > [to_1]$$
$$[to_2] \; ; \; party - \text{NONTHE}'$$

In this sentence (224), *been* is a participle and functions as a copula linking the participle *invited* to its subject 'X', which is coreferent with 'we'. The copular function of *been* is indicated by '=' in the notation, and its participle semantics by 'PF', which is placed after the sigma symbol for this embedded situation, thus indicating that the whole situation must be seen as perfect. A similar representation is made for the following sentence:

(225)   *She has been living in the city for three years.*

$$'\Sigma / \text{PR}$$
$$she = [have_1]$$
$$[have_2] \; ; \; \Sigma / \text{PF}$$
$$\text{X} = live > [in_1] \qquad\qquad > [for_1] > \text{PROGR}$$
$$[in_2] \; ; \; city - \text{THE} \; | \; [for_2] \; ; \; year / 3'$$

The same construction is found in other languages, for example in French:

(226)   *Le ciel a été illuminé par la foudre.*
        'The sky has been illuminated by the lightning.'

$$'\Sigma / \text{PR}$$
$$^a ciel - \text{THE} = [avoir_1]$$
$$[avoir_2] \; ; \; \Sigma / \text{PF}$$
$$^a\text{X} = [illuminer_2] > [par_1]$$
$$[par_2] \; ; \; foudre - \text{THE}'$$

Some speakers of English also use constructions where the perfect with 'have' occurs with a passive participle and a progressive (the so-called present passive perfect continuous). This is the case in the following example, where 'being invited', the second predicate, is presented as progressive:

(227)   *He has been being invited.*

$$'\Sigma / \text{PR}$$
$$he = [have_1]$$
$$[have_2] \; ; \; \Sigma / \text{PF}$$
$$\text{X} = [invite_2] > \text{PROGR}'$$

130   *Verb Constructions*

Essentially, this sentence means that at some point prior to the moment of speech but still relevant at the moment of speech the subject 'he' was continuously invited. In this case as well, the past participle *been* functions as a copula, but here it connects the passive progressive predicate *being invited* to the subject. This passive progressive (continuous) consists of the verb *be* in the progressive form combined with a past participle. The meaning of the whole construction can be paraphrased as follows: 'The subject (he) possesses the resultative (perfect) state in which he as the subject is in a constant state of unspecified people inviting him.'

Finally, in some cases the verb *have* itself occurs in the gerund, in which case the following representation can be given:

(228)   *I admit having done that.*

$$
\begin{aligned}
&{}^{\backprime}\Sigma/\,\mathrm{PR}\\
I = &[admit_1]\\
&[admit_2] \; ; \; \Sigma\\
&\qquad [have_1]\\
&\qquad [have_2] \; ; \; [_1do_1] > \mathrm{PF}\\
&\qquad\qquad [_1do_2] \; ; \; that{}^{\backprime}
\end{aligned}
$$

Sentence (228) illustrates that the construction indicates the subject's possession of the resultative state, expressed by the past participle at the reference point introduced by the matrix verb (see e.g. Egan 2008 for an analysis of the role of the matrix verb).

14.5.3   *Other Past Participle Constructions*

The example sentences in this section are constructions with a past participle and the verb *become* (Dutch *worden* and German *werden*). These verbs are given a bivalent notation because they refer to a subject that undergoes a change from one state into another. The subject of *become* is the direct object or 'undergoer' of the event expressed by the past participle verb, which is why the second valence of that verb is represented as the second valence of 'become'.

If we compare the construction with the copular verb *zijn* 'be' in (229) with the construction with *worden* 'become' in (230), we find a difference in structure: *worden* is considered to be bivalent because there are two stages involved (i.e. first there is the stage that Piet is not beaten and then there is the second stage, i.e. the result, that he is beaten), whereas the construction with 'be' only expresses the resulting stage. Although one could argue that the constructions with '*worden/werden/become* + past

14.5 Constructions with a Past Participle   131

participle' indicate that there is a process leading up to a resultative state, we argue that the focus is on the process rather than on the resultative state, and therefore it would be incorrect to represent 'PF' as part of the participial meaning in these cases.

(229) *Piet **was** door Jan geslagen.*
Piet was by   Jan beat-PP
'Piet was (had been) beaten by Jan.'

$$'\Sigma/PA$$
$$Piet = [slaan_2] > [door_1] > PF$$
$$[door_2] \; ; \; Jan'$$

(230) *Piet **werd**   door Jan geslagen.*
Piet became by   Jan beat-PP
'Piet was (being) beaten by Jan.'

$$'\Sigma/PA$$
$$Piet = [worden_1]$$
$$[worden_2] \; ; \; [slaan_2] > [door_1]$$
$$[door_2] \; ; \; Jan'$$

(231) *Er wurde vom   Lehrer gelobt.*
he became by.the teacher praise-PP
'He was praised by the teacher.'

$$'\Sigma/PA$$
$$er = [werden_1]$$
$$[werden_2] \; ; \; [loben_2] > [von_1]$$
$$[von_2] \; ; \; lehrer - THE'$$

(232) *Fraud became recognized as a major problem.*

$$'\Sigma/PA$$
$$fraud = [become_1]$$
$$[become_2] \; ; \; [recognize_2] > [as_1]$$
$$[as_2] \; ; \; problem - major - NONTHE'$$

An example with a more complicated structure is the Dutch pseudo-passive construction:

(233) *Er   wordt   door ons gewerkt.*
there becomes   by   us   work-PP
'Work is being done by us.'

For this sentence, Ebeling (1978: 429) gives a rather abstract representation, where the semantic contributions of *er* 'there' and *worden* 'become' are not

132 *Verb Constructions*

represented and the semantic contribution of the prepositional phrase with *door* 'by' is represented by the notation of a 'dominated' first valence:[9]

(233')

$$' \ldots \Sigma / \text{NOW}$$
$$< working > \text{PROGR} ; we \ldots '$$

However, we prefer a formalization that stays closer to the actual form-meaning structure of the construction, i.e.:[10]

(233'')

$$' \Sigma / \text{PR} / \text{ER}$$
$$\text{X} = [worden_1]$$
$$[worden_2] ; werken > [door_1]$$
$$[door_2] ; wij'$$

In this case too we have refrained from representing the semantic particle 'PF' (for 'perfective') because *werken* 'work' has a clear processual meaning due to the use of the bivalent verb *worden* 'become'.

---

[9] Note that the present progressive was represented by Ebeling with 'NOW' and 'PROGR'.

[10] For the notation of the presentative-locative *er* 'there', see the existential constructions in Section 15.2. Note that Ebeling (2006: 447–451) also represents 'ER' in the formalization, but similar to Ebeling (1978) he does not provide a representation of 'worden' and instead uses the abbreviation 'PROC', which stands for 'process'. As such, we stay closer to the actual form-meaning structure than Ebeling.

15 *Impersonal Constructions*

In this section we will analyse a number of impersonal and existential constructions in European and non-European languages. These are constructions where the subject-predicate structure is different from the nexus constructions with a regular subject-predicate pattern, as in *John is walking* or *the trees are high*.

15.1 Impersonal and Existential Constructions in European Languages

Impersonal constructions in English, Dutch and German are made with *it*, *het* and *es* respectively. When analysing the function and meaning of 'it' from a semiotactic point of view, the most important question is whether 'it' should be represented in the notations, which depends on whether or not we can find a referent for 'it'. In some examples, such as *it is boiling*, we find that 'it' refers to a specific referent (e.g. soup, water, the kettle, etc.) and we therefore analyse it as the subject of the sentence in a regular nexus situation:

$$'\Sigma/PR$$
$$it = boil'$$

The same analysis can be made for the following example (234), where 'it' could also be considered to refer to an entity, which in this case would be a non-identified situation or thing, e.g. air, temperature, day, etc.:

(234)   *It is warm today.*   (Dutch: *Het is warm vandaag*)

$$'\Sigma/PR$$
$$it = warm > today'$$

However, there are other examples where a referent for 'it/het/es' is more difficult to find, such as: *it is raining* (Dutch *het regent*; German *es regnet*). In other words, is there 'something' that 'rains' (or hails, snows)? On the one hand, it could be argued that in all occurrences 'it' functions as a subject in the

134 *Impersonal Constructions*

same way as represented for example (234) above, following the principle 'one form – one meaning', i.e. with 'it' as the first nexus member and the verb 'rain' as the second nexus member:

(235) *It rained yesterday.*

(235')

     'Σ/PA
   it = rain > yesterday'

Alternatively, one could maintain that in examples such as (235) 'it' cannot be taken to be the subject, because it is an element without meaning or referent and is only used grammatically. Huddleston and Pullum (2016: 1482) discuss special uses of *it*, including 'extrapositional and impersonal *it*'. For constructions where *it* is used as a 'dummy subject' with verbs and predicative adjectives denoting weather conditions, as in: *it is raining; it became very humid*, they write: "*It* does not represent a semantic argument and cannot be replaced by any other NP: it has the purely syntactic function of filling the obligatory subject position." This analysis leads to the conclusion that 'it' should not be represented, resulting in the following representation without a nexus, because there is no first nexus member, and with the predicate verb 'rain' represented directly below the sigma:

(235'')

     'Σ/PA
   rain > yesterday'

Likewise for the Dutch equivalent *Het regende gisteren*:

     'Σ/PA
   regenen > gisteren'

In other European languages an element such as *it* is not used in similar constructions expressing weather conditions, e.g. the following Russian example, where the verb is marked for the third person singular neuter, the so-called impersonal marking, which coincides in this case with the absence of a nominative subject.

(236) *Morosilo.*
     drizzle-3SG-N-PA
     'It was drizzling.'

Here again, there are two ways to analyse this construction: first, one can argue that the subject, although not linguistically expressed, is semantically-syntactically present and necessary to trigger the impersonal marking, and as such should be represented in the notation by 'X':

15.1 Impersonal and Existential Constructions in European Languages 135

(236')

$'\Sigma/PA$
X = *morosit"*

However, we argue that this is an impersonal construction without a subject. As such, there is no first nexus member and the situation is represented with only the predicate (a verb with a tense marking):

(236'')

$'\Sigma/PA$
morosit'

This template (a representation with or without X) can also be used for other so-called impersonal constructions in Russian, e.g. for constructions with an accusative logical subject that expresses physical experiences, or constructions with an instrumental (pro)noun that acts as a logical (meteorological) subject, often with an adversative character:

(237)   *Menja lixoradilo.*
        I-ACC fever-3SG-N-PA
        'I had a fever.' (lit. It fevered me.)

(237')

$'\Sigma/PA$
$X = [fever_1]$
$[fever_2] \; ; \; I'$

Another notation for this sentence, without the 'X' element, shows that there is no nexus because the first nexus member is not present and contains only the second valence of 'fever', with 'I' connected by the relation symbol for dominated valence:

(237'')

$'\Sigma/PA$
$[fever_2] \; ; \; I'$

We can likewise compose two different representations for the next example, namely one with a nexus and 'X' as the first nexus-member, and the other without the first valence of the verb:

(238)   *Berezu   svalilo   vetrom.*
        birch-ACC fell-3SG-N-PA wind-INSTR
        'The birch was felled by the wind.' (lit. It felled the birch by the wind.)

136   *Impersonal Constructions*

(238')

$$\begin{aligned}
&\quad\; '\Sigma\,/\,\text{PA} \\
&X = [fell_1] \qquad\qquad > \quad [\text{INSTR}_1] \\
&\quad\; [fell_2] \;\; ; \;\; birch \;\; | \quad [\text{INSTR}_2] \;\; ; \;\; wind'
\end{aligned}$$

(238'')

$$\begin{aligned}
&\quad\;\;\; '\Sigma\,/\,\text{PA} \\
&[fell_2] \;\; ; \;\; birch > [\text{INSTR}_1] \\
&\qquad\qquad\qquad\;\; [\text{INSTR}_2] \;\; ; \;\; wind'
\end{aligned}$$

Note that according to this approach the logical subjects in the accusative or instrumental case still preserve their prototypical syntactic function as indicating the second valence and the instrument respectively.

For constructions with a genitive logical subject in Russian, such as constructions with a monovalent verb and a noun indicating a quantity, a similar analysis can be given:

(239)   *Vody   pribyvalo.*
        water-GEN rise-3SG-N-PA
        'The water was rising.'

The notation proposed here represents 'water' as part of a larger entity 'X' as the first nexus member:

(239')

$$\begin{aligned}
&\qquad\qquad\qquad\; '\Sigma\,/\,\text{PA} \\
&X - [\text{GEN}_1] = rise \\
&\quad\; [\text{GEN}_2] \;\; ; \;\; water'
\end{aligned}$$

In such sentences, the genitive indicates the scope of the referent's involvement in the content of the utterance (see Jakobson 1990: 346–347). In this case it means that a particular quantity of water is involved.

A similar analysis can also be provided for 'existential genitive of negation' sentences. In the case of some so-called 'existential' monovalent negated verbs, Russian offers the choice between the regular personal subject-predicate construction, as in (240), and an impersonal construction with a noun in the genitive, as in (241) (see e.g. Babby 1980 for a detailed analysis). Because of the subtle difference in meaning between the genitive and nominative constructions, the sentences are given here with a broader context:

> *Tolstogo ves'ma interesovalo babidskoe dviženie sredi arabov, i on poprosil Abdo napisat' emu ob ètom dviženii, no **otvet ne prišël:** v 1905 godu egiptjanin skoropostižno skončalsja.*

15.1 Impersonal and Existential Constructions in European Languages   137

'Tolstoj was very interested in the movement of Babism among the Arabs, and he asked Abdo to write him about the movement, but **the answer did not come**: in 1905 his Egyptian friend suddenly died.'

(240)　　*otvet*　　　　*ne prišël*
　　　　　answer-NOM-M not come-3SG-M-PA
　　　　　'the answer did not come'

*Delo v tom, čto, kogda otec rassylal telegrammy iz Tobol'ska, čtoby menja, sirotu, kto-nibud' iz rodnyx prijutil, iz Kazani, gde žili sestry dvojurodnye, tetki, djadi, babuška, **otveta ne prišlo**.*

'The reason is that when my father sent a telegram from Tobol'sk, so that I, without family, could stay with one of my family members, from Kazan', where his cousins, aunts, uncles and grandmother lived, **no answer came**.'

(241)　　*otveta*　　　*ne prišlo*
　　　　　answer-GEN-M not come-3SG-N-PA
　　　　　'no answer came'

Note that the genitive is only used in negative sentences, whereas the corresponding construction with a nominative subject is also used in affirmative contexts.

Jakobson (1990: 347–348) tries to link the specific meaning of the existential genitive of negation construction to the meaning of the genitive in relation to the scope of the negation. He argues that in the case of the genitive, the referent is involved to an indefinite but perceptible extent. This means that in (241) *otveta ne prišlo*, the answer is denied as if removed from the content of the utterance, whereas in (240) *otvet ne prišel* only the action is denied. If Jakobson is correct, we could represent the two sentences given above as follows. In (240') we find the regular nominative-predicate construction with the negation applied to the action by gradation. In (241') the subject of the sentence is the participant in the genitive, which is negated:

(240')

$$\text{'}\Sigma/\text{PA}$$
$$answer = come > \text{NON'}$$

(241')

$$\text{'}\Sigma/\text{PA}$$
$$X - [\text{GEN}_1]/\text{NO} = come$$
$$[\text{GEN}_2] \; ; \; answer\text{'}$$

138   *Impersonal Constructions*

Alternatively, one might argue that the genitive of negation construction is impersonal, in which case the following representation could be given:[1]

(241'')

$$'\Sigma / PA$$
$$come - [GEN_1] > NON$$
$$[GEN_2] \; ; \; answer'$$

Regardless of whether one sees the construction as impersonal or not, an important question is whether the specific difference in semantics between the two constructions can be explained on the basis of their component parts or to put it differently, whether it is possible to provide a compositional approach to the construction. In answering this, it is important look more closely at the semantics of the constructions. Partee et al. (2012) have emphasized the importance of what they call the 'perspectival centre' in the explanation of the two constructions (cf. Padučeva 1992). They refer to Arutjunova (1976, 1997), who distinguishes three components in a 'classical' existential sentence: a 'Region of Existence', a name of an 'Existing Object', and an 'Existential Verb'. For example: *In the library* (Region of Existence) *is* (Existential Verb) *a book* (Existing Object). They argue that each construction is associated with a different perspectival centre:

- Nominative construction: the idea of existence is 'seen' from the perspective of the existing object.
- Genitive construction: the idea of existence is 'seen' from the perspective of the region of existence.

This difference in meaning can in fact be linked to the difference in syntactic-semantic structure. In the case of the sentence with the regular nominative-predicate structure in (240), we single out (i.e. presuppose) the existing object (the answer) and add the information about its non-existence:

'We are talking about an answer by letter by someone, but it did not come.'

In the case of the genitive in (241), however, there is no nominative entity that can be singled out, and instead the construction emphasizes that in a particular location (situation) particular things are absent:

---

[1] As also observed by Borschev and Partee (2002), different authors take different stances on whether the construction is personal or impersonal. A complicating factor is that because of the very different theoretical frameworks it is often difficult to compare the notion of subject across theories. For a discussion, we refer the reader to Borschev and Partee (2002).

'We were expecting at least one letter from Kazan', but not a single letter was there.'

Note that in many 'existential genitive of negation' sentences the region of existence is not made explicit linguistically but is 'triggered' by the construction itself. This semantic-specific contribution of the construction as a whole can be compared to the English *there* as found in existential sentences (cf. *There came no answer* as a translation of example (241)). In this construction, the idea of an absence of the existential entity is emphasized by the negated genitive meaning. The construction negates the idea of (even) partial involvement of the genitive referent. So even though it is probably not possible to provide a fully compositional account, it is possible to link the specific semantics of the construction to its syntactic-semantic structure.

15.2   Other Existential Constructions

In English and Dutch, existential sentences are typically made with *there* and *er* respectively. Jespersen (1965: 154–155) writes: 'Sentences corresponding to English sentences with *there is* or *there are,* in which the existence of something is asserted or denied – if we want a term for them, we may call them existential sentences – present some striking peculiarities in many languages.' What we will try to do here, with the aid of the semantic-syntactic analyses, is to reveal some of these peculiarities. According to Jespersen, by using the weak *there* in the place usually occupied by the subject, we hide away the subject and reduce it to an inferior position, because it is indefinite. He further explains that the word *there*, which is used to introduce such a sentence, though spelt in the same way as the local *there*, has really become as different from it as the indefinite is from the definite article. Its indefinite signification is shown by the possibility of combining it in the same sentence with the local (stressed) *there* or with *here*, e.g.:

(242)   *Er zijn veel mensen daar.*   (Dutch)

(243)   *There are many people there.* (English)

Although *there* and *er* are often called 'dummy subjects', from a semantic-syntactic point of view they cannot be analysed as subjects of the sentence because the verb agrees in number with the phrase that follows, which in these examples is the plural: *people/mensen.* Furthermore, if one analyses 'there' as the subject, the argument would be that 'many people' is a property of 'there', which is not appropriate. Instead we argue that 'there/er' has a weakened

140   *Impersonal Constructions*

locative meaning, setting the stage for the rest of the sentence, which expresses the existence or presence of 'many people' at some location. As such, occurrences of 'there' are represented as what we will call presentative-locative 'THERE', which is considered to pertain to the situation as a whole and is placed in the top sigma layer of the situation (whereas locative 'there' is placed on the subject-predicate level). The verb 'be' indicating existence or presence is represented as the predicate:

(243')

$$\text{'}\Sigma\,/\,\text{PR}\,/\,\text{THERE}$$
$$people - many = be > there'$$

In the following example we have an English existential construction with 'there is' followed by an indefinite pronoun, an infinitive and a dative.

(244)   *There is somewhere to go for me.*

$$\begin{array}{ll} & \text{'}\Sigma\,/\,\text{PR}\,/\,\text{THERE} \\ somewhere - [to_1] & = be > [for_1] \\ \quad\quad [to_2] \; ; \; \Sigma \quad | \quad\quad [for_2] \; ; \; I \\ \quad\quad X = go' \end{array}$$

This representation shows that the subject (first nexus member) of the sentence is 'somewhere', which is modified by the infinitive situation 'go' (connected by the convergent limitation relation with *to*, as explained in Section 14.2). The predicate (second nexus member) is the existential verb 'be present/exist'. Additionally, the nexus (subject + predicate) is further specified by the bivalent dative *for me*, connected by the gradation relation. This construction is coined 'existential construction' because it provides information about the existence or availability of a place that is associated with an event.

A similar meaning is expressed in Russian by the following sentence:[2]

(245)   *Mne   est'   kuda   idti.*
        I-DAT be-3SG-PR whereto go-INF
        'I have somewhere to go.'   (lit. whereto go is present/exists for me)

This Russian existential construction is given the same analysis as the English example (244) (albeit without the 'THERE' element), i.e. the subject is the interrogative pronoun *kuda* 'whereto', which is modified by the infinitive *idti*

---

[2] Quoted from Švedova (1967: 113).

15.2 Other Existential Constructions   141

'go', the predicate is *est'* 'be present/exist' and the dative is a further specification of 'subject – predicate', i.e. indicating the person for whom the 'place to go' exists. Due to the absence of an element such as the English *to*, the infinitive situation is linked directly to the pronoun by the divergent limitation relation:

(245')

$$
\begin{array}{l}
\quad\quad\quad '\Sigma/\text{PR} \\
somewhere \downarrow = be > [\text{DAT}_1] \\
\quad\quad -\Sigma \quad | \quad [\text{DAT}_2] \; ; \; I \\
\quad\quad \text{X} = go'
\end{array}
$$

An alternative analysis for this sentence could be to regard the infinitive situation as the subject of the sentence and the interrogative pronoun *kuda* as a further specification (location) of the predicate in the infinitive situation. This analysis would result in the following representation:

(245'')

$$
\begin{array}{l}
\quad\quad '\Sigma/\text{PR} \\
\Sigma = be \quad\quad\quad\quad > [\text{DAT}_1] \\
\text{X} = go > somewhere \quad | \; [\text{DAT}_2] \; ; \; I'
\end{array}
$$

With respect to the choice between analysing either the pronoun or the infinitive as the main element (head) in the existential constructions, the question is whether there are any other criteria to determine which analysis is correct. For instance, there is the matter of word order: one could argue that if the pronoun precedes the infinitive, the infinitive should be seen as a further specification of the pronoun rather than the other way around. Note that in some European languages this order does indeed seem to be meaningful. For the following examples in English we find that if we change the word order, the meaning of the sentence also changes:

(246)   *I have somewhere to go.*

(247)   *I have to go somewhere.*

Due to the semantic-syntactic difference between these sentences, they are represented in a different way, which we will show in the semiotactic notations. For the first sentence (246), we find a construction with the possessive verb 'have', where 'I' is the subject (first valence), 'somewhere' is analysed as the direct object (second valence) and the infinitive 'go' functions as a further specification of this object. As such, in this English sentence the pronoun functions as the head with the infinitive as its modifying element:

142   *Impersonal Constructions*

(246')

$$
\begin{aligned}
&{}'\Sigma\,/\,\mathrm{PR} \\
I = &[\mathit{have_1}] \\
&[\mathit{have_2}]\ ;\ \mathit{somewhere} - [\mathit{to_1}] \\
&\hspace{5.5em}[\mathit{to_2}]\ ;\ \Sigma \\
&\hspace{9em}X = \mathit{go}'
\end{aligned}
$$

In (247), however, we find a specific difference, namely that the verb *have* has become a monovalent verb because *to* is the bivalent element that connects to the infinitive 'go' and 'have' no longer expresses the meaning of possession but rather the meaning of a necessity or *must*, while 'somewhere' further specifies 'go', as a location:

(247')

$$
\begin{aligned}
&{}'\Sigma\,/\,\mathrm{PR} \\
I = &\mathit{have} > [\mathit{to_1}] \\
&\hspace{2.5em}[\mathit{to_2}]\ ;\ \Sigma \\
&\hspace{6em}X = \mathit{go} > \mathit{somewhere}'
\end{aligned}
$$

But what about the word order in Russian? Even though the word order in example (245) is indeed the most commonly attested order, deviations from the basic word order are certainly possible. We argue that for Russian it is difficult to take word order as a criterion for determining which of the two is the correct syntactic analysis, and further analysis is necessary to determine whether more objective criteria can be provided.

15.3   Existential Constructions in Japanese and Lepcha

In Japanese a noun marked with the dative particle *ni* and combined with the existential verb *aru* 'exist' is used to indicate the location of something, as in the first example below:

(248)   *koko ni   denwa   ga   aru*
here DAT telephone NOM exist-PR[3]
'Here is a telephone.'   (lit. in this place (a) telephone exists)[4]

$$
\begin{aligned}
&{}'\Sigma\,/\,\mathrm{PR} \\
\mathit{denwa} = &\mathit{aru} > [\mathit{ni_1}] \\
&\hspace{2.5em}[\mathit{ni_2}]\ ;\ \mathit{koko}'
\end{aligned}
$$

---

[3] Japanese has no verb inflection for person, number or gender.
[4] Japanese has no definite or indefinite articles.

15.3 Existential Constructions in Japanese and Lepcha 143

However, the same construction can also be used to express possession, e.g.:

(249) *kono kuruma ni   kaasutereo ga   aru*
       this   car   DAT car-stereo NOM exist-PR
       'This car has a car stereo.'   (lit. in this car (a) car stereo exists)

$$\begin{array}{l} '\Sigma/\text{PR} \\ sutereo \downarrow = aru > [ni_1] \\ \quad \smile kaa \quad | \quad [ni_2] \;;\; kuruma - kono' \end{array}$$

This possessive construction can be used even when the noun phrase marked by *ni* is a human being, as in the following example:

(250) *watashi ni   kuruma ga   aru*
       I   DAT car   NOM exist-PR
       'I have (a) car.' (lit. for me (a) car exists)

$$\begin{array}{l} '\Sigma/\text{PR} \\ kuruma = aru > [ni_1] \\ \qquad\qquad [ni_2] \;;\; watashi' \end{array}$$

Compared with the (free) English translation of this sentence, where 'I' is the subject of the predicate 'have', and 'car' is the direct object, the structure of the original Japanese sentence is different. In Japanese *kuruma* 'car', marked by the nominal particle *ga*, is the subject of the verb *aru*, which means 'exist'; furthermore, the 'possessor' *watashi* is marked by the dative particle *ni*, indicating a location or beneficiary. When not only the subject but also the thing possessed is animate, this must be someone who has a very close relationship with the possessor, such as a family member, relative or friend.

Thus, example (251) is acceptable because of the relationship between a mother and her children, but (252) (with a chauffeur) is very odd, and when the idea indicates existence, as in (253), this existential construction can certainly not be used.

(251) *watashi ni   kodomo ga   aru*
       I   DAT child   NOM exist-PR
       'I have children.' (lit. for me children exist)[5]

$$\begin{array}{l} '\Sigma/\text{PR} \\ kodomo = aru > [ni_1] \\ \qquad\qquad [ni_2] \;;\; I' \end{array}$$

---

[5] Although Japanese does have plural forms, they are not often used; *kodomo* may mean 'child' or 'children'. This sentence would preferably include the topical particle *wa*, which will be explained in Section 16.1.

144 *Impersonal Constructions*

(252) *?watashi ni untenshu ga aru*
'I have a chauffeur.' (lit. for me (a) chauffeur exists)

(253) **watashi ni haha ga moo arimasen*
'I don't have my mother anymore.' (lit. for me (a) mother does not exist)

In the Tibeto-Burman language Lepcha, an existential meaning can be expressed with the genitive case. Plaisier (2006: 76) quotes the following examples with the genitive suffix *-sá* and explains that this genitive may have the common function of expressing possession, as in (254), but may also express part-whole relationships and related semantic functions. If we compare the second example (255) with the Japanese constructions above, we find that instead of the dative particle in Japanese, in Lepcha the genitive can be used:

(254) *?áre kasu-sá   lí   go ma*
this 1SG.OBL-GEN house be AST
'This is my house.'

$$'\Sigma/PR/AST$$
this = house $\downarrow$
$$- I'$$

(255) *kasu-sá   ?ákup nyet nyí ma*
1SG.OBL-GEN child two be AST
'I have two children.'   (lit. (of) my children two exist)

$$'\Sigma/PR/AST$$
child $\downarrow$ */2 = exist*
$$- I'$$

16 *Other Constructions in Non-European Languages*

In this section a number of other constructions in non-European languages will be analysed. These constructions are different from the constructions in the European languages discussed in previous sections and we have analysed them to illustrate how the semiotactic notations can be helpful in acquiring a better understanding of the differences in structure between different types of languages. Since our analyses and semiotactic representations of some of the examples given in this section are based on the additional information provided by the sources, we fully accept the possibility that a deeper and more extensive study of these constructions could result in different outcomes. Although this section contains only a small selection of the many different structures that exist in languages all over the world, we have presented them here to illustrate how the semantic-syntactic approach can be applied to a wide range of different languages.

16.1   Compound Verbs

In Japanese, which is an agglutinative language, compound verbs are very numerous.[1] These compounds may consist of a 'verb + verb' combination (**verb incorporation**) or a 'noun + verb' combination (**noun incorporation**).

First we will discuss the verb-verb compounds. The words within these compounds may have a convergent or divergent compounding relation. If the subject of the sentence is performing both of the actions expressed by the two verbs simultaneously, as one combined action, the relation between them is convergent. A few examples are: *tori-ageru* 'take up' (*toru* 'take' + *ageru*

---

[1] The NINJA database list contains no fewer than 2,759 verb compounds (http://vvlexicon.ninjal .ac.jp/db).

145

146   *Other Constructions in Non-European Languages*

'raise'), *ake-hirogeru* 'open wide' (*aku* 'open' + *hirogeru* 'widen') and *mi-kaesu* 'look back' (*miru* 'look' + *kaesu* 'turn'). In the following example (256), the Japanese compound verb *tori-dasu* consists of two verbs, *toru* 'take' and *dasu* 'pull out', and both actions are performed by the same person at the same time, as one complex action.

(256)   *kare wa   poketto kara kuruma no   kagi o   tori-dashita*
        he   TOP pocket from car   GEN key ACC take-pull out-PA
        'He took the car key out of his pocket.'
        (lit. as for him, (he) took from (his) pocket (the) car key)

In the semiotactic representation (256') for this sentence, the topic 'he' is put first on the top layer before the sigma. Since an element that appears only once in the linguistic form cannot be placed twice in the representation, the subject (first nexus member) is represented by 'X', which refers back to the topic 'he'. The verb compound is presented with a convergent compounding relation and the verb *dasu* 'pull out', which carries the tense marking of the sentence, is the headword of the compound:

(256')

$$'he > \text{TOP} < \Sigma / \text{PA}$$
$$X = [pull.out \cup take_1] \qquad\qquad > [from_1]$$
$$[pull.out \cup take_2] \; ; \; key \downarrow \quad | \; [from_2] \; ; \; pocket$$
$$- \; car'$$

Note that the topical structure ('TOP') with *wa* is used most commonly in Japanese, whereas the use of the nominal particle *ga* is much more restricted because it places extra emphasis on the subject. The topical particle *wa* separates the preceding phrase from the rest of the sentence and places this phrase outside the domain and time frame of the situation that follows, so *kare* 'he' is singled out as a kind of introduction to what the speaker is going to talk about. However, the topic does have a syntactic relation with the rest of the sentence, and in this case it is coreferent with the subject of the sentence (but topics can have other grammatical relations and semantic roles as well, e.g. direct object). Therefore instead of the symbol '::' for syntactic sentence boundary, the relation of gradation (and reversed gradation) is used to connect the topic to the situation, in a manner similar to notation for coordination. (For a discussion on the topical particle *wa*, see Geerdink-Verkoren (2009: 119–122).)

In the next sentence we find an example of a divergent verb-verb compound, i.e. the Japanese combination *kiki-wasureru* 'forget to ask' (*kiku* 'ask' + *wasureru* 'forget'). In this case, the subject *watashi* 'I' does 'forget' but does not perform the act of asking; it is not a matter of: 'ask and forget', but of 'forget to ask'. Therefore, this compound is given a divergent notation:[2]

(257) watashi wa kare no namae o kiki-wasureta
       I   TOP he   GEN name ACC ask-forget-PA
       'I forgot to ask his name.'   (lit. as for me, (I) forgot to ask his name)

$$'I > \text{TOP} < \Sigma / \text{PA}$$
$$X = [\textit{forget} \downarrow \textit{ask}_1]$$
$$\cup$$
$$[\textit{forget} \downarrow \textit{ask}_2] \; ; \; \textit{name} \downarrow$$
$$\cup$$
$$- \textit{he}'$$

A Japanese compound verb may also consist of a 'noun + verb' combination, a construction also called noun incorporation. In the following example the relation between the noun and the verb is similar to the object-verb relation and is analysed as divergent compounding; the verb, as the headword, is put first in the representation.

(258) jibun   wa   chotto chūcho-shita
       I (myself) TOP briefly hesitation-do-PA
       'I hesitated for an instant.'

$$'I > \text{TOP} < \Sigma / \text{PA}$$
$$X = \textit{do} \downarrow > \textit{brief}$$
$$\cup \textit{hesitation}'$$

In Japanese such verb compounds constructed with a noun and the verb *suru* 'to do' are very numerous and productive; in fact many new combinations are still appearing in Modern Japanese, with (most commonly English) loanwords, such as *joggingu-suru* 'to jog', *doraibu-suru* 'to drive', *kisu-suru* 'to kiss', and *nokku-suru* 'to knock'.

There are other languages where compound verbs are very frequent, such as polysynthetic languages. Comrie (1989: 45) writes that incorporation refers to the possibility of taking a number of lexical morphemes and combining them together into a single word. He also explains that, while

---

[2] With the mathematical drawing tools used in this book for the semiotactic representations, it was technically difficult to produce the divergent notation in combination with the square brackets for the valences. The combined symbol '$\downarrow_\cup$' is therefore used to represent divergent compounding, but with the understanding that the two parts of the compound should be on two different vertical layers.

148   *Other Constructions in Non-European Languages*

the possibilities in English are limited, there are languages where this process is very productive, resulting in extremely long words, which would translate into English as a whole sentence, e.g. in Chukchi: *tə-meyŋə-levtə-pəyt-ərkən* 'I have a fierce headache'. However, as Comrie also points out, in contrast to Chukchi, other languages, such as Eskimo, may be polysynthetic but not incorporating.

In English compound verbs are less common; two examples are *stir-fry* and *kick-start*. These compound verbs also consist of two verbs and both actions are performed by the same person at the same time, as one complex action. As already described above for Japanese, in the semiotactic representations such compounds are given the notation of a convergent compounding relation, and the main verb that carries the tense notation comes first, e.g.:

(259)   *She stir-fried the pork and vegetables in a sesame sauce.*

$$\begin{aligned}
&{}^{\prime}\Sigma\,/\,\text{PA}\\
she = &[fry \cup stir_1] \qquad\qquad\qquad\qquad\qquad > \mapsto\\
&[fry \cup stir_2] \;;\; pork > and < vegetable\,/\,\text{PL} - \text{THE} \;\;|\\
\mapsto &[in_1]\\
&[in_2] \;;\; sauce \downarrow -\text{NONTHE}\\
&\qquad\qquad \cup sesame'
\end{aligned}$$

English also has compound verbs that consist of a noun and a verb, such as *baby-sit*. This compound is given a divergent notation because the noun and the verb do not have the same rank; the subject/agent performs only one action, e.g. in example (260) 'sit (with the baby)'. The verb carries the tense situation and as the head of the compound is put first in the syntactic representation.

(260)   *She babysits their kids on Saturday nights.*

$$\begin{aligned}
&{}^{\prime}\Sigma\,/\,\text{PR}\\
she = &[sit \downarrow baby_1] \qquad\qquad\qquad > [on_1]\\
&\quad\;\; \cup\\
&[sit \downarrow baby_2] \;;\; kid \downarrow /\,\text{PL} \;\;|\;\; [on_2] \;;\; night \cup saturday\,/\,\text{PL}\\
&\quad\;\; \cup\\
&\qquad\qquad\qquad - they'
\end{aligned}$$

We found another example on the Internet,[3] i.e. the compound verb *idiot-proof* in:

---

[3] www.grammar-monster.com/.

16.2 Relative Clauses 149

(261)   *We need to idiot-proof this program against some (very talented) idiots.*

$$
\begin{aligned}
&\text{'}\Sigma/\text{PR} \\
&we = [need_1] \\
&\qquad [need_2] \ ; \Sigma \\
&\qquad\qquad X = [\,proof \downarrow idiot_1\,] \qquad\qquad\qquad > \mapsto \\
&\qquad\qquad\qquad\quad [\,proof \downarrow idiot_2\,] \ ; \ program - this \mid \\
&\mapsto [against_1] \\
&\quad [against_2] \ ; \ idiot / \text{PL} - some'
\end{aligned}
$$

16.2   Relative Clauses

In Section 4.6 we discussed relative clauses with the bivalent relative pronouns 'who' and 'that'. However, relative clauses without a relative pronoun also occur. If we compare examples (262) and (263), we find that in the first sentence the bivalent pronoun *that* connects the relative clause to its headword.

(262)   *He is the man that I saw yesterday.*

$$
\begin{aligned}
&\text{'}\Sigma/\text{PR} \\
&he = man - \text{THE} - [that_1] \\
&\qquad\qquad\qquad\quad [that_2] \ ; \ \Sigma/\text{PA} \\
&\qquad\qquad\qquad\qquad\quad I = see > yesterday'
\end{aligned}
$$

However, in the following example, without a relative pronoun, the relative clause is connected directly to the headword with a divergent limitation relation:

(263)   *He is the man I saw yesterday.*

$$
\begin{aligned}
&\text{'}\Sigma/\text{PR} \\
&he = man - \text{THE} \downarrow \\
&\qquad\qquad\quad - \Sigma/\text{PA} \\
&\qquad\qquad\quad I = see > yesterday'
\end{aligned}
$$

In languages that do not have any relative pronouns, such as Japanese, the notation with divergent limitation (as represented above for example (263)) is the only option for representing relative constructions. Unlike in English, where the antecedent comes before the relative clause, in Japanese all modifiers and relative clauses precede the head noun. In the representation for the following Japanese example, quoted from Makino and Tsutsui (2008: 379), the headword is *oto* 'sound'. Note that in Japanese the use of a direct object with motion verbs is quite common, as will be explained in Section 16.4.

150   *Other Constructions in Non-European Languages*

(264)   *dareka   rooka   o   hashiru oto*
someone   hallway ACC run-PR   sound
'the sound of someone running through the hallway'

> '*oto* ↓
>   − Σ / PR
> *dareka* = [*hashiru₁*]
>   [*hashiru₂*] ; *rooka*'

In the next example, there is no coreference between the subject of the relative clause and the subject of the verb 'eat' in the main clause. The subject 'X' of the main verb *eat* refers to the topic *I*, whereas the subject of *make* in the relative clause situation is 'sister'.

(265)   *watashi wa   ane   ga   tsukutta tenpura o   tabeta*
I   TOP older.sister NOM make-PA tempura ACC   eat-PA
'I ate (the) tempura (that) (my) older sister made.'

(265')

> '*I* > TOP < Σ / PA
>   X = [*eat₁*]
>   [*eat₂*] ; *tempura* ↓
>   − Σ / PA
>   *sister* = *make*'

For this example sentence (265), we could also make a more elaborate representation, if we wished to demonstrate that there are two instances of coreference, i.e. between the topic 'I' and 'X' (the subject of 'eat'), and between a second 'X' representing the direct object of 'make' and 'tempura' (the direct object of 'eat'):

(265'')

> '[a]*I* > TOP < Σ / PA
>   [a]X = [*eat₁*]
>   [*eat₂*] ; [b]*tempura* ↓
>   − Σ / PA
>   *sister* = [*make₁*]
>   [*make₂*] ; [b]X'

Comrie (1989: 142) writes that relative clauses differ quite considerably in their syntactic structures across languages, and analyses the following example of one type of Turkish relative clause (between square brackets):

(266)   [*Hasan-ın Sinan-a ver-diğ-i*] **patates**-*i   yedim.*
Hasan of Sinan to give his   potato ACC I-ate
'I ate the potato that Hasan gave to Sinan.'

16.3 Negation in Japanese   151

Comrie explains that the syntactic structure of this Turkish sentence differs
considerably from its English translation. The verb form *ver-diğ-* is a non-finite
form of the verb *ver* 'give' + the nominalizing suffix *-diğ*; the nominalized verb
form[4] requires its subject ('Hasan') to be in the genitive, and the appropriate
possessive suffix (here *-i* 'his') to be on the verb noun. Thus a literal translation
of this 'relative clause + head noun' *Hasanın Sinana verdiği patates* would be:
'the potato of Hasan's giving to Sinan', which can be represented as follows:

(266')

$$
\begin{array}{l}
{}'\Sigma\,/\,\mathrm{PA} \\
I = [eat_1] \\
\quad [eat_2] \;\; ; \; potato \downarrow \\
\qquad\qquad\quad -\Sigma \\
\qquad\quad Hasan = give > [to_1] \\
\qquad\qquad\qquad\quad [to_2] \;\; ; \; Sinan{}'
\end{array}
$$

16.3   Negation in Japanese

As discussed in Chapter 7, negation may be analysed as referring to a specific
word or phrase within a situation, or to the situation as a whole. In Japanese it
is easier to determine the choice between them, because Japanese has two
kinds of negation: verbs and adjectives are negated by attaching the suffix *-nai*,
which has the same inflections as the verbal *-i* adjectives. This negation suffix
is used for the neutral (written) form, in informal speech and in subclauses. In
polite speech the affirmative suffix *-masu* becomes *-masen* when negated. This
polite form is used only for the finite verb of a sentence, expressing politeness
towards the person addressed, and is therefore considered to be part of the
speech act, not of the situation expressed by the utterance itself. Consequently,
for negation in Japanese there are two different semiotactic representations, as
the following examples will show.

In the first two sentences, which are in the neutral or informal form, the
negation 'NON' is directly connected by the gradation relation symbol '>' to
the verb. In (267) the verb in the subclause is negated (*isoga-nai*) and the
finite verb is a verb-verb compound. In example (268) we find the negation
suffix *-nai* on the verb in the relative clause [*tabako o noma-nai*].

---

[4] The representation (266') for this construction has been made from the viewpoint that the
'nominalized verb form' still (partly) functions as a verb; if this is not the case and it should
instead be analysed as a nominal, a different notation should be made (cf. also occurrences of the
English gerund as a noun or as a verb form).

152 *Other Constructions in Non-European Languages*

(267) *isoganai   to   basu ni   nori-okureru*
hurry-not-PR when bus DAT board-be late-PR
'When (you) don't hurry, (you'll) be late for the bus.'

$$
\begin{array}{l}
'\Sigma\,/\,PR \qquad\qquad\qquad\qquad\quad > [when_1] \\
X = be.late \cup board\ >\ [in_1] \qquad |\quad [when_2]\ ;\ \Sigma\,/\,PR \\
\qquad\qquad\qquad\qquad [in_2]\ ;\ bus\ |\qquad\qquad X = hurry\ >\, NON'
\end{array}
$$

(268) *tabako o   nomanai   koto   da*
tobacco ACC smoke-not-PR matter be-PR
'No smoking, please.'   (lit. (it) is a matter of not smoking tobacco)

$$
\begin{array}{l}
'\Sigma\,/\,PR \\
X = matter \downarrow \\
\qquad -\,\Sigma\,/\,PR \\
\qquad\quad X = [smoke_1]\ >\, NON \\
\qquad\qquad\ [smoke_2]\ ;\ tobacco'
\end{array}
$$

However, in the next example the negation suffix -*masen* is used, which is the form that expresses politeness ('POL') towards the person addressed, and as such is considered to belong to the speech act. Therefore, in the semiotactic representation 'NON' is placed on the top layer after the sigma symbol:

(269) *watashi wa paatii ni   ikimasen*
I   TOP party   DAT go-POL-PR-not
'I won't go to the party.'   (lit. as for me, (I) don't go to (the) party)

$$
\begin{array}{l}
'I > TOP < \Sigma\,/\,PR\,/\,POL > NON \\
\qquad X = go > [to_1] \\
\qquad\qquad\ [to_2]\ ;\ party'
\end{array}
$$

16.4   Transitive or Intransitive Constructions

In traditional English grammars a distinction is made between transitive verbs, which can have a direct object, and intransitive verbs, which are monovalent. Motion verbs are commonly classified as intransitive verbs, for example as in: *she walked in the park*. However, sentences with a so-called intransitive verb also occur in transitive constructions, e.g. *he walked the streets of London*. There are other languages where the classification into transitive or intransitive verbs is even less appropriate, such as Japanese, where the use of motion verbs in a bivalent construction regularly occurs. A location can be marked by the accusative particle *o*, which is the marker for the direct object (second valence of the predicate). However, this bivalent construction with motion verbs refers

16.4 Transitive or Intransitive Constructions   153

to a specific meaning, which differs from the meanings expressed when other particles are used.

Kuno (1973: 96–102) compares the following three examples containing the motion verb *aruku* 'walk'. In the first example (270) the dative particle *ni* is used to indicate the location. For static locations the dative particle *ni* has the meaning 'in', i.e. the place where someone or something exists (as in example (248) analysed above). However, when combined with a motion or action verb, this particle indicates the direction or goal of the motion: 'to; toward', e.g.:

(270) *hito   ga   michi ni   aruku*
       people NOM street DAT walk-PR
       'People walk to (the) street.'

$$'\Sigma\,/\,PR$$
$$people = walk > [to_1]$$
$$[to_2] \; ; \; street'$$

In the second example (271), the instrumental particle *de* indicates a dynamic location, i.e. the space in which the action or movement is taking place, without specifying the beginning, end or goal of the action:

(271) *hito   ga   michi de   aruku*
       people NOM street INSTR walk-PR
       'People walk (up and down/back and forth) in the street.'

$$'\Sigma\,/\,PR$$
$$people = walk > [in_1]$$
$$[in_2] \; ; \; street'$$

The third example is with the accusative particle *o*, marking *michi* 'street' as the second valence of the verb *aruku* 'walk'. The transitive construction indicates that the motion designated by the verb takes place over the entire dimension (or most of it), continuously and unidirectionally, thus expressing the meaning that the whole street is walked over, from beginning to end:

(272) *hito   ga   michi o   aruku*
       people NOM street ACC walk-PR
       'People walk through the street.'

$$'\Sigma\,/\,PR$$
$$people = [walk_1]$$
$$[walk_2] \; ; \; street'$$

154   *Other Constructions in Non-European Languages*

In the same way, we can compare the following examples quoted by Kuno containing the motion verb *hashiru* 'run' and three different particles: dative *ni*, instrumental *de* and accusative *o*:

(273)   *rooka   ni   hashiru*
hallway DAT run-PR
'to run to the hallway'   (probably from inside a room)

(274)   *rooka   de   hashiru*
hallway INSTR run-PR
'to run in the hallway'   (not necessarily for some distance)

(275)   *rooka   o   hashiru*
hallway ACC run-PR
'to run along (through) the hallway'   (for some distance)

16.5   Definite and Indefinite Constructions

There are languages that do not have definite or indefinite articles but have other tools to indicate whether something is referred to as definite or indefinite, as the examples quoted in this section will show. First, constructions in the Altaic languages Turkish, Manchu and Classical Mongolian are analysed, where (in)definiteness can be indicated by the presence or absence of case markings. Next, constructions in Mokilese, Ponapean, Tongan and Alaskan Yup'ik are discussed, where similar meanings can be distinguished by the use of either the transitive construction or noun incorporation.

As already discussed in Section 1.2, we use the notations 'THE' and 'NONTHE' for the semantic particles of definite and indefinite articles respectively. For other constructions that are taken to refer to such meanings in various languages, the notations 'DEF' and 'INDEF' are used in the semiotactic representations, even when there is no formal correlate other than what is indicated by the construction. Furthermore, we acknowledge the fact that the specific semantics of the form that signals definiteness may differ from language to language. As such, the notion of definiteness is a comparative concept in the sense of Haspelmath (2010) and needs to be supplemented with a language-specific analysis.

16.5.1   Turkish
Comrie (1989: 132) writes that there are many languages that have special marking of definite direct objects, and discusses the following examples in

16.5 Definite and Indefinite Constructions   155

Turkish, where only definite direct objects take the special accusative suffix, and all other direct objects are in the same suffixless form as is used for subjects.[5] In the first example the accusative suffix -*ü* indicates a definite object:

(276)   *Hasan öküz-ü aldı.*
         Hasan ox-ACC bought
         'Hasan bought the ox.'

$$'\Sigma / PA$$
$$Hasan = [buy_1]$$
$$[buy_2] \; ; \; ox / SING - DEF'$$

In the next example, with the indefinite particle *bir*, there is no case marking for the accusative:

(277)   *Hasan bir öküz aldı.*
         Hasan an ox bought
         'Hasan bought an ox.'

$$'\Sigma / PA$$
$$Hasan = [buy_1]$$
$$[buy_2] \; ; \; ox / SING - INDEF'$$

In the same sentence, but without *bir*, there is still the meaning of indefiniteness due to the absence of an accusative case marker, but there is no indication of how many oxen were bought:

(278)   *Hasan öküz aldı.*
         Hasan ox bought
         'Hasan bought an ox (or oxen).'

$$'\Sigma / PA$$
$$Hasan = [buy_1]$$
$$[buy_2] \; ; \; ox - INDEF'$$

---

[5] The relation between definiteness and case marking of the object (or its absence) is a cross-linguistic phenomenon that requires an explanation, but this is beyond the scope of this book. However, one might expect that since people across languages have similar communicative needs, similar patterns that fulfil these needs (apart from general cross-linguistic principles such as economy, iconicity, etc.) may occur in different languages.

156   *Other Constructions in Non-European Languages*

However, Comrie (1989: 134–135) also points out that this question of definiteness or indefiniteness is rather problematic, because the category of definiteness is not a discrete category across languages. For example, in sentence (277), the absence of the accusative marker was illustrated with the indefinite article *bir*. Yet, as the next example shows, the accusative suffix is allowed here, although the direct object introduced by the indefinite article *bir* is clearly indefinite:

(279)   *Hasan **bir** öküz-**ü** aldı.*
       Hasan an ox-ACC bought
       'Hasan bought an ox.'

Comrie argues that in describing definiteness cross-linguistically, there is a notion of continuum of definiteness (or specificity).[6] Definiteness in the highest degree means, as in English, that the speaker presupposes that the hearer can uniquely identify the entity being spoken of. Thus, comparing the Turkish examples (277) and (279), we find that they represent different realizations of the notion 'degree of definiteness/specificity'. Although these sentences are translated the same way into English, they are far from equivalent in the original language. Further study would be needed to determine how such subtle differences in meaning could be represented in the semiotactic notations.

16.5.2   Manchu

In Manchu the nominative case usually has zero expression, coinciding with the noun stem. According to Gorelova (2002: 163–172), the addition of case markers to noun stems becomes obligatory if the character of the semantic relation within the word combination is unclear. Furthermore, the 'zero-form' of nouns is used to express the meaning of 'non-specificity', e.g.:

(280)   *muke inengdari sain i   eye-mbi*
       water every.day good GEN flow-IMPF
       'Water every day flows well.'

$$'\Sigma\,/\,\text{IMPF}$$
$$water - \text{INDEF} = flow > good > everyday'$$

---

[6] Comrie (1989: 135) compares this notion to the notion of continuum of animacy, where people are more animate than animals, and animals more animate than inanimate objects.

16.5 Definite and Indefinite Constructions   157

Nouns in the zero-form (without an accusative case marking) can also indicate an indefinite direct object, as in the following example, where the subject is not mentioned:[7]

(281)   *emu hotun   sabu-mbi*
        one town-ø see- IMPF
        '(Someone) has seen a town.'

   $' \Sigma / $ IMPF
$X = [see_1]$
        $[see_2]$; *town* / 1 − INDEF'

Although in Manchu there is no strict explanation as to when the marker of the accusative is obligatory and when it can be omitted, it is clear that the appearance of the accusative is closely related with the category of definiteness. Therefore in (282) the use of the accusative particle *be* may be instigated by the demonstrative pronoun *tere* 'that':

(282)   *tere niyalma be   bi akda-mbi*
        that man   ACC I trust-IMPF
        'I trust that man.'

   $' \Sigma / $ IMPF
$I = [trust_1]$
        $[trust_2]$; *man* − *that*'

16.5.3   Classical Mongolian

According to Grønbech and Krueger (1993: 13), in Classical Mongolian the subject may be left unmarked or may be marked by the nominative particle *ber*, and direct object nouns may have an accusative suffix attached to their stem. In example (283), however, the subject and the direct object have no case markings, which indicates the absolute or indefinite case for both of them.

(283)   *bars   miqa   idemüi*
        tiger-ø meat-ø eat-PR
        'A tiger eats meat.'   (not a particular piece, but meat in general)

---

[7] The Manchu word *emu* is most often classified as the numeral 'one', which is why it is represented here as '*town*/1 − INDEF', indicating the meaning 'one unspecified town'. However, *emu* can indicate other meanings as well, such as a meaning similar to the indefinite article 'a', which could be represented as '*town* − NONTHE' (see also Hauer 2007: 131–132).

158   *Other Constructions in Non-European Languages*

$$'\Sigma / \text{PR}$$
$$tiger - \text{INDEF} = [eat_1]$$
$$[eat_2] \; ; \; meat - \text{INDEF}'$$

In the second sentence (284), the first noun *bars* 'tiger' is followed by the nominative particle *ber*, which emphasizes that the word is the subject and gives it a definite meaning. The direct object *miqa* is in the accusative case, which also relates to a definite meaning.

(284)   *bars ber   miqa-yi   idemüi*
         tiger NOM meat-ACC eat-PR
         'The tiger eats the meat.'   (a specific piece of meat)

$$'\Sigma / \text{PR}$$
$$tiger - \text{DEF} = [eat_1]$$
$$[eat_2] \; ; \; meat - \text{DEF}'$$

16.5.4   *Oceanic Languages Mokilese, Ponapean and Tongan*

Another way of making a distinction between definiteness and indefiniteness is by using noun incorporation (see also Section 16.1). Mithun (1984: 847–894) writes that a large number of languages scattered throughout the world use the morphological construction called noun incorporation, where a noun stem is compounded with a verb stem to yield a larger, derived verb stem. She further points out that all languages that exhibit such morphological structures also have syntactic paraphrases, and moreover that it would be inefficient for languages to preserve exactly equivalent expressions so systematically. A native speaker must therefore have a purpose in choosing one construction over another, although the purpose is not always the same in different languages.

One of the differences that can be expressed by using either noun incorporation or a syntactic paraphrase is (in)definiteness. Mithun argues that compounding has a significant effect on the role of the noun involved, e.g. *he is off berry-picking*, where the word *berry* does not refer to a specific berry nor to a particular bushful of berries, i.e. it is not marked for definiteness or number and one cannot say: 'Bob went the berries-picking' nor: 'I am those/three baby-sitting'. To show this difference, we first compare the following examples from Mokilese.[8] Mithun argues that the verb-noun bond is both semantic and syntactic. The sentence with an independent object, such as (285), would be used if the object is noteworthy in its own right; but the sentence with an incorporated object indicates an institutionalized activity of coconut-grinding, and as such this object does not refer to specific coconuts but rather modifies the type of activity under discussion. In the semiotactic notations this difference

---

[8] Micronesian Austronesian; Harrison 1976 in: Mithun 1984: 849.

16.5 Definite and Indefinite Constructions   159

is represented with a regular bivalent verb-object construction in the first example, and a divergent verb compound in example (286).

(285)   *Ngoah kohkoa oaring-kai.*
  I grind coconut-these
  'I am grinding these coconuts.'

  'Σ/PR
  $I = [grind_1]$
    $[grind_2]$; *coconut — this*/PL'

(286)   *Ngoah ko oaring.*
  I grind coconut
  'I am coconut-grinding.'

  'Σ/PR
  $I = grind \downarrow$
    $\cup coconut$ — INDEF'

Next we analyse two Ponapean examples,[9] where in the transitive sentence (287) the completive suffix *-la* immediately follows the verb *kang* 'eat', but in the incorporated object construction of (288), the suffix follows the entire verb-noun complex. According to Mithun, in the first sentence with the external object and a transitive verb, the completive indicates exhaustion or completion of the medicine; but with an incorporated non-referential object, as in (288), it simply indicates completion of the activity. More medicine may remain in the bottle.

(287)   *I kanga-la wini-o.*
  I eat-COMPL medicine-that
  'I took all that medicine.'

  'Σ/PA
  $I = [eat_1] >$ COMPL
    $[eat_2]$; *medicine — that*'

(288)   *I keng-winih-la.*
  I eat-medicine-COMPL
  'I completed my medicine-taking.'

  'Σ/PA
  $I = eat \downarrow >$ COMPL
    $\cup medicine — that$'

The last examples analysed in this section are two Tongan sentences quoted by Mithun.[10] Tongan has an ergative pattern of case marking by prepositional

---

[9] Rehg 1981 in: Mithun 1984: 850.
[10] Churchward 1953 in: Mithun 1984–851.

160   *Other Constructions in Non-European Languages*

particles: absolute case (ABS) is marked by 'a, and ergative case (ERG) by 'e
In (289), which contains an independent direct object, the subject is in the
ergative case. When the object is incorporated, as in (290), the subject is
absolutive.

(289)   *Na'e inu 'a   e   kavá 'e   Sione.*
         PAST drink ABS CONN kava ERG John
         'John drank the kava.'

$$'\Sigma/PA$$
$$John = [drink_1]$$
$$[drink_2] \; ; \; kava - \text{DEF}'$$

(290)   *Na'e inu kava 'a   Sione.*
         PAST drink kava ABS John
         'John kava-drank.'

$$'\Sigma/PA$$
$$John = drink \downarrow$$
$$\cup kava - \text{INDEF}'$$

Generally speaking, the analysis of a noun-verb incorporation is given when
the verb and the incorporated noun are morphologically compounded to form a
complex verb. However, for Tongan this analysis is problematic, because the
nouns are rather in 'juxtaposition' than morphologically compounded with the
verb. Ball (2005: 9) quotes the same examples given above as (289) and (290),
explaining that these examples illustrate the alternation between ordinary
transitive clauses and those with incorporation. In the second sentence, one
can observe the two basic properties of noun incorporation in Tongan: 1. case
markers or determiners do not appear before the incorporated noun in noun
incorporation; 2. the external argument is marked by the absolutive case in the
noun incorporation construction. This contrasts with the external argument in
(289), which is marked by the ergative case.

We refer the reader to Ball for a detailed discussion of all the arguments in
favour of the classification of noun incorporation in Tongan, and will quote
here only one of them, i.e. nominalization. Ball (2005:11) writes: 'The primary
evidence for considering the verb and incorporated noun as a single word
comes from the nominalization data. One of the few bits of derivation
morphology in Tongan is the place nominalizer affix, -*'anga*. Nouns with this
suffix denote a place where a certain state of affairs (perhaps characteristically)
occurs.' First he gives an example of a (simple) verb that can be nominalized
by this affix:

16.5 Definite and Indefinite Constructions   161

(291)   *pule-'anga*
rule-NMLZ
'kingdom, government' (Churchward, 1959, 420)

Second, Ball shows that the same affix can be used to nominalize noun-verb compounds, as in the following examples:

(292)   *inu-kava-'anga*
drink-kava-NMLZ
'place to drink kava'

(293)   *tō-talo-'anga*
plant-taro-NMLZ
'place to plant taro'

16.5.5   Alaskan Yup'ik
According to Bergsland (2010),[11] in Eskimo grammar an adverbial case is analysed as marking an indefinite object, for example singular *-mek* in Alaskan Yup'ik in the next example, with the subject 'woman' in the absolutive case (comparable to a nominative) and the verb in the simple singular (no suffix). A Yup'ik verb with no tense-indicating postbase may describe an action occurring either in the past or in the present, which is why no tense is represented in the semiotactic representations. For example, *ner'uq* may mean either 'is eating' or 'ate', depending on the context of the statement.

(294)   *arnaq   neq-mek ner'uq*
woman-ABS fish-ADV eat
'The woman is eating /ate (a) fish.'

$$
\begin{array}{c}
'\Sigma\\
woman - \text{DEF} = [eat_1]\\
\phantom{woman - \text{DEF} =} [eat_2] \; ; \; fish - \text{INDEF'}
\end{array}
$$

Bergsland also states that a definite object, on the contrary, is in the absolutive case, and then the subject is in the relative case,[12] as in the following example, where the verb has a suffix *-a*, which refers to both the subject and the object:

---

[11] Knut Bergsland (1914–1998): source retrieved from the Internet (see Bergsland 2010).

[12] Jacob Mey (1970: 48) writes that the Eskimo relative case is affixed to the subject noun of a transitive verbal construction, or to the 'non-head' of a complex noun phrase.

162   *Other Constructions in Non-European Languages*

(295)   *arna-m   neqa   nera-a*
         woman-REL fish-ABS eat- {she.it}
         'The woman is eating the fish.'
         (the fish is the woman's eaten one)

(295')

$$'\Sigma$$
$$woman - \text{DEF} = [eat_1]$$
$$[eat_2] \; ; \; fish - \text{DEF}'$$

Note that further study would be needed to determine how the special charac–
teristics of this construction, i.e. the relative case and the verb suffix *-a*, add
further meaning to the construction, and as such should be represented in the
semiotactic notation. If we wanted to represent the specific structure of this
sentence, we could then make the following representation, with 'the fish of
the woman' as the topic:

(295'')

$$'fish \downarrow -\text{DEF} \quad :: \quad \Sigma$$
$$- woman \quad | \quad she = [eat_1]$$
$$[eat_2] \; ; \; it'$$

16.6   Serial Verb Constructions

In this last section of non-European constructions, the structure of 'serial
verbs' in various languages will be analysed by quoting examples and argu–
ments from two sources. The first source is Tallerman (1998: 79–81), who
writes about what she calls 'verb serialization', occurring in Chinese, in
African languages and in many of the languages of New Guinea. She explains
that the type of complementation familiar from European languages involves
an embedded clause that is subordinate to a main clause, whereas verb
serialization involves stringing verbs together in a sequence in which no verb
is subordinate to another. In other words, in the verb structures in European
languages there is one finite verb and the other verbs are subordinate, while in
serial verb constructions all the verbs are finite and of equal rank. As yet, this
kind of structure has not been semiotactically analysed and represented. In
analysing a number of examples, we will try to discover what might be a
correct notation to represent this type of construction.

Tallerman first quotes the following example from the African language
Nupe, explaining that in the English translation there is a main clause with a
finite verb *Musa came* and an embedded infinitive construction *to take the*

16.6 Serial Verb Constructions   163

knife, whereas in the sentence in Nupe the two verbs are in the same (main) clause, forming a single predicate, and there is no subordinate clause:

(296)   *Musa bé   lá   èbi*
         Musa came took knife
         'Musa came to take the knife.'

In the semiotactic notations made so far, constructions with complex predicates, i.e. with two verbs inside the same situation and with the same subject, have been represented with either the relation for temporal gradation or with a compounding relation. However, in both of these relations one of the two elements is the headword of the combination, which is not the case in the serial verb constructions. Therefore the only other possible option seems to be to represent the serial verbs with the equipollent relation, which has been used to connect words of the same rank.[13] Until now, this relation has only been used to connect nouns, but we propose to use this relation to connect serial verbs as well. This view leads to the following representation for this sentence (296):

(296')

$$'\Sigma / PA$$
$$Musa = come \cdot [take_1]$$
$$[take_2] \; ; \; knife'$$

Tallerman lists four properties of verb serialization:

1. no words should intervene between the serial verbs (although in some languages the object of a transitive verb is placed between them)
2. the verbs must have the same subject
3. there is only one marker of negation for the whole construction
4. the serial verbs cannot be marked independently for tense, aspect or mood, but must share the same TAM (which is either marked on each verb, or else occurs only once)

One of the examples from the African language Yoruba, quoted by Tallerman, does indeed have a direct object between the two serial verbs, which is the exception mentioned in the first condition listed above:

---

[13] For the discussion on equipollent relations, see Section 2.3.

164 *Other Constructions in Non-European Languages*

(297) ó   mú   ìwé   wá
3SG took book came
'He brought the book.'

Although the serial verbs are of equal rank, and we do not know whether the word order is important for the meaning or not, we have decided to follow the word order of the verbs in the notation for this sentence, and also to take account of the fact that the direct object appears between the two verbs. We therefore propose to represent the direct object 'book' as the second valence of the first verb 'take', and connect the second verb 'come' to its first valence with the equipollent relation:

(297')

$$\begin{array}{l}
'\Sigma / PA \\
he = [take_1] \cdot come \\
\quad\quad [take_2] \; ; \; book'
\end{array}$$

By comparison, Japanese has a construction that also connects a bivalent verb with a motion verb to make one complex predicate, with a similar meaning, e.g.:

(298) *Jon ga   hon o   katte   kita*
John NOM book ACC buying come-PA
'John brought a book.'   (lit. John buying a book came)

The similarity between this example and (297) is that in both cases there is only one situation and the two verbs have the same subject and express one simultaneous action. However, the difference is that in the Japanese example the verbs are not of equal rank: there is a gerund verb form 'buying', followed by a finite (main) verb 'came', which carries the tense marking, thus the meaning is expressed: (while) buying (a book) he came'. Because of the gerund form, this construction is represented with a temporal gradation relation between the two verbs:

(298')

$$\begin{array}{l}
'\Sigma / PA \\
John = come \supset [buy_1] \\
\quad\quad\quad [buy_2] \; ; \; book'
\end{array}$$

Baker (2001: 140–141) also discusses serial verb constructions, for which he gives the following parameter: 'Only one verb can be contained in each verb phrase (English, etc.), or more than one verb can be contained in a single verb phrase (Edo, Thai, etc.)'. In other words, English has no exact equivalent for

16.6 Serial Verb Constructions 165

serial verb constructions that contain more than one verb associated with a single subject and (at most) a single tense auxiliary. He writes that serial verb constructions are found in West African languages, such as Edo and Yoruba, and in South-East Asian languages, such as Thai, Khmer and Vietnamese. Baker quotes the following example from Edo, for which we have given a notation similar to the one above for example (297), because the direct object also occurs between the two verbs.

(299) *Òzó ghá lè   èvbàré   khiẹ́n.*
       Ozo will cook food   sell
       'Ozo will cook the food and sell it.'

$$'\Sigma / FR$$
$$Ozo = will \cdot [cook_1] \cdot sell$$
$$[cook_2] \; ; \; food'$$

17 *Word Order and Propositional Contents*

Word order, or rather the order in which the syntactic constituents of a language are presented, is language-dependent. Although most languages have a certain preferred word order, there are languages (such as English and Dutch) with a fairly strict word order, and the order of the constituents is also used to convey grammatical information; however, in other languages (such as Russian and Japanese) the word order is more flexible, and grammatical indications are given mainly through case marking. In these languages, for example in Russian, word order is used primarily to convey notions of information structure, such as topic and focus. An important question in the semantic-syntactic analysis is how to take account of the word order. Since Semiotactics provides a 'static' formalization, which abstracts away from the way the syntactic structure is built up, it is difficult to take word order into account, at least in those cases where differences in word order reflect different information structures.

We will first illustrate the topic of word order with reference to English and the notion of 'subject'. Traditionally, in a nexus relation a distinction is made between the subject (first nexus member) and the predicate (second nexus member). The term 'first nexus member' reflects that in Germanic languages the subject often occupies the first position in the sentence, before the predicate. The subject singles out an entity and the second nexus member provides information about this entity. Although this definition works well for the majority of cases in English, it is more difficult to apply to sentences where both nexus members are entities. Let us compare the following sentences:

(300)   *All three winners were Russians.*

(301)   *His work is his passion.*

In (300) it is clear that 'all three winners' singles out an entity and the word 'Russians' provides information about this entity, i.e. their nationality. In (301), however, it is difficult to determine on the basis of the semantics of the sentence and its components which meaning singles out an entity and which meaning

Word Order and Propositional Contents   167

provides information about this entity. In this case, word order is the only criterion for stating that 'his work' is the subject and 'his passion' the predicate.

In Russian, word order is more difficult to take into account in the analysis to determine the nexus structure, because a sentence can be presented in many different orders without changing the meaning. The basic marker of grammatical relations in Russian is not the word order, but rather the morphology. Comrie (1989: 78) gives example (302), where the first name *Tanja* is in the nominative (feminine singular) form -*a* and the second name, from the citation form *Maša,* has the accusative (feminine singular) ending -*u*:

(302)   *Tanja ubila Mašu.*
'Tanya killed Masha.'

Changing the word order does not affect the distribution of the grammatical roles and any of the six possible permutations of the three words *Tanja, ubila, Mašu* is a grammatical Russian sentence with the meaning 'Tanya killed Masha'. However, although the sentences with the different word orders have the same semantic roles and grammatical relations, they are not equivalent, because they differ in terms of the pragmatic roles expressed, i.e. at the level of 'topic' and 'focus'; the topic comes at the beginning of the sentence and the focus at the end. For instance, in the following question-and-answer pairs we find that the preferred word order in the answers varies in Russian, whereas in English the order necessarily remains the same:

(303)   *Kto ubil Mašu?*   — *Mašu ubila Tanja.*
'Who killed Masha?'   — 'Tanya killed Masha.'

(304)   *Kogo Tanja ubila?*   — *Tanja ubila Mašu.*
'Whom did Tanja kill? — 'Tanya killed Masha.'

In the semiotactic analysis such pragmatic differences between topic and focus are difficult to represent, because the syntactic roles and relations are the same. However, some instances of word order can be represented by using existing syntactic relations, for example extraposition, when a part of the sentence is presented by a comma or by intonation as a topic:

(305)   *I don't like this, John.*

$$'\Sigma / \text{PR} :: John$$
$$I = [_2do_1] > \text{NON}$$
$$[_2do_2] \; ; \; \Sigma$$
$$X = [like_1]$$
$$[like_2] \; ; \; this'$$

168   *Word Order and Propositional Contents*

In other cases there is no other element, such as a punctuation mark or intonation, just a difference in word order, as in the following examples. We can show this difference in word order in the representation by using the reversed gradation symbol in (307), to demonstrate that it is still the event 'I saw' that is modified by 'yesterday', and not the other way around: it is not the case that 'yesterday' is modified by the event 'I saw', which would be represented if we used the regular gradation symbol here (*'yesterday $>$ I $=$ [see$_1$]'):

(306) *I saw him yesterday.*

$$'\Sigma/\text{PA}$$
$$I = [see_1] > yesterday$$
$$[see_2] \; ; \; he'$$

(307) *Yesterday I saw him.*

$$'\Sigma/\text{PA}$$
$$yesterday < I = [see_1]$$
$$[see_2] \; ; \; he'$$

In the same way, we can maintain the original word order in the representation of the example sentence (84) analysed in Section 4.6, repeated here as (308) by using the reversed gradation symbol '$<$':

(308) *When he leaves, I will leave too.*

$$'[when_1] \qquad\qquad < \quad \Sigma/\text{PR}$$
$$[when_2] \; ; \; \Sigma/\text{PR} \quad | \quad I = [will_1] > too$$
$$he = leave \; | \qquad [will_2] \; ; \; \Sigma$$
$$X = leave'$$

However, it is open to debate how far one should go in representing such differences in word order; it all depends on the extent to which differences in meaning are attributed to word order. Furthermore, Semiotactics is not specifically designed to account for various semantic ('pragmatic') differences in word order (combined with different accentuations), as is the case in Russian, for example. As such, the model abstracts away from pragmatic-semantic discourse phenomena, such as topic and focus.

The matter of word order also relates to an issue we touched upon earlier in this book, namely the question of to what extent the formalization should make a distinction between the propositional content (associated with the state of affairs expressed below the sigma) and meanings that relate to the speaker's attitude with respect to the propositional content. In our discussion of auxiliaries such as *do* (Chapter 8) or modal verbs (Section 14.1), we have opted for a representation that mirrors as closely as possible the syntactic relations that can be seen in the form, at the expense of a formalization that makes a distinction between propositional content and other meanings that are not part of the propositional content. Note that this approach differs from the one proposed by Ebeling (2006), who argues that meanings such as 'yesterday' or 'certainly' should be placed next to the sigma because they involve a speaker's perspective on the propositional content in the same way as tense, aspect or modality markers.

However, there are other elements that are taken to pertain to the speaker's attitude to his/her utterance for which we propose another notation. These elements are called 'Speaker's Aside' by Jespersen (1984: 79), e.g. *strange to say, oddly enough, talking of golf.* In Huddleston and Pullum (2016: 773) phrases such as *frankly, briefly, confidentially,* etc. are classified as 'speech act-related adjuncts', i.e. adjuncts that relate not to the situation or proposition expressed in the clause, but to the speech act performed in uttering the clause. Huddleston and Pullum also point out that, depending on their arrangement in the utterance, the same adjuncts may also occur as 'situational adjuncts', and hence in fact refer to an element within the sentence. A distinction must therefore be made between them: when the adjuncts are distinctly separated from the rest of the sentence by a comma, or a pause in spoken language, they can be taken to refer to the speaker's attitude, but when they are embedded inside the sentence or clause, they are analysed as referring to another element in the sentence or clause. The following examples are compared:

(309)   *Frankly, it was a waste of time.*

(310)   *Ed spoke frankly about his feelings.*

In example (309) *frankly* is separated from the rest of the sentence and expresses the speaker's attitude. In the semiotactic notation for this sentence, *frankly* (in the basic form 'frank') is represented as an extraposition, placed before the sigma and connected by the symbol '::' for syntactic boundary. Since what is modified by the adverb 'frankly' is not expressed linguistically, the symbol 'X' is inserted, which can be taken to refer to the speaker's utterance:

(309')

$$'X > \_frank :: \Sigma / PA$$
$$it = waste - [of_1]$$
$$[of_2] ; time'$$

170   *Word Order and Propositional Contents*

However, in sentence (310) *frankly* is taken to refer to 'Ed's' way of speaking and as such is represented in the situation as adding extra information to 'subject + predicate' and connected with the gradation relation:

(310')

$$
\begin{array}{l}
'\Sigma/\text{PA} \\
Ed = speak > frank > [about_1] \\
\qquad\qquad\qquad [about_2] \; ; \; feeling \downarrow / \text{PL} \\
\qquad\qquad\qquad\qquad\qquad - he'
\end{array}
$$

This difference in function is not always related to the position in the sentence To give an example, in the following sentence *honestly* has the same function of expressing the speaker's attitude as in (309), but occurs as part of the syntactic sentence, because in this case the subject 'I' coincides with the speaker.

(311)   *I honestly don't care.*

$$
\begin{array}{l}
'\Sigma/\text{PR} \\
I = [_2do_1] > \text{NON} > honest \\
\quad [_2do_2] \; ; \; \Sigma \\
\qquad\quad X = care'
\end{array}
$$

If we have the same construction but with the subject in the third person: *he honestly doesn't care*, 'honestly' could in principle pertain to the attitude of the third person subject or to the attitude of the speaker, even though the second interpretation is usually marked by a pause: *he, honestly, doesn't care*. This latter construction would be indicated in the representation with the symbol for apposition (⊢). Note furthermore that in our approach the difference between adverbs that can indicate an attitude of the speaker or a specification of the verbal meaning is not represented in the syntactic notation. An example in Dutch is *natuurlijk*, which can mean 'naturally/of course' or 'naturally/in a natural way' (e.g. *hij loopt natuurlijk*, which can express the meaning 'of course he walks' or 'he walks naturally (in a natural way).' In our model, the difference in function between these meanings can be indicated by postulating polysemous meanings: '$_1$natuurlijk' and '$_2$natuurlijk'. In spoken language these different meanings are accompanied by different intonational means and sentence stress (*hij LOOPT natuurlijk* ('of course') versus *hij loopt NATUURLIJK* ('in a natural way')). These clues should be seen as linguistic signs, although as yet we have not incorporated them into the Semiotactics model.

To summarize, when such adjuncts are separated from the rest of the sentence by a comma (or by intonation or a pause), we propose to treat these

Word Order and Propositional Contents 171

complex constructions as one formal sentence consisting of several syntactic sentences (see Chapter 10). We will illustrate this view by giving the semiotactic notation for the following sentence from Hengeveld (1990: 13), analysed by Ebeling (2006: 474) as consisting of three syntactic sentences: (i) *honestly*, (ii) *you certainly danced beautifully yesterday* and (iii) *if I may say so*. This results in the following representation, taking account of both the word order of the sentence and the IC relations between the different parts:

(312)   *Honestly, you certainly danced beautifully yesterday, if I may say so.*

$$
\begin{array}{l}
\text{'X} > honest :: \Sigma/\text{PA} \ :: \ \text{X} \hspace{4cm} > \to \\
\hspace{2cm} you = dance > beautiful > certain > yesterday \ | \\
\mapsto [if_1] \\
\hspace{0.5cm} [if_2] \ ; \ \Sigma/\text{PR} \\
\hspace{1.5cm} I = [may_1] \\
\hspace{2cm} [may_2] \ ; \ \Sigma \\
\hspace{3cm} \text{X} = say > so'
\end{array}
$$

To come back to the central issue raised at the beginning of this section, the formalization presented in this book is able to deal with word order as a means of conveying information structure in only a limited number of cases (e.g. topicalization), and in most instances it does not account for word order or information structure. For this, the model should be further developed. Ebeling (2006: 168, 172) notes, for example, that it would be possible to indicate the semantic correlate of sentence accent with the abbreviation 'ADD', which stands for 'added information' (e.g. *I am working TODAY*; '...today^{ADD}...'), and that presentational word order could be indicated by numbering the elements in the formula according to the order in which they occur. Whether or not this is really informative is an issue for further discussion.

Conclusion: The Syntactic Theory from a Semantic Perspective

In this book we have presented a universal semantic approach to syntax, which is based on more than a century of thinking about syntax, especially the work of Otto Jespersen, culminating in the work of Carl Ebeling. The basic principles of Semiotactics are quite simple and straightforward, and follow from the idea that language is a means of communication that works in the same way in different languages:

- Form-meaning units are the basis of language
- Syntax deals with the relations between meanings
- There is a limited set of universal syntactic relations that connect meanings.

Other important concepts in Semiotactics are the principle of compositionality and the difference between semantics (which deals with meanings) and pragmatics (which deals with interpretation of meanings). These basic principles of the theory were discussed in Part I of this book. We also explained that the theory of Semiotactics includes a method to formalize the syntactic relations between the meanings of a construction, so that a formalization can be provided for every part of grammar. As such, every construction is shown to have a particular meaning and a particular syntactic arrangement, making it transparent how meanings interact with each other to form a combined constructional meaning.

Although Semiotactics starts out from the Saussurian sign (form-meaning correlate), our discussions have clearly shown that the syntactic formalization does not always have a one-to-one correspondence to the form-meaning elements in the sentence. In some cases we have preferred to indicate the syntactic relationship between meanings by using syntactic symbols in the formalization, at the expense of using the semantic correlate of the form. To take the English infinitive and gerund as an example, we did not provide a formalization of these semantic particles as e.g. 'INF' or 'GER', but rather indicated the semantic contribution of the forms by using different syntactic

Conclusion   173

symbols, as for *I like to walk* v. *I like walking*, analysed in Section 14.3. In other cases we have argued that the syntactic formalization describes the relations between meanings and does not necessarily correspond to the way these are materialized in the actual form of the expression. A good example of the difference between the syntactic representation and the actual way the expression is built up, is how the plural and definiteness are represented, as discussed in Section 2.4. For constructions like *the high trees*, where the plural form is marked on the noun and the adjective is a separate word, the syntactic formalization is built up as: 'tree – high / PL – THE', indicating that:

- From the set of trees, the subset of high trees is selected
- This subset functions as a 'specimen' and it is indicated that this specimen is plural
- This plural specimen is indicated to be definite.

Thus, the formalization given here does not take into account that number is marked on the noun. Finally, in some cases there may be a conflict between representing various aspects of a particular meaning in the syntactic representation. In such cases more than one formalization is theoretically possible, as the discussion on modal epistemic verbs like *must* in Section 14.1 revealed, where we gave arguments both for representing the semantic contribution of these forms at the top level next to the sigma symbol ('Σ') and for representing them below the sigma. A strong point of representing these meanings next to the sigma is that this reflects their semantic contribution, which relates to the speaker's attitude to the situation as a whole. A negative point is that this formalization does not show that *must* behaves like a bivalent form, where the infinitive is the second valence. Similarly, we have argued that we prefer to formalize the semantic contribution of 'by' in a passive clause, even though it could be argued that the way in which the actor of a passive clause is materialized in language is not only arbitrary but also gives the language user no choice other than to follow the linguistic structure. As such, we have opted to stay closer to the actual linguistic structure in our representations and provide formalizations that are relatively language-specific. Instances such as these show that in each individual case a careful decision has to be made about how to analyse and represent a construction. The formalization itself, which is an integral part of the theory, forces the linguist to do so.

In Part II we have provided an application of the theory, analyzing English and other European languages, and also various non-European languages. This application clearly illustrates that Semiotactics is a truly universal syntactic theory that can be successfully applied to any language. It shows how very

174   *Conclusion*

different languages can be, yet at the same time reveals that the same syntactic patterns can be found cross-linguistically. In our view, the analyses presented here show how fruitfully this semantic-syntactic approach can be applied to syntax, also in the case of very complex constructions. However, we would also like to emphasize that in some cases it can be difficult to provide fully objective criteria for choosing one specific syntactic analysis over another when more than one option seems possible. This is why we have given the arguments for alternative analyses, in addition to the ones that we prefer.

Semiotactics is a theory that aims to analyse and help explain semantic-syntactic structures of individual languages. However, because of its universal basis it can also serve as a starting point for cross-linguistic comparison. Cross-linguistic comparison presupposes that there is a basis for comparison to start with, such as descriptions in a standardized format and a clear classification of the various methodological statuses of linguistic concepts: which relations and units are universal and which are language-specific? To be even more precise: which relations and units are universal because their existence is a corollary of the applied definition of language? And which are universal because they have been observed to occur in all languages? Semiotactics deals with these preliminary issues with the ambition of facilitating cross-linguistic comparison. Furthermore, even though *Semiotactics* is a theory of synchronic linguistics, it may also be helpful for scholars who study the development of constructions and syntax over time.

With this work we hope to encourage linguists working with other languages to analyse various constructions in these languages by using the semiotactic approach, and to discover whether, and if so how, the theory could be further extended and if necessary adapted. The aim of this book is to introduce the theory of Semiotactics in an accessible way and to allow its readers to become familiar with the specific formalization of the theory. This is why we have also provided a guide explaining how to apply the instructions for making the semiotactic representations in practice (Appendix B).

Appendix A

Relation Symbols

⊢	- apposition
∪	- compounding
−	- convergent limitation
↓	- divergence
|	- division sign (no syntactic relation)
;	- dominated valence
•	- equipollent
::	- extraposition
>	- gradation
...	- incomplete representation
=	- nexus
X	- non-specified element
<	- reversed gradation
SE{ }	- set expression
Σ	- situation
/	- stratification
^{a}X	- superscript for quasi-divergence
⊃	- temporal gradation
~	- temporal limitation
[ ]	- valences
↦	- division sign for semiotactic notations which are too wide to fit the paper size

176   *Appendix A*

Analysed Examples

Alaskan Yup'ik
  arna-m neqa nera-a, 162
  arnaq neq-mek ner'uq, 161
Avava
  ier sapm, 80
  kopm iru, 81

C. Mongolian
  bars ber miqa-yi idemüi, 158
  bars miqa idemüi, 158
Chukchi
  tə-meyŋə-levtə-pəγt-ərkən, 148

Dutch
  (Kan het dat Daan thuis is?) Ja dat kan., 106
  Deze pen schrijft lekker., 86
  druppel bloed, 82
  een frisdrank, 21
  een frisse drank, 21
  een kaalhoofdige man, 101
  een kaalkop, 101
  een oude vriend, 16
  Elke doos woog zes kilo., 100
  Er wordt door ons gewerkt., 131
  Het is warm vandaag., 133
  Het regende gisteren., 134
  Hij gaf me een kop thee., 81
  Hij is dronken gevaarlijk., 27
  Ik dronk een kop thee., 81
  Ik ga lunchen., 117
  kop thee, 82
  Piet moet rijk zijn., 108
  Piet was door Jan geslagen., 131
  Piet werd door Jan geslagen., 131
  twee glazen rode wijn, 98
  twee rode wijn, 98
  twee rode wijnen, 99
  Vier koffie, twee bier, één mineraalwater, 99

Edo
  Òzó ghá lè èvbàré khièn., 165
English
  a bald-headed man, 66
  a black bird, 21
  a blackbird, 21
  a bookshop, 91
  a lone wolf, 64
  a man of honour, 96

Analysed Examples 177

A mouse!, 34
a silversmith, 22
a typical William Shakespeare play, 96
a wheelchair, 22
a wide-brimmed hat, 66
All three winners were Russians., 166
Be quiet., 36
big young dog, 15
blueberries, 91
bright young men, 92
burning hot soup, 93
burning hot wood, 93
Can you help me?, 110
Captain Smith, 92
Come in., 36
cooperative prices, 94
cooperative society, 94
Did he come?, 70
Each day is different., 100
Ed spoke frankly about his feelings., 169
Every cloud has a silver lining., 100
Four coffees, two beers, one mineral water!, 99
four pieces of wood, 98
Frankly, it was a waste of time., 169
Fraud became recognized as a major problem., 131
granddad young, 20
Had I known I would have told you., 61
He agreed to help me., 112
He ate an apple., 44
He ate the whole day., 44
He avoided talking to her., 121
He bought it. For his nephew., 74
He can play the piano., 108
He can't come., 108
He did come., 70
He didn't come., 70
He does no harm., 126
He has been being invited., 129
He has sold the books., 128
He has walked., 128
He helped me finish on time (by doing the bibliography for me)., 118
He helped me to finish on time (by taking the children away for the week-end)., 119
He is a blackshirt., 103
He is here., 30
He is living in London., 124
He is older than me., 45
He is older., 45
He is the man I saw yesterday., 149
He is the man that I saw yesterday., 149
He is walking., 123

178 *Appendix A*

English (cont.)

He must be home., 105
He told me it was very interesting., 63
He told me that it was very interesting., 63
He waits for the train., 42
He waits on the platform., 41
He walks!, 37
He walks., 36
He was a good-natured man., 101
He woke up screaming., 123
her warm mother's heart, 96
His appetite was gone., 124
his new captain's uniform, 96
his poor mother's heart, 95
His work is his passion., 166
Honestly, you certainly danced beautifully yesterday, if I may say so., 171
I admit having done that., 130
I am going to entrust you with a secret., 116
I am really leaving, John, you can't stop me now., 75
I believe that this party can, and will, win the next election., 57
I consider it a treat to dine here., 59
I don't like this, John., 167
I gave a book to John., 47
I gave John a book., 47
I have nothing to say., 58
I have somewhere to go., 141
I have to go somewhere., 141
I honestly don't care., 170
I like my tea cold., 27
I like to watch., 120
I like walking., 121
I met Lawrence, the novelist, not the Colonel., 73
I need you to change my life., 119
I remember going to the beach every summer as a child., 121
I remember him coming back early., 121
I remember his coming back early., 122
I saw him be impolite., 118
I saw him to be impolite., 118
I saw him yesterday., 168
I saw John and Paul there., 55
I shall make the travel arrangements for you., 109
I want to walk., 56
I was asked to leave., 126
I'm bringing some friends with me., 99
If only I could!, 57
Is she a singer or an actress?, 55
Is this accurate or not?, 56
It is boiling., 133
It is warm today., 133
It rained yesterday., 134

Jenny, you must not play in the street!, 107
John and Tom are friends., 53
John reads a book., 39
John shouted and everybody waved., 60
John Smith will be the next President., 109
John was attacked by Peter yesterday., 124
John's bicycle, 19
John's hat, 94
Johnny, you may leave the table., 108
King Edward, 92
my book, 18
nice weather, 25
No harm is done., 26
No, you can't., 74
not a big dog, 67
not particularly well constructed plot, 26
not unkind, 68
not very kind, 67
old man, 15
Peter attacked John yesterday., 125
Peter is not kind., 68
Peter was not kind to me yesterday., 69
right away, 64
Samuel Johnson, 22
secretary to the premier, 97
Shall I help you?, 108
She babysits their kids on Saturday nights., 148
She does her homework every night., 70
She finally decided on the blue car., 41
She has been living in the city for three years., 129
She has written various articles., 128
She is a redhead., 102
She left crying., 122
She stir-fried the pork and vegetables in a sesame sauce., 148
Shelley's are better than Keats's., 95
terribly cold weather, 26
The Amazon river, 92
the big dog, 17, 24, 30
the big dogs, 24
The blue-eyed girl had red hair., 100
The book that you gave me is very interesting., 63
the butcher's, 95
the butcher's shop, 95
The cantata, by Bach, was beautiful., 73
The cat in the tree is grey., 40
The cat sat in the tree., 41
The cat sits on the chair., 41
The company rented the second floor for a whole year from the institute for just one hundred
    dollars a month., 43
the Crown Inn, 92

180   *Appendix A*

English (cont.)
   The dog barks., 29
   The dog is big., 30
   the faces of the girls, 97
   the King of England's castles, 97
   the man here, 94
   the man in the moon, 97
   The man was bitten by the dog., 84
   The man who is coming there, do you know his name?, 75
   The man who owns the bar is John., 62
   The man, who owns the bar, is John., 62
   the old man, 25
   the old men, 25
   the River Thames, 92
   the then government, 94
   the two young dogs, 23
   There are cats everywhere., 30
   There are many people there., 139
   There is somewhere to go for me., 140
   These chairs were made by my uncle., 126
   They are kissing each other., 78
   This hat is mine., 95
   This is the game to watch., 117
   This pen writes smoothly., 86
   This question is difficult to answer., 117
   three pairs of reading glasses, 98
   Three points are important., 34
   Three points is enough., 34
   To resist is futile., 114
   To see is to believe., 116
   Tommy deserved not to be hated., 127
   Two men are carrying three tables., 85
   two of us, 80
   unkind, 67
   very big dog, 25
   We don't have much time., 99
   We have been invited to a party., 129
   We need to idiot-proof this program against some (very talented) idiots., 149
   We saw him run., 110
   We went to his house but he wasn't there., 60
   When he leaves, I will leave too., 60, 168
   Will you help me move this heavy table?, 109
   William Shakespeare's plays, 95
   Yesterday I saw him., 168
   You must eat something., 106
   young granddad, 20

French
   J'ai vu le château., 128
   La tarte est faite par Anne., 126

Analysed Examples 181

Le ciel a été illuminé par la foudre., 129
un été terriblement sec, 93

German
ein schwarzes Pferd und vier weisse, 94
Er wurde vom Lehrer gelobt., 131

Japanese
dareka rooka o hashiru oto, 150
hito ga michi de aruku, 153
hito ga michi ni aruku, 153
hito ga michi o aruku, 153
isoganai to basu ni nori-okureru, 152
jibun wa chotto chūcho-shita, 147
Jon ga hon o katte kita, 164
kare wa poketto kara kuruma no kagi o tori-dashita, 146
koko ni denwa ga aru, 142
kono kuruma ni katsutereo ga aru, 143
rooka de hashiru, 154
rooka ni hashiru, 154
rooka o hashiru, 154
tabako o nomanai koto da, 152
watashi ga Jon ni hon o ageru, 48
watashi ni kuruma ga aru, 143
watashi ni wa kodomo ga aru, 143
watashi wa kare no namae o kiki-wasureta, 147
watashi wa ane ga tsukutta tenpura o tabeta, 150
watashi wa paatii ni ikimasen, 152

Lepcha
kasu-sá ʔákup nyet nyí ma, 144
ʔáre kasu-sá lí go ma, 144

Manchu
emu hotun sabu-mbi, 157
muke inengdari sain i eye-mbi, 156
tere niyalma be bi akda-mbi, 157

Mokilese
Ngoah ko oaring., 159
Ngoah kohkoa oaring-kai., 159

Nupe
Musa bé lá èbi, 163

Ponapean
I kanga-la wini-o., 159
I keng-winih-la., 159

Russian
Berezu svalilo vetrom., 135
Ja dal emu knigu., 51

182   *Appendix A*

Russian (cont.)
Ja idu obedat'., 117
Ja rezal xleb nožom., 49
Ja ždu avtobus/ avtobusa., 52
Ja zvonil emu., 51
Menja lixoradilo., 135
Mne est' kuda idti., 140
Mne ne ponjat' ego., 50
Morosilo., 134
On byl starše čem ja., 46
On byl starše menja., 47
On byl studentom., 49
On dal mne knigu., 50
On javljaetsja studentom., 32
On pomogal mne., 50
On pošel ko mne., 50
On predstavljaet soboj studenta., 33
On režet nožom., 51
On student., 32
Oni celujutsja., 78
Orkestr gremit basami., 50
otvet ne prišël, 137
otveta ne prišlo, 137
Tanja ubila Mašu., 167
Vody pribyvalo., 136
Xleb režetsja Olegom., 49, 52

Spanish
Mi hermano es muy activo., 31
Mi hermano está enfermo., 31

Tongan
inu-kava-'anga, 161
Na'e inu'a e kavá'e Sione., 160
Na'e inu kava'a Sione., 160
pule-'anga, 161
tō-talo-'anga, 161
Turkish
Hasan bir öküz aldı., 155
Hasan bir öküz-ü aldı., 156
Hasan öküz aldı., 155
Hasan öküz-ü aldı., 155
Hasan-ın Sinan-a ver-diğ-i patates-i yedim., 150

Yoruba
ó mú ìwé wá, 164

Appendix B

How to Construct a Semiotactic Representation

The semiotactic representation for an utterance is built up by positioning the elements according to their functions (the syntactic part) and placing relation symbols between them to connect their meanings (the semantic part). Thus the two are combined. To illustrate how the semiotactic formalization is made, we will now demonstrate step-by-step how the representation for the following sentence is built up.

This man bought two interesting books for his young daughters in the bookstore yesterday.

We start (and end) each representation with an apostrophe, followed by the sigma symbol 'Σ', which represents the situation expressed by the whole sentence and is used as a frame to which all the sentence parts are attached. Next we must determine whether this sentence has a subject-predicate construction, i.e. a nexus situation, which is clearly the case in this sentence. Therefore, the nexus symbol '=' is placed directly beneath the sigma symbol:

$$'\Sigma \atop =$$

The next step is to insert the first nexus member (subject) and the second nexus member (predicate), which in this case are 'this man' and the verb 'buy' respectively. Since the verb is in the past tense, we will connect 'PA' to the sigma with the stratification relation '/'. The subject 'man' is modified by the property 'this', which is connected to 'man' by the limitation relation '−':

$$'\Sigma \,/\, \text{PA}$$
$$man - this = buy$$

The verb 'buy' has two valences, i.e. [buying] and [bought], which are represented on two layers in a vertical column and are connected to the two

184   *Appendix B*

direct participants of the action. The first participant 'this man' is already
present in the notation as the first nexus member, and the second participant
is the direct object 'two interesting books', connected by the symbol ';' for
'dominated' valence. Furthermore, the entity 'book' is modified by the
property 'interesting', which is indicated by the symbol '−' for limitation.
The numeral '2' is represented with the stratification symbol '/', and since
'2' already indicates more than one, the notation 'PL' (for 'plural') is not
needed:

$$'\Sigma/\text{PA}$$
$$man - this = [buy_1]$$
$$[buy_2] \ ; \ book - interesting / 2$$

Now we can add the beneficiary of the action, i.e. 'his young daughters', which
is connected by the bivalent preposition 'for'. The first valence of 'for'
connects to the subject + predicate (thus modifying the act of buying) with
the gradation relation '>'. The second valence of 'for' connects to 'his young
daughters' with the symbol ';' for 'dominated' valence. The property 'young'
is connected by convergent limitation '−' to 'daughters' and the genitive 'his'
is represented by the divergent limitation relation (with the symbols for divergence '↓' and limitation '−'). The plural is represented by 'PL', connected with
the stratification symbol. The division sign '|' is placed between two elements
which, although they are on the same line, have no syntactic relation between
them:

$$'\Sigma/\text{PA}$$
$$man - this = [buy_1] \qquad\qquad\qquad > \mapsto$$
$$[buy_2] \ ; \ book - interesting / 2 \ |$$
$$\mapsto [for_1]$$
$$[for_2] \ ; \ daughter - young \downarrow / \text{PL}$$
$$- he'$$

The last part of the sentence that has to be represented in the notation is the
locative phrase 'in the bookstore'. The preposition 'in' is given the same
bivalent notation as 'for', i.e. the first valence is connected by the gradation
relation '>' and the second valence connects with the dominated valence
symbol ';' to 'the bookstore'. The word 'bookstore' is analysed as a
divergent ('↓') compounding ('∪') relation, with 'store' as the headword.
The definite article is represented by 'THE', connected by the limitation
relation '−'. The time phrase 'yesterday' is connected to the event with the
gradation symbol '>'. After the last word in the representation, another

How to Construct a Semiotactic Representation   185

apostrophe is added, to indicate that the representation ends here. Thus, the
entire representation for this sentence is:

$$
\begin{array}{l}
\qquad '\Sigma\,/\,\mathrm{PA} \\
man - th\text{-}is = [buy_1] \qquad\qquad\qquad\qquad\qquad > \mapsto \\
\qquad\qquad\quad [buy_2] \; ; \; book - interesting\,/\,2 \mid \\
\mapsto [for_1] \qquad\qquad\qquad\qquad\qquad > [in_1] > yesterday \\
\quad\; [for_2] \; ; \; daughter - young \downarrow\,/\,\mathrm{PL} \mid \; [in_2] : store \downarrow -\mathrm{THE} \\
\qquad\qquad\qquad\qquad - he \quad\mid \qquad\qquad\quad \cup book'
\end{array}
$$

References

Apresjan, Ju. (2009). *Issledovanija po semantike i leksikografii. Tom I. Paradigmatike*. Moskva: Jazyki slavjanskoj kul'tury.

Arutjunova, Nina D. (1976). *Predloženie i ego smysl*. Moskva: Nauka.

(1997). *Bytijnye predloženija. Enciklopedija 'Russkij jazyk'*. Moskva: Bol'šaja Rossijskaja Enciklopedija, 57–59.

Babby, Leonard. (1980). *Existential Sentences and Negation in Russian*. Ann Arbor, MI: Karoma Publishers.

Baker, Mark. (2001). *The Atoms of Language*. New York: Basic Books.

Ball, Douglas. (2005). Tongan Noun Incorporation: Lexical Sharing or Argument Inheritance. In: Stefan Müller, ed., *Proceedings of the 12th International Conference on Head-Driven Phrase Structure Grammar, Department of Informatics, University of Lisbon*. Stanford, CA: CSLI Publications, 7–27.

Bartsch, Renate. (1998). *Dynamic Conceptual Semantics*. Stanford, CA: CSLI Publications.

Bergsland, Knut. (2010). Eskimo-Aleut Languages. Retrieved 02–03-2017 from: http://universalium.academic.ru/239056/Eskimo-Aleut_languages.

Borschev, Vladimir and Partee, Barbara H. (2002). The Russian Genitive of Negation in Existential Sentences: The Role of Theme-Rheme Structure Reconsidered. In: Eva Hajicová, Petr Sgall, Jirí Hana and Tomáš Hoskovec, eds, *Travaux du Cercle Linguistique de Prague (nouvelle série)*. Amsterdam: John Benjamins Publishing Company, 185–250.

Bresnan, Joan, ed. (1982). *The Mental Representation of Grammatical Relations*. Cambridge, MA: The Massachusetts Institute of Technology Press.

Broekhuis, Hans and Keizer, Evelien. (2012). *Syntax of Dutch: Nouns and Noun Phrases, Volume I*. Amsterdam: Amsterdam University Press.

Comrie, Bernard. (1989). *Language Universals & Linguistic Typology*. Chicago: The University of Chicago Press.

Croft, William. (2001). *Radical Construction Grammar*. Oxford: Oxford University Press.

(2003). *Typology and Universals*. Cambridge: Cambridge University Press.

Croft, William and Cruse, D. Alan. (2004). *Cognitive Linguistics*. Cambridge: Cambridge University Press.

Crowley, Terry. (2006). *The Avava Language of Central Malakula (Vanuatu)* (John Lynch, ed.). Canberra: Pacific Linguistics 574.

Culicover, Peter W. and Jackendoff, Ray. (2005). *Simpler Syntax*. Oxford: Oxford University Press.

Dik, Simon C. (1997). *The Theory of Functional Grammar*. Berlin: Mouton de Gruyter.

Duffley, Patrick. (1992). *The English Infinitive*. London: Longman.

Ebeling, Carl L. (1954). On the Semantic Structure of the Russian Sentence. *Lingua* IV, 207–222.

(1978). *Syntax and Semantics. A Taxonomic Approach*. Leiden: Brill.

(1980). How Many Valences? In: Voz'mi na radost': *To Honour Jeanne van der Eng-Liedmeier*. Amsterdam: Slavic Seminar, 361–371.

(1994). Een inleiding tot de syntaxis *[An Introduction to Syntax]*. Leiden: The Hakuchi Press.

(2006). Semiotaxis. Over theoretische en Nederlandse syntaxis *[Semiotactics. On Theoretical and Dutch Syntax]*. Amsterdam: Amsterdam University Press.

Egan, Thomas. (2008). *Non-finite Complementation*. Amsterdam: Editions Rodopi B. V.

Fillmore, Charles, Kay, Paul and O'Connor, Catherine. (1988). Regularity and Idiomaticity. In: Grammatical Constructions: The Case of Let Alone. *Language*, 64, 501–538.

Fortuin, Egbert. (2000). *Polysemy or Monosemy: Interpretation of the Imperative and Dative-Infinitive Construction in Russian*. Amsterdam: ILLC Dissertation Series.

(2011). Meaning without Form. In: Hetty Geerdink-Verkoren and Aone van Engelenhoven, eds, *Searching the Invariant. Semiotactic Explorations into Meaning*. Munich: Lincom Europa, 17–32.

(2014). The Existential Construction in Russian: A Semantic-Syntactic Approach. In: E. L. J. Fortuin, P. Houtzagers, J. Kalsbeek, S. Dekker, eds, *Dutch Contributions to the Fifteenth International Congress of Slavists. Minsk. August 20–27, 2013. no. 40*. Amsterdam: Rodopi, 25–58.

Geerdink-Verkoren, Hetty. (2009). *A Semiotactic Approach to Modern Japanese*. Munich: Lincom Europa.

Geerdink-Verkoren, Hetty and van Engelenhoven, Aone, eds (2011). *Searching the Invariant. Semiotactic Explorations into Meaning*. Munich: Lincom Europa.

Gil, David. (1992). Scopal Quantifiers: Some Universals of Lexical Effability. In: Michel Kefer and Johan van der Auwera, eds, *Meaning and Grammar: Cross-Linguistic Perspectives*. Berlin: Mouton de Gruyter, 303–346.

Goldberg, Adele E. (1995). *Constructions: A Construction Grammar Approach to Argument Structure*. Chicago: University of Chicago Press.

Gorelova, Liliya M. (2002). *Manchu Grammar*. Leiden: Brill.

Grønbech, Kaare and Krueger, John R. (1993). *An Introduction to Classical (Literary) Mongolian*. Wiesbaden: Harrassowitz Verlag.

Haspelmath, Martin. (2008). Frequency vs. Iconicity in Explaining Grammatica Asymmetries. *Cognitive Linguistics* 19(1), 1–33.

(2010). Comparative Concepts and Descriptive Categories in Cross-Linguistic Studies. *Language* 86(3), 663–687.

(2015). Ditransitive Constructions in the World's Languages. *Annual Review of Linguistics*, 1(1), 19–41.

188   References

Hauer, Eric. (2007). *Handwörterbuch der manchusprache*. Wiesbaden: Harrassowitz Verlag.

Hawkins, John A. (1978). *Definiteness and Indefiniteness. A Study in Reference and Grammaticality Prediction*. London: Croom Helm.

Helden, Andries van. (2017). Not the Last Word on the Short Form: A Deictic Approach. In: René Genis, Eric de Haard, Radovan Lučić, eds, *Definitely Perfect: Festschrift for Janneke Kalsbeek (= Pegasus Oost-Europese Studies, 29)*. Amsterdam: Pegasus, 255–291.

Hengeveld, Kees. (1990). The Hierarchical Structure of Utterances. In: *Layers and Levels of Representation in Language Theory: A Functional View*. Jan Nuyts, A. Machteld Bolkestein and Co Vet. (eds). Amsterdam: John Benjamins Publishing Company, 1–24.

Hoffmann, Thomas and Trousdale, Graeme, eds, 2013. *The Oxford Handbook of Construction Grammar*. Oxford and New York: Oxford University Press.

Honselaar, Wim and Keizer, Evelien. 2011. Lexical Stratification. In: *Searching the Invariant. Semiotactic Explorations into Meaning*. Hetty Geerdink-Verkoren and Aone van Engelenhoven, eds. Munich: Lincom Europa, 73–84.

Huddleston, Rodney and Pullum, Geoffrey K. 2016 [2002]. *The Cambridge Grammar of the English Language*. Cambridge: Cambridge University Press.

Hudson, Richard A. 1984. *Word Grammar*. Oxford: Basil Blackwell.

(1992). So-Called 'Double Objects' and Grammatical Relations. *Language, 68(2)*, 251–276.

Iwasaki, Shoichi and Inkapiromu, Preeya. 2005. *A Reference Grammar of Thai*. Cambridge: Cambridge University Press.

Jakobson, Roman. 1990 [1937]. Contribution to the General Theory of Case. In: *On Language*. Linda R. Waugh & Monique Monville-Burston, eds. Notes: 533–537. Cambridge, MA: Harvard University Press, 332–385.

Janda, Laura A. 1993. *A Geography of Case Semantics. The Czech Dative and the Russian Instrumental*. Berlin: Mouton de Gruyter.

Jespersen, Otto. 1965 [1924]. *The Philosophy of Grammar*. New York: W. W. Norton & Company.

(1984 [1937]). *Analytic Syntax*. Chicago: The University of Chicago Press.

(1940). *A Modern English Grammar on Historical Principles. Part 5*. London: George Allen and Unwin.

Kortlandt, Frederik. 1980. Temporal Gradation and Temporal Limitation. In: *Studies in Slavic and General Linguistics, 1* [Fs. Ebeling], 237–246.

(2008). Russian Syntax and Semantics. In: *Russian Linguistics* 32: 115–123. Springer.

Kroeger, Paul R. 2004. *Analyzing Syntax: A Lexical-Functional Approach*. Cambridge: Cambridge University Press.

Kuno, Susumu. 1973. *The Structure of the Japanese Language*. Cambridge MA: The Massachusetts Institute of Technology Press.

Leech, Geoffrey, Cruickshank, Benita and Ivanič, Roz. 2001. *An A-Z of English Grammar and Usage*. Harlow: Pearson Education Limited.

Makino, Seiichi and Tsutsui, Michio. 2008. *A Dictionary of Basic Japanese Grammar*. Tokyo: The Japan Times.

References   189

Matthews, Peter H. (1996) [1981]. *Syntax*. Cambridge: Cambridge University Press.
Mel'čuk, Igor A. 1988. *Dependency Syntax: Theory and Practice*. Albany. NY: SUNY Press.
Mey, Jacob. (1970). Possessive and Transitive in Eskimo. *Journal of Linguistics*, 47–56.
Mithun, Marianne. (1984). The Evolution of Noun Incorporation. *Language*, 60(4), 847–894.
Padučeva, Elena V. (1992). O semantičiskeskom podxode k sintaksisu i genitivnom sub"ekte glagola BYT'. *Russian Linguistics* 16, 53–63.
Partee, Barbara H., Borschev, Vladimir, Paducheva, Elena V., Testelets, Yakov and Yanovich, Igor. (2012). The Role of Verb Semantics in Genitive Alternations: Genitive of Negation and Genitive of Intensionality. In: *The Russian Verb. Oslo Studies in Language* 4(1). A. Grønn A. Pazel'skaya, eds, 1–29. Retrieved from: www.journals.uio.no/index.php/osla/article/view/229/286]
Plaisier, Heleen. (2006). *A Grammar of Lepcha*. (PhD) Leiden: Leiden University.
Pollard, Carl and Sag, Ivan A. (1994). *Head-Driven Phrase Structure Grammar*. Chicago: University of Chicago Press.
Romeu, Juan. (2015). *Ser, Estar* and Two Different Modifiers. In: *New Perspectives on the Study of Ser and Estar*. Isabel Pérez-Jiménez, Manuel Leonetti and Sylvia Gumbel-Molina, eds. Amsterdam: John Benjamins Publishing Company, 51–84.
Rosch, Eleanor. (1973). Natural Categories. *Cognitive Psychology* 4(3), 328–50
Saussure, Ferdinand de. (1966). *Course in General Linguistics* [orig. (1916) *Course linguistique générale*]. Charles Bally, Albert Sechehay and Albert Riedlinger (Eds). Lausanne: Payot.
Seuren, Pieter, A.M. (1996). *Semantic Syntax*. Oxford: Blackwell.
Shopen, Timothy. (1985). *Language Typology and Syntactic Description· Volume 1, Clause Structure*. Cambridge: Cambridge University Press.
Stainton, Robert J. (2006). Neither Fragments nor Ellipsis. In: *The Syntax of Nonsententials: Multidisciplinary Perspectives*. Ljiljana Progovac, Kate Paesani, Eugenia Casielles and Ellen Barton, eds. Amsterdam: John Benjamins Publishing Company, 93–116.
Švedova, N. Ju. (1967). Paradigmatika prostogo predloženija v sovremennom russkom jazyke. In: *Russkij jazyk. Grammatičeskie issledovanija*. (Reprinted in: Švedova, N. Ju. 2005. *Russkij jazyk. Izbrannye raboty*. Ross. akad. nauk; Otdelenie istoriko-filolog. nauk; *In-t russkogo jazyka im. V. V. Vinogradova*. Moskva: Jazyki slavjanskoj kul'tury (Studia Philologica), 55–115).
Sweet, H. (1913). *Collected Papers*. Arranged by H. C. Wild. Oxford: Clarendon Press.
Tallerman, Maggie. 1998. *Understanding Syntax*. London: Arnold Publishers.
Tesnière, Lucien. (1959). *Éléments de syntaxe structurale*. Paris: Klincksieck.
Wells, Rulon S. (1947). Immediate Constituents. *Language* 23, 81–117.
Wierzbicka, Anna. 1988. *The Semantics of Grammar*. Amsterdam: John Benjamins Publishing Company.
Zipf, George. (1949) *Human Behavior and the Principle of Least Effort: An Introduction to Human Ecology*. New York: Hafner.

190 *References*

Websites:

corpus.byu.edu/bnc
grammarmonster.com
vvlexicon.ninjal.ac.jp/db
www.ruscorpora.ru/en

Index

abstraction 76
actant 43
adjective 16, 25, 48
adjective modifier 16
   appositive reading 16
   restrictive reading 16
adjective-noun 16, 20
adjunct 26
adverb 25
and 53, 60
apposition 17, 73
appropriate referents 7, 12
argument roles 44
assemblage 12
assertive mood 38

Bahuvrihi 66
be, copula 30
be, exist 30
become 130
binominals 82
bivalent 33, 42–3
bivalent preposition 40
bivalent verb 39
but 60
by 84

case 48
   absolute, Tongan 160
   absolutive , Alaskan Yup'ik 161
   accusative 48
   accusative pronoun 110
   accusative subject, Russian 135
   accusative, C. Mongolian 157
   accusative, Japanese 152–3
   accusative, Manchu 157
   accusative, Russian 32, 49, 51, 167
   accusative, Turkish 155

dative 48
dative participant, Russian 50
dative pronoun, Russian 50
dative, Japanese 47, 142, 153
dative, Russian 51
ergative case, Tongan 160
genitive 19, 48, 94
genitive construction, Russian 136
genitive subject, Russian 136
genitive, Lepcha 144
genitive, Russian 47, 52
genitive, Turkish 151
instrumental 48
instrumental, Japanese 153
instrumental, Russian 32, 49, 51
locative 48
nominative 48
nominative construction, Russian 136
nominative, C. Mongolian 157
nominative, Manchu 156
nominative, Russian 33, 167
relative, Alaskan Yup'ik 161
Russian cases 48
case marking 42
comparative 45, 47
complex meaning 39
compositional 8
compound 20, 33
compound verb 148
compound verbs, Japanese 145
compounding 10, 20, 91
   convergent compounding 21
   divergent compounding 22
COND 61
conditional 61
conjunction 26, 46, 60
construction 14
container 81, 98

191

192 Index

CONTR 67
convergence 9, 15, 28
convergent 9, 28
coordination 53
copula 30
coreference 57

DECL 34, 37
declarative 37
DEF 17, 154
definite 11, 154
definite article 17
definiteness 11, 17, 154
dependent preposition 41
derived referent 7
distinctive feature 5, 28, 39
ditransitive 42, 47
ditransitive constructions 42
divergence 9
divergent 9, 28
do 70
domination 28
door 84
double-object constructions 42

ellipsis 57
  VP-ellipsis 72
elliptical 34
EMPH 70
emphasis 11, 70
entity 8, 39
epistemic modality 105
equipollent 22, 91, 163
er 139
estar 31
EXCL 34
exclamative 11, 37
existential construction, Russian 140
existential constructions 133
existential sentences 139
extraposition 74, 167

feature 5, 9
focus 166
formalization 11
form-meaning 13, 48, 83

generic time 31
genitival adjunct 95
genitival compounds 96
gerund constructions 120

gerund, Japanese 164
give 47
gradation
  reversed gradation 26, 60, 168
  temporal gradation 26, 123, 164
gradation relation 10, 25–6, 41, 60

have 127
homonymous 5

IC 9
IC structure 12, 26
idiomatic expressions 22
if 56
immediate constituent 9, 15
IMP 36
imperative 36
impersonal constructions 133
incorporation 20
  noun incorporation 145, 158
  noun incorporation, Tongan 160
  verb incorporation 145
INDEF 17, 154
indefinite 154
indefinite article 17
indefiniteness 17, 155
individual time 31
infinitive 56
  as primary 115
  as secondary 115
  as tertiary 115
  bare infinitive 109, 118
  to-infinitive 109, 118
infinitive constructions 109
inherent feature 5
interpretation 6, 85
interrogative 37
intonation 13
intonational contour 34, 74
intransitive verb 42, 84, 152
inversion 61
it 133

languages
  Alaskan Yup'ik 161
  Avava 80
  Chukchi 148
  Classical Mongolian 157
  Dutch 21, 27, 81, 86, 98, 100–1, 106, 1⊂3,
    116, 130–1, 133, 139, 170
  Edo 165

Eskimo 161
French 93, 129
Georgian 81
German 94, 130, 133
Japanese 47, 142, 145–6, 149, 151–2, 164
Lepcha 144
Manchu 156
Mokilese 158
Nupe 162
Ponapean 159
Russian 32–3, 46, 48, 51, 78, 117, 134, 136,
  140, 167
Spanish 31
Tongan 159
Turkish 150
Yoruba 163
lexemes 43
limitation
  convergent limitation 15–16, 19
  divergent limitation 18
  temporal limitation 19, 27, 31
limitation relation 10, 15, 41
linguistic sign 5
location 40–1

meaning 6, 12, 85
  constructional meaning 72, 82
metalanguage 14, 40
metaphor 5, 7
metonymic 15
metonymic relation 86
metonymy 5, 7
middle passive 86
minimal pairs 83, 113, 118
modal verbs 105
modification 10
monotransitive 42
monovalent 33, 42
mood 29, 35
morpheme 14
MUT 79
mutually 79

narrated event 35
negation 67, 70
negation, Japanese 151
nexus 10, 28
  first nexus member 28, 166
  nexus complex 29
  nexus symbol 28
  second nexus member 28, 166

no 23
nominal construction 100
nominal predicate 30
NON 67, 70
non-referential 18
NONTHE 17
noun
  collective noun 82
  countable noun 24
  uncountable noun 24
number 23
numeral 48, 97

object
  direct object 42–3
  direct object, Manchu 157
  direct object, Turkish 154
  indirect object 42–3
object complement 42, 111
of 80, 97
or 53
orientation 15
orientation point 35

PA 35, 37
participant 42, 47
  direct participant 39, 51–2, 164
  peripheral participant 51–2
participant roles 44
participle 48
passive construction 124
past participles 124
past tense 35
perfective 124
PF 124
phrase structure 2
PL 24
plural 14, 17, 24
POL 152
polysemous 5, 82, 86
polysemy 5
possessive 18
potential referents 17
PR 35, 37
pragmatics 6
predicate 28, 43
preposition 40, 47
prepositional phrase 39–40, 43, 47, 96
present tense 35
presentative-locative 140
PROGR 123

194   *Index*

progressive constructions 122
progressive relation 15, 23
projection 39
pronoun 48
  indefinite pronoun 140
  possessive pronoun 19, 122
  relative pronoun 61, 75, 149
proper names 18
property 8, 25, 28
propositional content 169
prototype 6
punctuation marks 13

Q 34, 37, 70
quantifiers 99
quantities 97
quasi-divergence 58
questions 37, 70

raising to object 111
REAL 37
realis 37
reciprocal 78
referential 18
reflexive 78
regressive relation 25
relation symbol 12
relative clause, Japanese 149
relative clause, Turkish 150
relative clauses, 149

SE 64
semantic doubling 34, 57
semantic particles 10, 14
semiotactic 8
semiotactic representations 14
sentence
  formal sentence 34, 74
  syntactic sentence 74
ser 31
serial verbs 162, 165
set expression 64
set level 23
sigma symbol 29
SING 24
singular 11, 24
situation 28, 30, 34–5
speaker's aside 169
speaker's attitude 35
specimen set 36

splitting 25
square brackets 39
stratification 10, 23–4, 36
subject 28, 42–3
subject-predicate 10, 29
subject-verb agreement 35
subset 15–16, 19, 36–7
symbol 'X' 56
syntactic boundary 169

temporal dimension 29, 33
tense 29, 35
than 46
THE 17, 23
there 139–40
TOP 146
top layer 35, 37
topic 146, 166
topical particle, Japanese 146
topicalization 171
transitive verb 39, 152
trivalent 42, 47

un- 14
universal relations 10

valence
  complementary valence 39
  dominated valence 39
  dominating valence 39
  first valence 39, 42
  oblique valence 43
  second valence 39, 42
  third valence 42, 50
valence addition 44
valence reduction 44, 47
valences 39, 42
verb agreement 34
verb inflection 14
verb serialization 162
voice
  active voice 6, 126
  passive voice 6, 85, 126

when 60
word order 12, 166
word order, Russian 167
worden 130

zijn 130